Dictionary of International Trade Finance

Mike Hammett

Series Editor: John O E Clark

Financial World Publishing
IFS House
4-9 Burgate Lane
Canterbury
Kent
CT1 2XJ
United Kingdom

T   01227 818687
F   01227 479641
E   editorial@ifslearning.com
W   www.ifslearning.com

Financial World Publishing publications are published by The Chartered Institute of Bankers, a non-profit making registered educational charity. The Chartered Institute of Bankers believes that the sources of information upon which the book is based are reliable and has made every effort to ensure the complete accuracy of the text. However, neither CIB, the author nor any contributor can accept any legal responsibility whatsoever for consequences that may arise from errors or omissions or any opinion or advice given.

Typeset by Kevin O'Connor

Printed in Spain

© The Chartered Institute of Bankers 2001
ISBN 0-85297-576-7

FINANCIAL
WORLD
Publishing
THE CHARTERED INSTITUTE OF BANKERS

Preface

This book is intended to provide access to the terms of trade finance for students and professionals in the growing world of internatonal trade, and its interaction with banking and the stock exchange. It should also assist private investors and people who read financial journals and the financial pages of daily newspapers. Like its companion volume, the *Dictionary of International Investment and Finance Terms*, it does not limit itself merely to well-established terms. It also includes definitions of the everyday jargon, acronyms and newly adopted words (many from the United States) that are now common in national and international financial dealings.

The Dictionary of International Trade Finance is one of a series of publications complied from The CIB's unique database of dictionary definitions that relate to various aspects of finance and their applications. As a result, some definitions appear in more than one book – as they should to maintain a comprehensive coverage of the subject within a single self-contained volume. The dictionaries in the series published to date include:

Dictionary of International Accounting Terms
0-85297-575-9
Dictionary of International Banking and Finance Terms
0-85297-632-1
Dictionary of International Business Terms
0-85297-574-0
Dictionary of International Insurance and Finance Terms
0-85297-631-3
Dictionary of International Investment and Finance Terms
0-85297-577-5
Dictionary of International Trade Finance
0-85297-576-7

Mike Hammett BA, FCIBS, ACIB, PGCE

Chief Examiner for the Chartered Institute of Bankers in Scotland in International Trade Finance and Services, and for European Union and International Business (at the Post-Associate/Post-Graduate level).

Formerly Head of a Documentary Bills & Credits Department in Nigeria, Lecturer in Export and Import Finance at the Napier University, Edinburgh, and The Chartered Institute of Bankers' Assistant Examiner for Finance of International Trade.

Has written a number of books and articles on export finance and exporting and undertaken funded research in the UK, France and Switzerland.

Acknowledgements

I would like to thank the following people for their very willing and invaluable help. John Forsyth, Senior Ship Manager, George Gibson & Co. Ltd., Leith, Edinburgh; David McLintoch, Manager, Risk Management Services, Clydesdale Bank PLC, Glasgow. Also my wife Glennys for all her patient support – including not killing me whenever I deserved it.

John O E Clark

John O E Clark is a writer and editor who regularly contributes to dictionaries, encyclopedias and other types of information books for publication in Britain and abroad. He specializes in explaining technical subjects to students and other non-experts, and to people whose first language is not necessarily English.

A

A1 In the best condition. In marine insurance, a ship that is well maintained is shown in Lloyd's Register of Shipping as being A1.

AAA Abbreviation of the Association of Average Adjusters.

AAA The most favourable risk rating.

AAR Abbreviation of *against all risks*.

abandon To withdraw from a deal by paying a premium or "penalty" that has been agreed in advance.

abandonment The situation when a ship runs aground and the cost of recovery is deemed by the loss adjuster to be too high, and the insurer treats it as a total loss. If, however, the ship and/or its cargo are recovered later, they will then belong to the insurer.

abatement A reduction. The term is used in the USA to describe the cancellation, in whole or in part, of a government levy.

ability to pay The ability to pay the principal and interest for a long-term loan.

absolute liability The legal principle that that a party that causes loss or harm is liable, whether or not it acted with wrongful intent or negligently. It is also called strict liability.

absolute purchasing power parity The theory that the exchange rate between two countries equalizes the price of a basket goods in the two countries (but as the composition of the goods and the price indices can vary substantially and because some goods may not be traded or are subject to tariffs, it is unlikely that the theory will apply in reality).

absolute quota A limit, imposed by government, on the amount of goods that may be imported in a particular period.

absorbing a cost Not to pass on a cost to a customer.

Abu Dhabi United Arab Emirates currency: dirham (AWD), divided into 100 fils.

accelerated depreciation The practice of depreciating an asset at a rate greater than the actual decline in its value in order to obtain tax concessions. It need not occur throughout the life of an asset; a substantial proportion of its total value is often written off in the first year, and reduced allowances for depreciation are made thereafter.

acceleration clause A provision that an unpaid balance will become due if there should be any default, e.g. failure to pay the principal and/or interest.

acceptance The action of accepting a bill of exchange for payment. The signing (usually across the face) by the drawee of a term bill of exchange is a promise to make payment at maturity.

acceptance bill A bill of exchange that the drawee/acceptor accepts by signing it on its face. He thereby commits himself to paying it on maturity (the due date). It is also called an acceptance note.

acceptance by intervention *See acceptance for honour.*

acceptance draft A bill of exchange that the drawee/acceptor accepts by signing it on its face. He thereby commits himself to paying it on maturity (the due date).

acceptance for honour The situation when a bill of exchange is turned down (or protested) and is then accepted by another party, thereby saving the honour of the *drawer*. It is also known as acceptance *supra protest* or acceptance by intervention.

acceptance (or accepting) house A merchant bank that specializes in wholesale/corporate international trade finance. For a fee it will add its own name to a bill of exchange as a recommendation that the party upon whom it is drawn is of a good financial standing. *See also acceptance house credit.*

acceptance house credit A with recourse finance facility used by large-scale exporters and importers. They can draw a bill of exchange on their own or another bank discounted "at a fine rate". It is consequently a cheaper rate than smaller-scale traders could obtain.

acceptance market The section of the money market that deals in accepted bills of exchange.

acceptance note An alternative term for *acceptance bill.*

acceptance report A declaration by a buyer certifying the progress made by a supplier up to a specified point in time. It is employed where a percentage of a letter of credit sum is payable against an acceptance, or progress, report. If satisfied, the buyer certifies the supplier's declaration that the contract conditions have been fulfilled and the object supplied is working properly.

acceptance supra protest See *acceptance for honour*.

accepting bank The bank nominated in a letter of credit to accept drawings under that credit.

Accepting Houses Committee A committee that represents the London acceptance houses. Its members receive preferential terms on bills sold to the Bank of England.

acceptor The person accepting a bill of exchange.

accident insurance Insurance cover of the loss of any limbs or eyes etc. in the event of an accident. It also covers compensation to the policyholder's dependants in the event of death.

accidental loss An insurable risk covering any financial loss caused by the damage or destruction resulting from a sudden, unexpected or unusual event.

accommodating transactions In international trade, below-the-line items employed to offset any imbalances (such as those caused by a country's trade deficit).

accommodation Money that is lent to someone for a brief period.

accommodation bill A bill of exchange signed in order to help another person to raise a loan. The signatory (or accommodation party) is acting as a guarantor and does not normally expect to pay the bill when it falls due. Accommodation bills are also known as kites, windbills or windmills.

accommodation credit A with recourse finance facility used by large-scale exporters and importers. They can draw a bill of exchange on their own or another bank discounted "at a fine rate" (i.e. cheaper).

accommodation payment A euphemism for a bribe. See *kickback*.

accord and satisfaction When one party has discharged its obligations under a *contract*, it may choose to release the other party from its obligations. When this is done for a new *consideration*, the release is known as accord and satisfaction.

account Very generally, a note kept of any financial transaction. It is often abbreviated to a/c, acc. or acct.

  1. It is used in banking to designate an arrangement made to deposit money with a bank or other kind of financial institution. Used in this sense it may be of many differing types, usually indicated by a qualifying word, depending on the conditions of withdrawal, level of

interest, minimum amount of money in the account, or other factors (examples include *current* account, *deposit* account, *savings* account, etc.).

2. It is a record of financial transactions and, in this sense, is often termed accounts.

accountancy The body of knowledge relating to financial matters. It is also the work done by an *accountant*, involving knowledge of the law as it affects financial matters (e.g. the tax laws), **book-keeping** and the preparation of **annual accounts**.

accountant Any person practising accountancy, whether qualified or not. The term may be prefixed with various other terms, denoting the specialism of the accountant (e.g. *cost* accountant, *management* accountant), that accountant's position within a business (e.g. *chief* accountant), or his or her professional qualifications (e.g. *certified* accountant, *certified public* accountant, *chartered* accountant).

accounting Very broadly, the activity of recording and verifying all monies borrowed, owed, paid or received.

accounting concepts The basic concepts by which sets of accounts are made up. The four generally accepted accounting concepts are the *accruals* concept, *consistency* concept, *going concern* concept and *prudence* concept. They are also called accounting principles.

accounting cost The total expenditure required to undertake an activity. *See also* **economic cost**.

accounting equation The principle that capital plus liabilities equals the total resources of a company.

accounting exposure A risk arising from the translation of assets and liabilities into foreign currency. It is also known as translation exposure.

accounting period The time for which accounts are prepared, such as a year for a company's financial accounts or a month for internal management accounts.

accounting principles Another term for *accounting concepts*.

accounting rate of return (ARR) The anticipated net profit from an investment, calculated as a percentage of investment.

accounting ratio One of several ratios that are considered important in assessing the financial viability of a project or company.

account management group A sub-section of an agency specializing in a field such as marketing that concentrates on all the work done for a particular client or clients.

account payable The amount that an importer/buyer owes to his supplier, used particularly with open account terms.

account receivable The amount owed to an exporter/supplier by its customer, used particularly with open account terms.

account rendered An unpaid balance that appears in a statement of account.

account sales A statement that shows the gross proceeds of the sales of an overseas consignment that has been sold by an overseas agent, less the expenses incurred and the agent's commission.

accounts receivable finance. With recourse finance, a method whereby an exporter can borrow money from a bank in exchange for/on the strength of unpaid invoices (accounts receivable).

account stated An account consisting of items that both parties concerned have agreed as being correct; any balance is thereby also agreed.

account statement A written summary of all the amounts withdrawn and all deposits credited to a customer's account within a given period and showing the balance as at the date of the statement. Statements covering transactions between correspondent banks or with business clients are often prepared daily.

accredited Term that describes someone who is authorized to act on behalf of a company or individual.

accretion The increase in the value of a bond from its original price on purchase at a discount to its par value on redemption.

across the board tariff reductions An agreement between the members of GATT to make a fixed percentage reduction in tariffs in all member countries.

accrual The gradual increase by addition over a period of time. *See also accrued charges.*

accruals concept Principle used in accounting by which income and expenditure are taken into the profit and loss account for the period in which they occur. This method of accounting is useful in that it pulls together receipts and the costs incurred in generating them, avoiding the lag between the time income is received and the time liabilities become due. *See also accounting concepts.*

accrued charges Charges that have not yet been accounted for or paid. For example, if a demand for rent is made in arrears, it must appear on the accounts as an accrued charge, because the service has already been used, but not paid for.

accrued interest Interest that has been added by time of the sale of a financial instrument.

accumulated depreciation In accounting, the total value of an asset that has been written off so far.

accumulated profits The amount shown in an appropriation of profits account carried forward to the next year's accounts, after paying dividends and taxes etc. and then allotting some proportion to reserve.

accumulating shares Additional ordinary shares issued to equity holders in lieu of a dividend. They are consequently attractive for capital growth, rather than for regular income. Tax is normally deducted from the declared dividend as usual and then the net dividend is used to purchase additional ordinary shares.

accumulation Something that is allowed to increase in value, such as a retained profit accumulated if a company's total dividend payments are less than the total of the profits it has made or interest it has continued to receive.

ACH Abbreviation of *automated clearing house.*

acid test ratio *See liquidity ratio.*

ACK In computer transmissions, an abbreviation of acknowledgement, sent as a message to confirm the arrival of error-free data.

acknowledgment A verification that a signature on a document is legitimate and has been authorized. It can also mean that a paying bank has received a financial instrument that cannot be paid immediately.

acquisition The take-over of control of one company by another or by an individual (usually by buying a major stake in the equity).

acquisition cost The charge incurred in commission etc. in buying any kind of security.

ACT Abbreviation of advance corporation tax.

act of bankruptcy 1. Attempting to leave the country to avoid creditors; 2. Giving away property in order to defraud creditors; 3. Failing to comply with a bankruptcy notice filed by a creditor. By acting in any one of these ways a person may make him/herself liable to bankruptcy proceedings.

act of God Any event so out of the ordinary that it could not have been prevented by any amount of human care and forethought, e.g. lightning, freak tidal waves or floods etc., which relieves a contractor, such as a freight carrier, of any liability for losses suffered as a result of it.

act of war Any act causing loss or damage as a result of conflict between nations. Such risks are excluded from most insurance policies, although an extra premium may be payable to cover the risk.

active Busy, in action, constantly changing, as in e.g. active account or active stock.

active account A bank account on which deposits and withdrawals regularly occur.

active market Any market where there is large volume of trading. The spread between the buying and selling prices is usually closer in an active market than when there is a lot smaller volume of trading. It consequently results in much greater stability.

active partner A partner working for a firm.

actuals Any physical commodity, such as copper, timber, wheat, wool etc., usually involving physical delivery as distinct from a financial instrument, which does not usually or necessarily do so.

active stock Shares that are frequently traded on a financial exchange.

actual total loss The total destruction or loss of an insured item or damage sufficient to make it no longer of any use.

actuary A statistician employed by an insurance company to calculate the likelihood of risk and advise insurers on the amount of premium to be charged for each type of risk and how much to set aside to cover it.

ACV Abbreviation of *air-cushion vehicle*.

ADB Abbreviation of *Asian Development Bank*.

addendum An appendix or supplement to a document, such as a bill of exchange, which can be used for endorsements.

add-on market See *aftermarket*.

add-on sales Further sales made to an existing customer.

address commission The commission paid to a shipping *agent* in return for seeing that a cargo is loaded onto a ship.

adequacy of coverage The extent to which any asset is protected by insurance or hedging .

adjudication The act of giving judgement in a dispute.

adjudication of bankruptcy A court order declaring a person or company bankrupt. *See also bankruptcy.*

adjudication order A court order declaring someone bankrupt. Also known as *adjudication of bankruptcy.*

adjust In finance, to correct figures or make allowance for interest changes, as in forward contracts.

adjuster *See loss adjuster.*

adjustment An alteration, such as the addition of a discount or subtraction of a premium to allow for the interest differential in a forward contract.

administration Broadly, the sum of actions involved in the organization or management of a company (*see administration expenses*). In law, however, administration is either the winding-up of the estate of a deceased person in the absence of an executor or in the event of intestacy, or it is the winding-up of a company. Both cases involve the court appointment of someone to act as *administrator.*

administration expenses One of the general expenses. In company accounting, it is a blanket term covering expenses incurred in the overall management of a company, but not positively attributable to any particular department or operating arm.

administration order A County Court order requiring the administration of the estate of a debtor, who usually has to pay the debts by instalments in order to avoid bankruptcy.

administrative receiver A person appointed by the court to manage a company's assets on behalf of debenture holders or other secured creditors.

administrator 1. A person appointed (usually by the court) to manage someone else's property. 2. A person appointed by the court to manage the affairs of someone who has died without making a will (intestate). Proof of his or her authority is a letter of administration issued by the court.

admission temporaire carnet An international customs document covering the temporary export of some types of goods, such as commercial samples, which may be allowed into the country (if it is a signatory to the international convention) without having to pay any duty, because they will be taken out again shortly after the end of the international fair etc. at which they are to be exhibited/demonstrated.

ADP (ISO) code Andorra. It has no currency of its own – there are mainly Spanish peseta in circulation. It will adopt the euro/cent from 2002.

ADR Abbreviation of *American depositary receipts*.

ADR The European agreement on the international carriage of dangerous goods by road.

ad referendum When referring to a contract, an indication that while the contract has been agreed and signed, there are still some matters to be discussed.

ad valorem Latin for according to the value. In taxation, it indicates that tax is calculated as a percentage of the value of the transaction, rather than being charged at a fixed rate. For example, value added tax (VAT) is paid as a percentage of the value of the goods or services sold.

ad valorem **duty** A customs and excise duty on high-value goods based on the value of an imported item rather than on either its quantity or its weight.

advance 1. A loan granted by a bank or other financial institution. 2. Part-payment for work contracted made ahead of total payment, before the goods or services contracted for have been rendered. Sometimes, if payment depends on sales, the advance is set against those sales.

advance compensation An alternative term for *forward purchase*.

advance payment bond A guarantee to a buyer that advance payments for incomplete work will be repaid in the event of the seller subsequently defaulting. It is often used where there is a lot of work entailed before the delivery of the goods etc. to the buyer. A major risk to an exporter, for example, is that a contract may be frustrated by some event occurring after the advance payment has been received, but before the delivery of the goods or the completion of the contract.

adventure A commercial or financial risk.

adverse Bad or, at the very least, unhelpful.

adverse balance   In general, an account balance that shows a loss or liability. More especially, it is short for adverse *balance of trade*.

advertising   A range of activities that surround the practice of informing the public of the existence and desirability of a product. The main purpose of advertising is to boost sales or, in the case of national bodies and charitable organizations, to provide information or to solicit contributions.

advertising agency   A company that specializes in planning and carrying out *advertising* campaigns.

advertising allowance   An expense paid by an exporter to an agent to allow him or her to arrange local advertising.

advice note   A notice from an exporter giving details of goods ordered or delivered. It includes their marks and numbers, if there is more than one package. It either accompanies or precedes the shipment, and precedes the invoice. *See also delivery note*.

advice of acceptance   A document from a collecting bank to the bank from which a collection order was received that acknowledges receipt of funds and gives details of any charges incurred.

advice of fate   *See advise fate*.

advice of non-acceptance   A document from a collecting bank to the bank from which a collection order was received that gives notice of non-acceptance or non-payment. It is also termed advice of non-payment.

advice of non-payment   *See advice of non-acceptance*.

advise fate   A request from a collecting banker to a paying banker to confirm that the bill of exchange/cheque to which it refers has been honoured. This confirmation cannot be given until the paying banker receives the bill/cheque. It is a speedy method of confirmation, also called advice of fate.

advising bank   A correspondent bank, usually in the exporter's country (and not necessarily his or her own), used by an issuing bank to notify the opening of a letter of credit.

Advisory Committee on Export Policy (ACEP)   A US organization that resolves disputes between federal agencies, chaired by the US Department of Commerce.

A

Advisory Committee on Trade Policy and Negotiations (ACTPN)   A committee appointed by the US president to advise on trade policy and related matters, such as trade agreements.

advisory funds Funds for investment deposited with a bank but which can be invested only after consultation with the depositor.

AED (ISO) code United Arab Emirates – currency: dirham.

AFA (ISO) code Afghanistan – currency: afghani

AFBD Abbreviation of *Association of Futures Brokers and Dealers.*

AfDB Abbreviation of *African Development Bank.*

against all risks (AAR) In marine insurance, a term that indicates that a vessel and its cargo have been insured against all insurable eventualities. It is roughly equivalent to fully comprehensive insurance of motor vehicles.

affidavit A written statement made under oath before an authorized person, such as a commissioner of oaths or a notary public.

affiliate Any of two or more companies that have loose ties with each other.

affiliated company A company that is associated in some way with another company. Of no legal standing in the UK, the term has confusingly two opposite meanings in the USA. It may be a company that controls another company, or a company that is controlled by another company.

affirmation of contract The confirmation by behaviour that a contract is valid, as opposed to trying to get out of it for some good reason. It may be by declaration of intention, inferred from, say, selling goods bought under the contract, or allowing time to elapse without pursuing a remedy.

affreightment A contract for the transportation of goods, covered by a *charter party* or a *bill of lading* etc.

Afghanistan currency: afghani (AFA), divided into 100 pule.

afloat Describing goods that are on their way from their port of departure to a specified port of destination. It can affect their price on a commodity market.

à forfait finance Alternative term for forfaiting (from the original French).

African Development Bank (AfDB) A bank specifically created to assist the development of African nations.

after-acquired property Possessions obtained by a bankrupt after bankruptcy has been declared. See **bankruptcy**.

after date Written on a bill of exchange, an indication that the bill will become due a certain (specified) period after the date on the bill, e.g. "60 days after date". See also **at sight**.

after-hours dealing Trading on official exchanges outside normal trading hours. As a result, prices might change considerably between the previous day's closing and the beginning of the next.

aftermarket Trading in stocks and shares after they have made their initial debut on the market. The aftermarket may also be the market in components and services arising after a product has been sold. It is also known as the add-on market.

after-sales service The continued servicing of goods (often under guarantee), sold by a manufacturer, exporter or his or her agent, effective for a specified period during which the service is free in respect of parts and/or labour, often followed by a maintenance contract for which the buyer has to pay. It can be a very important element in establishing good relations between an exporter and his customers.

after sight See **at sight**.

after-sight bill A bill of exchange that becomes payable at a certain date after presentation for acceptance (e.g. after 30 or 60 days, etc.).

AG Abbreviation of the German **Aktiengesellschaft**.

against all risks (AAR) In marine insurance, a term that indicates that a vessel and its cargo have been insured against all insurable eventualities. It is roughly equivalent to fully comprehensive insurance of motor vehicles.

against the box In a *short* sale the individual selling short actually owns the stock sold short, but for some reason does not wish to or cannot deliver the particular stock owned in order to settle the sale with the buyer.

AGD (ISO) code Antigua – currency: East Caribbean dollar.

agency 1. A person or company that represents another in a particular field. 2. A contractual agreement by which one party agrees to represent another, the agent's word becoming as binding in the affairs of the other as if the latter had acted on his or her own behalf.

agency bill A bill of exchange that is drawn on, and accepted by, the London branch of a foreign bank.

agenda A list of matters to be discussed at a meeting or a course of action to be taken.

agent A person or company that has entered into a contract of *agency* with another party, called the *principal*, and acts as its representative, usually in buying and selling goods or services. Normally an agent does not own the principal's property, but must obey the principal's instructions.

agent bank A bank officially appointed to supervise a loan granted by a syndicate.

Agent/Distributor Service (ADS) A US organization that, for a fee, helps to find foreign representatives for US exporters.

agent for exporter An authorized forwarding agent of an exporting company.

agent of necessity A situation that arises when an agent acts to safeguard the principal's interests, without the principal's permission. It can arise only when (a) the principal cannot be reached, (b) there is a contract of agency already in existence between the two parties, and (c) immediate action is absolutely necessary. If these conditions exist, the agent's actions are legally binding on the principal.

agent's lien The right of an agent in certain circumstances to retain the property of the principal (for example, in lieu of payment).

age schedule A listing of invoiced sales in date order on the principle that the longer the debt is outstanding the less likely it will ever be paid. In this way it provides a useful analysis of bad debts.

aggregation risk When trading in securities takes place in more than one market, the possible multiplying of risk.

agio A premium, such as 1. A commission or charge made by a bank or a bureau de change in return for converting cash from one currency to another; or 2 .The price increase over and above the market price of traded goods and attributable to the extra costs involved in countertrading.

AGM Abbreviation of *annual general meeting*.

agorot A subdivision (1/100) of the Israeli shekel.

agreement A verbal or written contract between two or more parties to explain the way they intend to act in respect of each other.

agribusiness The industry that encompasses and includes farming and all commercial aspects of agriculture.

agricultural bank A bank specializing in granting loans for agricultural development. It is also known as a land bank.

agricultural disarmament A reduction in protectionist practices, such as price subsidizing, in agriculture.

Agricultural Marketing Service (AMS) A service that the US Department of Agriculture provides by guaranteeing contract specifications of products exported to overseas buyers.

AIBD Abbreviation of *Association of International Bond Dealers*.

aids to trade Activities (often services) that assist other businesses, such as advertising, banking, insurance and transport.

aid trade provision (ATP). Subsidized loans and credits that are offered to developing countries on condition that goods and services are purchased from companies of the country granting the aid. It is also known as *tied aid*.

AIM Abbreviation of *alternative investment market*.

air consignment note An alternative name for *air waybill*.

air-cushion vehicle (ACV) A vehicle that rides on a cushion of air (by land or air), e.g. a hovercraft.

air freight The carrying goods by air or the cost of sending goods by air.

air-pocket stock Stock whose price suddenly falls, usually after rumours of the company's poor performance.

air waybill (AWB) A document used for carriage of cargo by air, itemizing the goods and constituting evidence of the existence of a contract to make the shipment. (It is thus similar to a sea waybill, but not quasi-negotiable as an ocean bill of lading would be.)

Aktiengesellschaft (AG) Teutonic (German, Austrian, parts of Switzerland, Luxembourg and Liechtenstein) equivalent to a UK public limited liability company (plc).

Albania currency: Albanian lek (ALL), divided into100 qindarka.

Algeria currency: Algerian dinar (DZD), divided into 100 centimes.

aligned documentation An A4 documentation system based on standardized forms. All the documentation needed for any particular consignment can be run off from a master copy. Blank new forms are commercially available, but nowadays are more likely to dealt with by *electronic data interchange*.

ALL (ISO) code Albania – currency: Albanian lek.

alligator spread Profit made on an option that is instantly snapped up by the broker as commission, leaving nothing for the investor.

all-in Including everything, most often used to describe a price or service.

allocation The allotment of a fully or partly subscribed issue, e.g. for eurobonds.

allocation under lines of credit Finance provided by Canada's Export Development Corporation to foreign importers of Canadian goods and services.

allocatur A certificate of approval of costs incurred in an action (e.g. liquidation) for taxation purposes.

allonge A slip attached to a bill of exchange that provides extra space for the noting of endorsements. Allonges were most useful when bills of exchange moved freely from one holder to another, but now are less common.

all-or-none order An instruction to buy or sell a security directing a futures broker not to carry out the order unless it can be fulfilled in its entirety.

allotment Broadly, the sharing out of something, usually funds, among a group of people such as a syndicate.

allotment of shares When a company issues shares by publishing a prospectus and inviting applications, allotment is the assignment of shares to each applicant. In cases where the issue is oversubscribed, shares are allotted in proportion to the quantity requested and so applicants do not always receive the number of shares they originally requested. *See also* **application and allotment**.

allotment subscribed The allocation (and hence reduction) of a security, such as a eurobond, apportioned to the individual subscriber in an oversubscribed issue.

allowable expenses Expenses that are tax-deductible.

allowance   1. A reduction in the amount owed made by an exporter/ supplier to allow for any damages or shortages. 2. Money that is allotted (allowed) to individuals for a specific reason, or a provision made for unusual or uncertain events. 3. An amount deducted for one of various reasons before income is calculated for tax purposes.

all risks   An obsolete term (yet one still occasionally seen) describing insurance cover of all claims for the many risks covered (but in fact not all – usually excluding such special risks as war and strikes or goods perishing) and consequently subject to the highest premiums. Now referred to as an *Institute Cargo Clause A*.

alpha   A Stock Exchange categorization of the top 100 most actively traded shares with a large capitalization value. *See also beta; delta; gamma.*

alternate director   A person who shares a directorship with another. Each member of the pair has a vote on the board.

alternative investment market (AIM)   A London market that helps smaller companies to raise capital.

alternative payee   A bill of exchange or cheque can be made payable to either of two people, each of whom is an alternative payee.

amalgamation   The coming together or unification of two or more companies.

ambulance stock   Securities recommended to a client whose investment portfolio has done badly. The practice is especially common in Japan.

amendment   An addition to or a change in a document. If properly authorized, it has the same authority as the original document.

American depositary receipts (ADRs)   Receipts issued by US banks declaring that a certain number of a company's shares have been deposited with them. ADRs are denorninated in dollars and although they usually refer to non-American companies, they are traded on the US markets as US securities.

American Express (AMEX)   An international credit company based in the USA.

American Express card   A plastic card issued by American Express, used as a no-limit debit card by its holders. It is not a true credit card because long-term credit is unavailable, and debts must be paid by a given due date.

American Institute of Underwriters The American organization that uses similar clauses to the UK Institute of London Underwriters cargo clauses in marine insurance.

American option A currency option that can be exercised at any time prior to and including the expiry date of the option. It originated in the USA and its use is not restricted in anyway geographically. *See also European option.*

American Stock Exchange (AMEX) The New York stock exchange that deals in stocks and bonds of smaller companies.

AMEX Abbreviation of *American Express* and *American Stock Exchange.*

AMH Abbreviation of *automatic materials handling.*

amortization The reduction of a debt by regular payments covering both current interest obligations and the full repayment at maturity.

amortize To pay off a debt by means of payments over a period of time. More specifically, in accounting, the cost of a fixed *asset* is written in to the profit-and-loss account over a period of years, rather than being taken into account when it is first bought. The cost of the asset has been amortized when this period is over. *See depreciation.*

amortizing mortgage A mortgage in which all the principal and interest has been repaid, usually by equal payments, by the end of the mortgage term. Although the payments are equal, early payments are made up mostly of interest, whereas later payments are mostly repayments of the principal.

amount differs A banker's statement on a bill of exchange or a cheque when returning it unpaid because the amount in words differs from that in figures.

AMS Abbreviation of *Agricultural Marketing Service.*

analysis Determination of the composition or the significance of something. It can be a detailed study or investigation often culminating in a report, upon which executives may base their decisions.

analysis certificate A requirement of a documentary letter of credit where a certificated confirmation of the chemical analysis of goods by a competent organization is needed.

analysis-paralysis What happens when managers spend their time having endless meetings and writing interminable reports, but never making any decisions. It is characterized by a desire for more and more statistics and information.

analyst A person who undertakes *analysis*.

ancillary credit business Business that does not directly provide credit but is engaged in credit brokerage, debt adjusting, debt counselling, debt collection or the operation of a credit reference agency.

Andorra It has no currency of its own – there are mainly Spanish pesetas in circulation (ADP) as well as (also French francs). It will adopt the euro/cent from 2002.

ANF Abbreviation of *arrival notification form*.

ANG (ISO) code Netherlands Antilles – currency: Netherlands Antilles guilder.

Angola currency: kwanza (AOK), divided into 100 lwei.

announcement day The day when a new bond issue is publicly announced.

annual accounts A report submitted annually showing the current financial state of a company and the results of its operations for that year. *See also annual report.*

annual charges For taxation purposes, that part of a person's or company's income that has been paid after tax has been deducted. For example, a covenant to a person is deemed by the Inland Revenue to have been paid net of tax.

annual general meeting (AGM) A shareholders' meeting, required by UK law to be held yearly by every public company. An AGM is normally used to discuss the *annual report* and accounts, to announce *dividends* and to elect *auditors* and *directors*. It is often the only opportunity that shareholders have to air their views. *See public company*. *See also extraordinary general meeting.*

annual increment The amount by which money (often a salary) or the costs of goods increase in the course of one year.

annualize To convert interest on a short-term to an annual basis, e.g. a security or commission etc. earning ½% a month would be seen to be earning the equivalent 6% p.a. by multiplying the monthly rate by 12. It can be a useful method of producing MAT (moving annual total) figures.

annualized percentage rate (APR) Also known as annual percentage rate, the rate of *interest* charged on a monthly basis (e.g. on a hire purchase transaction) shown as a yearly *compound interest* rate.

annual report A document required by UK law to be released annually by public companies, describing the company's activities during the previous year. It usually includes the company's balance sheet for the year.

annual value Income that accrues annually from the possession of, say, property or a portfolio of shares. A distinction is normally made between net annual value and gross annual value, the former being the annual income from a possession after expenses of ownership have been deducted, and the latter being the income before expenses have been taken into account.

annul To make void in law, to cancel.

antedate To put on a document, e.g. an invoice, a date that is already past. *See also* **postdate**.

anticipation Broadly, the payment a debt or any other liability before it falls due, usually with a view to saving on interest payments.

anticipatory hedge The policy of an investor who expects to deal in the spot market at a future date and tries to protect against a change in the spot price by hedging now.

Antigua currency: East Caribbean dollar (AGD), divided into 100 cents.

anti-trust laws Legislation in the USA enacted to prevent the formation of *monopolies*. It is similar to the Monopolies and Mergers Act in the UK.

AOB Abbreviation of any other business. AOB normally appears at the end of an agenda and provides an opportunity for the discussion of any matters not already dealt with or arising too late for inclusion on the formal agenda.

AOK (ISO) code Angola – currency: kwanza.

APACS Abbreviation of *Association for Payment Clearing Services.*

APCIMS Abbreviation of Association of Private Client Investment Managers and Stockbrokers.

applicant In international trade, the party, usually an importer, who requests his or her bank to open a letter of credit in the beneficiary's favour.

application and allotment A system whereby a company may issue shares.

It is done by publishing a prospectus, inviting applications from institutions and individuals to buy shares, and then allotting them to those who take up the offer. *See also allotment of shares.*

application for a letter of credit A written request addressed by a buyer/importer to a bank to open a letter of credit.

application of the arrangement (OECD) Term that applies to all *official support* for exports of goods and/or services, or to financial leases, that have repayment terms of two years or more. It also applies to official support in the form of *tied aid.*

appointment In international trade, the action of designating an agent to act on someone's behalf. The appointment can either be formally by deed, in writing, or even verbal.

apportion 1. To share out. The term is normally applied to costs. 2. The allocation (and hence reduction) of a security, such as a eurobond, apportioned to the individual subscriber in an oversubscribed issue.

appreciation The strengthening of a currency (or any other commodity) in response to market demand.

appropriation The act of putting aside (funds) for a special reason. There are three specialist meanings of the term:

1. In the shipping of produce, the appropriation is the document by which the seller identifies to the buyer the relevant unit in the shipment.

2. In company accounting, it is the division of pre-tax profits between corporation tax, company reserves and dividends to shareholders. The term works in the same sense in a partnership.

3. If a *debtor* makes a payment to a *creditor* and does not specify which debt the payment is in settlement of, the creditor may appropriate it to any of the debts outstanding on the debtor's account. This is often known as appropriation of payments.

See also appropriation account.

appropriation account An account that shows net profits (current and carried forward) and how they are split between dividends and reserves.

APR Abbreviation of *annualized percentage rate.*

arb Shortened form of *arbitrage.*

arbitrage (currency arbitrage).

1. Dealing between two (international) financial centres to make a profit (or 'turn') on rates of exchange, resulting from a temporary difference in the exchange rates quoted in the two centres. *See locational arbitrage.*

2. Creating funds in currency X by borrowing in another currency Y and converting it to the currency X in a swap deal.

arbitrage (general) Practice of dealing on two markets almost simultaneously in order to profit from differing *exchange rates.* Arbitrage may take place when dealing in *commodities, bills of exchange* or currencies. It also occurs in situations where prices and returns are fixed and in this sense arbitrage may be contrasted with *speculation* in that there is little risk involved. In the USA, the term is often shortened to arb. *See also reverse arbitrage; soft arbitrage.*

arbitrager (or **arbitrageur**) A person who practises *arbitrage.*

arbitration In disputes arising out of a *contract*, the parties involved may either go to court or appoint someone (an arbitrator) to settle the dispute. The agreement to go to arbitration does not preclude either of the parties later taking legal proceedings if it desires. *See also umpirage.*

arbitration clause Clause in a contract, particularly between an importer and an exporter or an employer and a trade union, that details the procedure to be taken to settle disputes. *See arbitration.*

ARBs Abbreviation of *arbitragers.*

Argentina currency: peso (ARP), divided into 100 centavos.

ariary Madagascar currency unit. 1 ariary = 5 Malagasy francs.

arithmetic mean The simple arithmetical average achieved by adding all the individual numbers together and dividing their total by the number of items being added. Thus, e.g., the arithmetic mean of 8, 12, 19, 23, and 28 is 90 divided by 5 = 18. A disadvantage of the mean is that it is very adversely affected by extreme values and may therefore be unrepresentative. For example, consider the average salary of these people: one person on £5,000,000, one person on £60,000, four people on £40,000, and four people on £20,000. The mean is £5,300,000 divided by 10 = £530,000, giving the impression that nine of them ought to be a lot better off than they actually are!

ARM Abbreviation of adjustable-rate mortgage.

Armenia currency: dram.

ARP   (ISO) code Argentina – currency: peso.

ARR   Abbreviation of *accounting rate of return*.

arrangement   (general) The settlement of any financial matter. More specifically, a deed of arrangement is an agreement between a *debtor* and some or all of his or her *creditors*, reached in order to avoid the debtor's *bankruptcy*. Arrangement may he encountered in various forms: as a letter of licence, deed of inspectorship, *assignment* of property, or a deed of composition. It may take place either before or after a bankruptcy petition has been presented to the courts.

Arrangement   (OECD) In guidelines for officially supported export credits, a "gentlemen's agreement" among its *Participants*. Although not an OECD Act, it is incorporated into European Community law and receives the administrative support of the OECD Secretariat. *See also arrangement on guidelines for officially supported export credits; application of the arrangement*

arrangement fee   A fee charged by a bank for certain services, such as setting up a bridging loan.

arrangement on guidelines for officially supported export credits   The OECD countries coordinate their policies on export credits granted to a foreign buyer of exported goods or services to ensure an orderly credit market and the arrangement seeks to prevent countries from competing to offer the most favourable financing terms for exports. It therefore tries to prevent an export credit favourable financing terms or "subsidy" race. *See also Arrangement; application of the arrangement.*

arrears   Money owed but not yet paid. *See also advance.*

arrestment   Scottish term for *attachment.*

arrival notificaton form (ANF)   A written advice to a consignee that goods have arrived and can be collected.

arrived ship   A vessel that has arrived at the agreed port (either for loading or unloading) and been notified to the person responsible for the cargo.

articled clerk   A kind of apprentice, generally working in one of the professions, such as law or accounting.

artificial currency   A substitute for a physical or real currency, e.g. SDRs (Special Drawing Rights). The ecu (European currency unit) was an artificial currency until it was converted into a real currency.

ASAP   Informal abbreviation of as soon as possible.

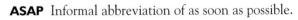

ASB   Abbreviation of *Accounting Standards Board*.

AsDB   Abbreviation of *Asian Development Bank*.

Asian Development Bank (ADB)/(AsDB)   An international bank established in 1966 to facilitate economic growth among developing Asian countries.

Asian option   An option on foreign exchange or commodity prices that additionally pays the difference gained between its strike price and the average price of the underlying asset, calculated over the option's life. It is also called an average-rate option.

asked price   A US term for *offer price*.

asking price   The price at which foreign exchange, foreign bank notes or other securities are offered for sale.

as per advice   A term normally found as a note on a bill of exchange, indicating that the *drawee* has already been notified that the bill has been drawn on him or her.

assay   The testing of a metal or ore to determine the proportion of precious metal it contains. Assay most often applies to metals used in coinage, and to gold and silver. Metals assayed are stamped with a hallmark or an assay mark.

assay master   An official who is responsible for the testing and grading of precious metals.

assented bond   A bond whose holder has agreed to reduce interest payments or to reduce the payment of the principal amount for a rescheduling or other type or reorganization.

assented stock   In a situation where a company is threatened with a take-over, assented stocks or shares are those whose owner is in agreement with the take-over. In these circumstances, there may arise separate markets in assented and non-assented stock. Assented stock may also be stock whose owner is in agreement with a proposed change in the conditions of issue.

assessment   The act of calculating value, such as for a tax assessment.

asset   Something that belongs to an individual or company and which has a value, e.g. buildings, plant, stock, but also *accounts receivable*. There are several types of assets for business purposes, and they are usually classified in terms of their availability for exchange.

asset-backed Describing investments that are related to tangible assets, e.g. property, so that the investment participates in growth that can easily be determined. *See **tangible assets**.*

asset-based financing A loan secured by a company's assets, especially its accounts receivable or its stock.

asset card US term for a ***debit card***.

asset cover A measure of a company's solvency equal to the ratio of its net assets to debt. High asset cover implies that a company is more than marginally solvent.

asset management Broadly, the efficient control and exploitation of a firm's assets. The term is most commonly used to describe the management of any ***fund*** by a fund manager.

asset play Activities of a company, the major part of whose value is based on its assets rather than its operations.

asset stripping The practice, normally frowned upon, whereby a company is bought so that the buyer may sell off its assets for immediate gain.

assets-to-equity ratio The value of assets owned by a company compared to the total of issued capital and reserves.

asset value The total value of the assets of a company.

asset value per share The value of the assets of a company, minus its liabilities, divided by the number of shares.

assignee The gainer of a title or interest that has been transferred by an assignor.

assignment The legal transfer of property, right or obligation from one party to another. Assignment takes place most commonly where a ***contract*** is involved.

assignment in blank The formal assignment of a transferable asset, such as a eurobond. The name of the new holder and the date of the transfer are left in blank.

assignment notice In exchange-traded options, a document usually issued by a clearing house to an option writer stating that an option has been exercised by the holder.

assignment of letter of credit The transfer of the proceeds of a letter of credit (or part of them) to another person (assignee) as advised by the beneficiary to the bank, which promises to pay the proceeds to the assignee before paying the balance to the original beneficiary.

assignor The individual transferring a title or other interest to a third party.

associate A company or individual linked in some way to another, as in, e.g., an associate company.

associate company A company that is partly owned by another, which has a stake of less than 50%.

associate director A director who is a member of the board but lacks full voting powers. The position is normally held by able but comparatively junior managers; it rewards their enthusiasm and reinforces their commitment without giving them real power.

associated operation An operation that is somehow linked to another within a company. Associated operations within a company may, e.g., manufacture similar products or use similar production methods.

association A group of people or companies with a common interest. For example, a trade association is a group of companies operating in the business who come together to provide information and services to each other. Association is also what happens when a company is formed.

Association for Payment Clearing Services (APACS) An organization established in 1985 for managing and controlling the main payment clearing systems and methods of money transmission in the UK.

Association of British Factors (ABF) An organization established in 1977 of representatives of companies whose main business is providing full factoring services.

Association of Futures Brokers and Dealers (AFBD) The professional body governing the activities of the personnel working in the financial futures market within the UK. In 1991 it became part of the *Securities and Futures Authority*.

Association of International Bond Dealers (AIBD) An organization, established in Zurich in 1969, which in 1991 changed its name to the *International Securities Market Association*.

AST Abbreviation of *automated screen trading*.

as-you-like option Also termed a call-or-put option, an option whose form can be changed to another form, at the holder's choice and within a certain time limit.

at A subdivision (1/100) of Laotian kip.

ATA carnet Abbreviation of an *admission temporaire carnet*.

ATA convention International convention that permits commercial travellers to take samples and so on into a country temporarily without paying duty. They use a temporary admission (ATA) carnet for this purpose.

at best Short for the best possible price, an instruction to a broker to buy or sell shares or commodities at the best price available. See *at limit*.

at call Money at call has been borrowed but must be repaid on demand. *See also* **at short notice**.

at limit An instruction to a broker to buy or sell shares or commodities with a limit on the upper and lower prices.

ATM Abbreviation of *automatic telling* (US *teller*) *machine*.

at market An alternative term for the best possible price (*see* **at best**).

ATP The European agreement covering the international carriage of perishable foodstuffs by road.

at par A term that denotes that the price of a financial instrument is equal to its nominal, or face, value. *See also* **parity**.

ATS (ISO) code Austria – currency: schilling. The 1999 legacy conversion rate was 13.7603 to euro. It will fully change to the euro/cent from 2002.

at short notice Describing money that is borrowed for a very short period of time, say 24 or 48 hours, usually at a low **interest** rate. *See also* **at call**.

at sight A note on a bill of exchange indicating that the payment is due on presentation of the bill.

attachment An act of court whereby the court is able to recover money owed by a debtor by ordering a person owing money to the debtor to pay that money direct to the court. *Arrestment* is the equivalent of attachment in Scottish law.

at the highest possible price An instruction to a broker in which the seller does not authorize any maximum or minimum price for the fulfilment of the order. In a limited market, such as a more exotic foreign currency, it will be carried as soon as possible.

at the lowest possible price An instruction to a broker in which the buyer does not authorize any maximum or minimum price for the fulfilment of the order. In a limited market, such as a more exotic foreign currency, it will be carried as soon as possible.

at-the-money Describing an option whose strike price is equal to the price of the underlying instrument.

at the money option An option where the strike price equals the market price of the asset (e.g. in a currency market it will equal spot).

at the opening order On futures and options exchanges, a market when there is a range of prices at the opening of business.

attorney In the UK, someone who is legally authorized to act for another, or a person practising at the bar. In the USA, however, the term is more often used to denote a lawyer.

attractive stock Ordinary shares that promise a good return.

at warehouse Describing *goods* or *commodities* that are waiting at a warehouse either to be bought or delivered to a customer. A price at warehouse (or ex warehouse) does not normally include freight charges. *See also* **futures; spot goods.**

auction A method of selling goods in public. The auctioneer acts as an agent for the seller, offers the goods and normally sells to the highest bidder (for which service the auctioneer charges a *commission*).

auction ("forced sale") Exported goods that have not been taken up by the importer are frequently disposed of by auction to mitigate the exporter's loss and/or to pay for unpaid duties/storage and any other outstanding charges. Also port authorities frequently dispose of unclaimed goods this way.

auction sales A method of selling that is particularly suitable for non-standardized goods and hence popular in commodity markets. They are arranged at specific times.

auction system An order-driven stock exchange system in which brokers and dealers bid for stock using open outcry (or an auction), as on the New York Stock Exchange.

AUD (ISO) code Australia – currency: Australian dollar.

audit The examination of the accounts of a company. It is a legal requirement in the UK that the accounts of all companies over a certain size (in terms of annual turnover) be scrutinized annually by a qualified *auditor*.

auditor A person appointed by a company or other organization to perform an *audit*.

audit trail A system whereby each stage of a transaction is formally recorded.

aurar A subdivision (1/100) of an Icelandic krona.

Australia currency: Australian dollar (AUD), divided into 100 cents.

Austria currency: schilling (ATS) divided into 100 groschen. The 1999 legacy conversion rate was 13.7603 to the euro. It will fully change to the euro/cent from 2002.

authenticate To state that something is true, such as an authorized signature on a certificate as when an *auditor* signs a company's accounts, thereby authenticating them.

authority Broadly, the given power to act in a certain way. Hence, a banker receives an authority from a client to operate the account in a certain way, or an *agent* receives authority to act in such a way on behalf of his or her principal.

authorized capital The amount of capital a company is authorized to raise through the issue of shares, as set down in the company's articles of association.

authorized cheque signatory A director or member of staff who has the authority to sign cheques on behalf of an organization (such as a company or association). Usually the risk of fraud is reduced by requiring two authorized signatures on every cheque.

authorized share capital Alternative term for *authorized capital*.

automated clearing house (ACH) A computer system used by the US Customs Service for making electronic transfer of funds (instead of using cheques or cash) for paying duty and taxes on imported goods.

Automated Pit Trading (APT) A computerized trading system that initially supplemented the open outcry market at the London International Financial Futures Exchange (LIFFE). Its main use was after 1620 hours (when the floor market closed) until 1800 hours (when the exchange closed).

automated screen trading (AST) A system that uses computers to display prices and to deal in securities.

automatic debit transfer A service provided in the UK by Girobank that, for a small charge, allows a business to collect regular sums of money from a large number of customers.

automatic exercise An exchange-traded options mechanism automatically implementing in-the-money options on the final date.

automatic materials handling (AMH) A computerized system designed to move materials and components from one location to another in a factory or warehouse.

automatic (or **automated**) **telling machine (ATM)** A machine that issues cash to customers of a bank or other such financial institution, usually by inserting a *cash card* and using a personal identification number (PIN). It is also called a cash dispenser or, colloquially, a hole in the wall.

aval An unconditional, irrevocable, divisible and assignable guarantee on a bill/note usually on behalf of the drawee/issuer, signed by the guarantor and stating to whom the guarantee is given to pay on the due date.

avalor An internationally recognized bank or government institution acting as a guarantor.

average 1. Damage to a means of transport or its cargo. 2. A single number or value that indicates the general tendency of a collection of numbers or value. The average of *n* values is the sum of the values divided by *n*. It is also called the mean or arithmetic mean.

average adjuster A specialist in dealing with maritime losses and apportioning them among underwriters.

average available earnings The *profit* available for distribution to shareholders.

average balance Sum of the daily balances of a bank account over a period of time divided by the number of days in the period.

average bond A bond issued by a bank or an insurance company guaranteeing that a cargo owner will pay his or her contribution to the general average loss, once it has been determined by the *average adjuster*. It allows the goods to be disposed of in the meantime without having to await the decision (particularly useful for, e.g., perishable or fashionable goods or for cashflow).

average cleared credit balance The average balance on a credit account used to estimate the allowance that can be made against the cost of maintaining the account (before the actual commission charge is known).

average cost pricing The determination of a price in accordance with the average cost of producing a good. The manufacturer makes neither a profit nor a loss.

average deposit The cash deposited by a consignee as a security to cover being able to take up and dispose of his or her goods while waiting for an *average adjuster* to assess the individual contributions. For higher value consignments it is more normal to arrange an average bond in lieu of having to part with the cash and adversely affect the consignee's cashflow.

average due date The average of different due dates for a number of outstanding amounts to be paid, such as for bills of exchange. *See due date*.

average price An alternative term for *target price*.

average-rate option An option on foreign exchange or commodity prices that additionally pays the difference gained between its strike price and the average price of the underlying asset, calculated over the option's life. It is also called an Asian option.

average revenue The total amount of money received divided by the number of units of a product sold.

average term The date in the middle of the normally six monthly repayments of an export credit.

averaging The method of adding holdings of a commodity when its price falls so as to reduce the average purchase price (or vice versa).

aviation broker A broker who arranges everything to do with aircraft from chartering to bookings, freight, insurance, etc.

aviation insurance The insurance of aircraft, air cargo, loss, injury, and damage to life and baggage, etc.

avoirdupois System of weights used in the UK and USA (using, e.g., pounds and ounces), now almost completely replaced by the metric system.

award A judicial order given as payment or compensation, such as damages.

AWB Abbreviation of *air waybill*, a document issued for transport by airfreight.

AWD (ISO) code Abu Dhabi United Arab Emirates – currency: dirham.

AXD (ISO) code Dubai United Arab Emirates – currency: dirham.

axe To stop abruptly or to cut back (normally for financial reasons).

AYD (ISO) code United Arab Emirates (others) – currency: dirham.

Azerbaijan currency: manat.

A

B

back 1. A term used adjectivally to refer to the past. 2. To endorse a bill of exchange or cheque. 3. To lend money to a project to enable it to start or to continue operating.

back date To date a document with a date previous to that on which it was actually signed. Back dating indicates that the provisions of the document become effective on the back date rather than the date on which the document was signed.

back dating In accounting, assigning value to an entry (credit or debit) on a date that is earlier than that on which the entry is actually made.

back duty Also known as back tax, a retrospective tax levied on profits or goods on which no tax was paid at the time.

backed note A receiving note that authorizes a ship's master to take goods on board. It is endorsed by a shipbroker and is proof that freight will be (or has been) paid.

back freight The cost of returning goods, usually incurred where the buyer has refused to pay for them and no alternative payment is otherwise foreseeable. It is usually a very expensive admission of defeat and impossible if the goods are perishable.

back interest An alternative term for *accrued interest*.

back month On financial futures markets, describing those contracts that are being traded for the month that is farthest away in the future.

back tax An alternative term for *back duty*.

backer A person or institution that financially supports projects or operations.

backhander An informal term for a bribe or unofficial payment in cash for a favour or for work done.

backing away The failure of a securities dealer to carry through a deal at the price he or she has quoted. It is usually frowned upon in all markets.

back-to-back credit 1. A new credit opened on an already existing non-transferable letter of credit (the original credit or "prime credit") in favour of another beneficiary, i.e. back-to-back. 2. Two letters of credit that cover a single shipment of goods, involving a middleman. In both cases the exporter is acting not as a supplier (whose identity is often concealed), but as a middle person and the original credit is either not transferable or cannot comply with the ICC's UCPDC rules. He or she will offer the original/prime credit as security for the issue of the second. *See also* **countervailing credit**.

back-to-back loan A type of loan between companies in different countries (and perhaps in different currencies) employing a bank or finance house that uses funding from a third party to provide the loan.

backwardation 1. In a commodity or financial market, the situation where the forward or futures price is less than the spot price. It can arise because of excessive present demand, which is anticipated to fall later. *See also* **contango**, which is the opposite effect. 2. In stock markets, the situation where the highest bid price is higher than the lowest offer price, in theory enabling a purchase from one market maker to be sold to another immediately at a profit.

backward vertical integration Also called upstream vertical integration or simply backward integration, the amalgamation of a company that operates at one stage of production with another that is located farther back in the chain. For example, a manufacturing company may amalgamate with a company that provides its raw materials.

BACS Abbreviation of **Bankers Automated Clearing Services**, a company that processes automated credits, direct debits and standing orders, as well as other types of payments.

bad debt A debt that has not been, and is not expected to be, paid. Invoiced sales may be sold to a *factoring* company to avoid this being a serious problem to a company (especially a new or inexperienced one).

badges of trade Criteria that distinguish between trading and investment. For example, dealings on the commodity market are usually regarded as trade for UK tax purposes, whereas dealings in securities may not be.

bad paper A bill of exchange that is never likely to be honoured.

bad title A claim to property that does not bestow ownership, e.g. by a holder of a bill of exchange who cannot claim to a holder in due course.

BAF Abbreviation of *bunker adjustment factor*.

bag A package of flexible material, ranging from paper and plastic to jute etc. with an opening at the top. It is appropriate for goods such as

B

flour, cement, fertilizer, etc., but is vulnerable to breakage and other damage, such as leakage, sweating, etc.

Bahamas currency: Bahamian dollar (BSD), divided into 100 cents.

Bahrain currency: Bahrain dinar (BHD), divided into 1000 fils.

baht The standard currency unit of Thailand, divided into 100 satang.

bail bond A document that guarantees the amount of bail (i.e. surety money) required for the temporary release of a an accused individual or prisoner, or for a ship.

bailee A person, such as a banker, to whom goods are entrusted for safe keeping. *See bailment.*

bailing out Describing the act of rescuing an individual or company from financial distress.

bailment The act of placing goods into the care of someone else. The person who places the goods is the bailor and must be the rightful owner. The bailee is the person who receives the goods.

bailor A person who leaves goods with somebody (the bailee) for safe keeping. *See bailment.*

baiza A subdivision (1/1000) of the Omani rial.

balance The difference between the total of all the credit entries and all the debit entries on an account.

balance an account To close an account or to calculate its balance, plus interest, accumulated up to the day of such a calculation.

balance carried forward A balance moved forward from one closing accounting period to the next, thereby commencing a new accounting period.

balanced budget A budget where revenues are enough to offset expenditures.

balance due on notice of readiness to ship A method used as a compromise to *cash with order* where a largish sum is involved. The exporter accepts an initial deposit with the buyer's promise to pay the rest once the goods are about to be shipped (in other words at a time when it would be much more difficult for either the seller or the buyer to pull out of the deal).

B

balance of payments A list of all the transactions conducted within a given period of time (usually a year) by one country with all the other countries with which it deals.

balance of trade Also known as the visible balance, the difference between the value of a country's visible imports and visible exports. When the value of visible imports total more than the value of visible exports, the situation is known as an adverse balance of trade. *See also balance of payments* .

balance sheet A statement that shows the financial position of a company in respect of its assets and liabilities at a certain time.

balance ticket An alternative term for *certification of transfer*.

bale A method of packing by tightly wrapping bundles and binding them with cords or hoops. It is appropriate for goods such as cotton, hay, paper, etc. It is also used as a quantitative measure, such as of 500 lb of American cotton. It provides cheap, but limited, protection.

balloon A large irregular part-payment of a loan, made when funds are available. Such an arrangement is termed a balloon loan.

balloon interest A higher rate on securities that have later maturities.

balloon mortgage A mortgage in which a lump sum has to be paid at the end of the mortgage period to pay off the outstanding principal and interest. It is also called a non-amortizing mortgage.

balloon payment The full and final payment payable by the borrower in a lump sum on the maturity date of a loan.

Baltic and International Maritime Council (BIMCO) An organization that represents the interests of its many international shipowning members. It provides a lot of services (such as help in compiling *standard charter parties*) and many advisory services.

Baltic Exchange One of the oldest centres for chartering freight (by sea or air). Located in London, it has more than 700 members who are concerned with freight handling.

Baltic freight index In the US *Journal of Commerce*, a daily listing of price trends for chartering ships to carry freight.

Baltic International Freight Futures Exchange (BIFFEX) A facility for the purchase and sale of freight futures, transferred to *London Futures and Options Exchange* in 1991.

banco Funds held on account by a bank, as opposed to cash.

B

Bangladesh   currency: taka (BDT), divided into 100 poisha.

bani   A subdivision (1/100) of the Romanian leu.

bank   An institution that carries on the business of banking and is so authorized by the central bank (in the UK the Bank of England). *See also* **merchant bank**.

bank bill   A bill of exchange or draft accepted for payment by a bank. It can be used by the drawer or payee as collateral, or it may be sold or discounted. Such bills are very important to some nations' own money markets.

bank bond   A bond that has been issued by a bank, as opposed to a surety or insurance company.

bank charges   (payment of) Because a principal is normally responsible for an agent's costs, the bank charges for a collection are normally the seller's responsibility and for a letter of credit the buyer's responsibility, but this is subject to negotiation.

bank clearing   The system whereby banks settle mutual indebtedness arising from payment transfers between themselves.

bank commission   A charge for special services or for risk coverage added to the interest on bank loans.

bank draft   A cheque written by a bank that may be drawn on either the issuing bank itself or on a third bank. It is also termed a banker's draft.

banker's acceptance   A bill of exchange drawn on and accepted by a bank. With the bank's backing it can qualify as a money-market instrument and qualify for a "finer rate" (in other words the payee obtains a cheaper form of finance).

Bankers Automated Clearing Services Ltd (BACS)   A company established in 1986 whose name is based on its previous title, Bankers Automated Clearing House. It processes automated credits, direct debits and standing orders, as well as other types of payments.

banker's direct guarantee   A system that avoids the imposition of local charges and often permits the insertion of an *English/Scots law clause*, thus enabling the bond or guarantee to be cancelled after its expiry date (some foreign laws do not otherwise allow this).

banker's draft   An alternative name for a *bank draft*.

B

bank facilities guarantee   A guarantee from one bank to another that a loan or any other facility will be repaid. A subsidiary company may need one, for example, where it needs to use local banking facilities abroad.

Bank for International Settlements (BIS) An international bank that acts as agent and trustee for various international organizations. It also acts as an interbank clearing house. The Bank of England is the agent of BIS in London.

bank giro A system for transferring funds between accounts held at different banks, usually by means of international credit transfers.

banking centre A place where a bank is domiciled or represented by a business office.

banking covenant A formal agreement between a bank and a company borrowing from it, defining limits within which the company can act (for example, it may put a ceiling on any borrowing from another source).

Banking Directives Directives of the EU that are aimed at streamlining banking practice across European borders. For example, the Second Directive of 1989 allows banks to operate in any country as long as they are authorized in their own. In 1993 this facility was extended to companies dealing in investment products.

bank payment order An order from a customer to a bank instructing it to make a payment in favour of a third party.

bank rate The official rate of interest charged by the central banks as lender of the last resort. The term has fallen out of use in the UK, to be replaced by *minimum lending rate*.

bankruptcy The state of being unable to pay one's debts, as determined by a court of law.

Barbados currency: dollar (BBD), divided into 100 cents.

bareboat charter A type of ship charter in which the hirer pays all expenses during the charter period.

bargain In Stock Exchange jargon, any deal struck that involves the buying and selling of shares.

barometer A selection of data to depict larger trends, e.g. the FTSE 100 or the currency exchange index.

barratry The fraud or gross negligence of a ship's master or crew to the detriment of its owners or users.

B

barrel A cylindrical container ordinarily bulging out in the middle, conventionally made of wood with metal hoops around them, but which can be made of many other materials including metal and plastic. It is also used as a measure of capacity, often varying from 30 to 40 gallons. It is appropriate for liquid or fatty/oily goods such as beer, lard, petroleum, etc. It is subject to leakage and to rust, if made of ferrous metal.

barrier to entry A set of economic and other conditions that make it difficult to set up a business, i.e. to enter the market.

barter The simple exchange of one set of goods for another with no money changing hands (*see countertrade*).

base currency Every exchange rate consists of a quoted currency against a base, or reference currency. For example, if the euro is quoted at 1.1052 - 1.1096 to the US dollar the US dollar is the base currency.

base rate The rate of interest charged by UK banks on loans to their prime corporate customers. It represents the minimum amount of interest a bank charges on a loan and higher quotations reflect any increased current market pressures and/or the risk involved in the loan.

basis The difference between the spot price and a futures contract price.

basis point A unit used to measure the rate of change of investment payments for bonds or notes. Each basis point is equal to 0.01%, e.g. 25 basis points is 0.25%.

basis risk The risk that the price of a derivative instrument will vary from that of the underlying commodity.

basket of currencies A group of currencies against which the value of some other currency is measured.

basket pegger A country that uses the average of a group of foreign currencies (rather than a single currency) to fix its exchange rate.

batch processing In finance, the sending of large numbers of payment messages in *transaction envelopes*.

BBD (ISO) code Barbados – currency: dollar.

BC Abbreviation of *buyer credit* (an ECGD-supported finance facility).

BCF (ISO) code Benin – currency: CFA franc.

BDT (ISO) code Bangladesh – currency: taka.

B

b/e Abbreviation of *bill of exchange* (or draft).

BEAC Abbreviation of Banques des Etats de l' Afrique Centrale – the Central bank for many French-speaking equatorial African countries such as Cameroon, Central African Republic, Chad, etc.

bear A pessimistic financial exchange dealer or analyst who believes that prices will go down.

bear call spread An options market tactic to arrange a combination of calls and puts at different strike prices in order to benefit as the price of a security or commodity' falls. It involves the sale of a call option with a low strike price and the purchase of one with a high strike price. *See also **bull call spread** .*

bear closing A situation that occurs when a dealer sells a commodity that he or she does not own and then buys it back, at a lower price, thus making a profit or reducing his or her loss.

bearer bill Also called a bearer note, a bill of exchange, cheque or other negotiable instrument that is payable to the bearer (or is endorsed in blank).

bearer bond A bond payable to the bearer rather than to a specific, named individual. It usually has detachable coupons that are sent to the issuer for regular interest payments.

bearer note *See bearer bill.*

bearer securities Securities that are payable to the bearer and are thus easily transferable.

bearer scrip A temporary document that acknowledges acceptance of an offer form and money for a new issue, which is exchanged for a bearer bond when the bond is available (or when all instalments have been paid).

bearer stocks Like bearer bonds, securities that are payable to the bearer, not to a named holder.

bear market A lengthy period of falling prices, usually resulting from a pessimistic economic outlook.

bear put spread An options market tactic to arrange a combination of calls and puts at different strike prices in order to benefit as the price of a security or commodity falls. Involves the purchase of a put option with a high strike price and the sale of one with a low strike price. *See also **bull put spread**.*

B

bear spread A type of options trade which takes a view that prices are likely to fall.

beenz A global e-currency, facilitating cost-effective real-time payments on the Internet that will be linked with mondex in the future.

BEF (ISO) code Belgium – currency: Belgian franc. The 1999 legacy conversion rate was 40.3399 to the euro. It will fully change to the euro/cent from 2002.

beggar-my-neighbour A policy of self-aggrandisement at the expense of competitors, especially by nations. It is outlawed by the International Monetary Fund (IMF).

Belarus (also known as Belorussia, Byelorussia) currency: rouble, divided into 100 kopecks.

Belgium currency: Belgian franc (BEF), divided into 100 centimes. The 1999 legacy conversion rate was 40.3399 the euro. It will fully change to the euro/cent from 2002.

Belize currency: dollar (BZD), divided into 100 cents.

below par A market price that has fallen below the nominal value at which the share was issued or below the spot rate for a currency etc.

beneficiary 1. The party, usually an exporter, in whose favour a letter of credit is issued. 2. A person who gains money or property from some financial transaction, such as an insurance policy.

Benin currency: CFA franc (BCF); there is no subdivision.

bequest The disposition of assets according to the terms of a will.

Bermuda currency: Bermudan dollar (BMD), divided into 100 cents.

Berne Union Short form of *International Union of Credit and Investment Insurers* (because it is domiciled in Berne under the Swiss Civil Code). It is an international forum for discipline and consultation in export credit and investment insurance.

berth A ship's designated place at a wharf or the mooring of a ship in its berth. It also refers to the space needed for a ship to swing at anchor.

best execution rule A requirement that a dealer must obtain the lowest available price when buying for a client and the highest possible price when selling.

B

best price An order to buy or sell something at the best price available at the time. In a limited market, such as a more exotic foreign currency, it will be carried as soon as possible.

best to deliver   The bond or gilt issue matching the deliverable criteria of a futures contract that costs least to purchase in the cash market.

beta   1. A measure of the relative volatility of a security's price. A balanced portfolio is likely to have a factor of about 1. One with only half the movement of the market as a whole will have a factor of 0.5, while conversely one with double the degree of change will have a factor of 2, and so on. 2. A Stock Exchange classification for second-line shares, as opposed to the less numerous highly-capitalized alpha (first-line) or more numerous delta (third-line) shares.

BGL   (ISO) code Bulgaria – currency: Bulgarian lev.

BHD   (ISO) code Bahrain – currency: Bahrain dinar.

Bhutan   currency: ngultrum.

bid   An offer to buy something (e.g. a currency) at a certain price. A seller may make a certain offer and a prospective buyer may make a bid. The bid cancels out the offer.

bid bond   A bond required from a company tendering for a contract to assure the prospective buyer that it will comply with the terms of the tender should it be accepted.

bidding ring   A group of stock market or other dealers who act in concert to drive prices up or down. The practice is illegal.

bid-offer spread   The difference between the *bid price* and the *offer price* offered by a *market maker*.

bid price   The price a market maker is prepared to buy at (e.g. for a currency).

BIF   (ISO) code Burundi – currency: Burundi franc.

BIFA   Abbreviation of British International Freight Association.

BIFFEX   Abbreviation of *Baltic International Freight Futures Exchange*.

Big Bang   The popular term for the deregulation of the London Stock Exchange on 27 October 1986. Among the changes implemented were the admission of foreign institutions as members of the exchange, the abandonment of rigid distinctions between stockbrokers, jobbers and bankers, and the abolition of fixed commissions.

Big Mac index   The *Economist's* index as to whether currencies are at their

B

correct levels on a purchasing-power parity basis. The Big Mac PPP is the exchange rate at which hamburgers would cost the same in the USA as in other countries. Intended light-heartedly, it is taken more seriously in some circles as having some genuine guidance value.

bilateral clearing agreement A trading agreement between two countries, neither of which has a hard currency, in which transactions are entered in clearing units, instead of a fixed currency. It is also called a bilateral clearing arrangement.

bilateral clearing arrangement Another name for *bilateral clearing agreement.*

bilateral deal An alternative term for a *countertrade* agreement.

bilateralism/bilateral trade Trade restricted to that between two countries.

bill 1. A list of charges to be paid on goods or services. In this sense the usual US term is check. 2. A document, issued by a bank, promising to pay someone a certain amount of money. It is in this sense that the US meaning of the term is a banknote. 3. A document describing goods, most often used in dealings with customs. 4. Short for *bill of exchange.*

bill for collection A bill of exchange presented to a bank for collection (and not for discounting).

bill guarantee A signed commitment to pay a bill of exchange should the specified signatory not do so.

bill holdings A collection of bills of exchange deposited with a bank.

billing cycle (or invoicing cycle) The posting of bills/invoices or statements at regular intervals during a period of e.g. a month to even out the administrative work involved.

bill of entry A shipper's detailed statement of the type and value of goods submitted through customs.

bill of exchange A document indicating that one party (the drawee, e.g. an importer) agrees to pay a certain sum of money on demand or on a specified date, to the drawer (e.g. an exporter). A familiar bill of exchange is a cheque.

bill of imprest An order that entitles its bearer to have money paid in advance.

B

bill of lading A document signed by the captain of a ship or his deputy detailing the transfer of goods from a (foreign) supplier to a buyer at a prescribed port of destination. It may be used as a document of title.

bill of sale A document certificating the transfer of goods (but not real estate) to another person. Goods transferred in this way may not become the property of the receiving party but may be redeemed when the bill is paid.

bill of sight A document passed to a customs inspector by an importer who is unable to describe in detail the imported goods. When the goods are landed a full description must be given, a process known as perfecting the sight.

bill portfolio A collection of bills of exchange deposited with a bank.

bill rate The rate at which a bill of exchange is discounted. *See* **discount**.

bill renewal A method of prolonging the validity of a bill of exchange by postponing the expiry date.

bills in a set Traditionally in international trade bills of exchange are made out in triplicate and sent to the drawee/importer separately to prevent loss. These copies are known as bills in a set. (This practice is gradually disappearing as more and more are being sent electronically.)

bills payable Bills of exchange that are held and must be paid at some future date.

bills receivable Bills of exchange that are held and payment is due to be received at some future date.

BIMCO Abbreviation of *Baltic and International Maritime Council*.

BIP Abbreviation of the ECGD's *bond insurance policy* covering contract bonds and guarantees.

birr The standard currency unit of Eritrea and Ethiopia, divided into 100 cents.

BIS Abbreviation of *Bank for International Settlements*.

B/L Abbreviation of *bill of lading*.

b/l Abbreviation of *bill of lading*.

black 1.To forbid or boycott trade in certain goods or with certain trading partners. 2. An account that is said to be in the black is in credit. If it is not in credit it is in the red.

blacklist A list of companies, products or people that are considered to be undesirable and so to be avoided.

B

blacklist certificate In a sense the complete opposite of a certificate of origin in that the exporter is required to certify that the goods do not originate from a specified country. Many Arab importers have asked for a blacklist certificate in the past, specifying that the goods are not of Israeli origin, nor have passed through any agency originating in/ specifically related to Israel.

black market A wholly illegal market; one that is illicit and uncontrolled. Black markets deal in scarce or stolen goods, and frequently come into existence in times of war because the goods are rationed or because the market is exceptionally high – in which case counterfeit or imitation goods often appear. Trading is often by barter.

Black-Scholes model A mathematical options-pricing model devised to measure whether options contracts are adequately valued. The model takes into account many factors such as level of interest rates, volatility, price, and the time remaining before the option expires.

blank In general, any form that has not been filled in or not filled in completely, such as a blank draft.

blank agreement An agreement that covers many, if not all, items concerning one party's relationship with another

blank bill/draft A bill of exchange/draft transferred by the drawer without all the details having been filled in (the drawer will still be liable having left the recipient thereby free to fill it in as he or she wishes).

blank cheque 1. A cheque transferred by the drawer without all the details having been filled in (the drawer will still be liable having left the recipient thereby free to fill it in as he or she wishes). 2. Colloquially, to give someone a blank cheque describes the placing of considerable trust in another party.

blank endorsement A bill of exchange endorsed (i.e. signed on the back) leaving the (any) name of the transferee to be filled in later.

blanket assignment The ceding (assignment) of all present and future claims of a debtor on third parties.

blanket credit line A fixed amount or limit of credit set up for a borrower. It is the amount of outstanding credit that may not be exceeded at any time. Such lines are usually set up for companies or countries.

blank rate A fixed charge that covers a series of transactions or services.

B

blank transfer A transfer form that is left blank as regards the name of the transferee, so that in the case of any security the lender will have the right to complete it and sell the security should the borrower default on the loan.

blended rate The situation in which a lender, to avoid continuing an old loan at an old low rate, offers the borrower the chance to renew it at a rate somewhere between the old and the current market rate.

block discounting A method of finance to ease a supplier's cashflow problems. A factor or other similar type of finance house buys blocks of invoices (i.e. unpaid debts) from a supplier and pays for a large proportion of them in advance. As the block becomes due the factor settles any outstanding balance after it has deducted its charges.

blocked account A bank account that becomes subject to restrictions, especially those imposed by governments.

blocked currency A currency that may not be removed from a country, sometimes for political reasons.

blocked period A period during which certain securities are not placed at the owner's free disposal, such as those that are held as collateral for a loan.

B/L tonne Short for bill of lading tonne. It is either 1000 kilgrammes or 1 cubic metre, whichever works out to be the greater weight/ measurement. It is alternatively called a *freight tonne*.

blue month The month with the greatest trading activity in products such as *futures* and *options*.

BMD (ISO) code Bermuda – currency: Bermudan dollar.

BND (ISO) code Brunei – currency: Brunei dollar.

board 1. Goods loaded onto a ship or aircraft. 2. A group of people who run a company, society or trust, such as a board of directors.

Board of Trade A UK committee whose main responsibilities included commercial relations with other countries, supervision of shipping, publication of statistics about UK industry, and acting as a go-between for the government with UK industry. In 1972 it was incorporated into the new *Department of Trade and Industry*.

bogus Fake or counterfeit.

bolivar The standard currency unit of Venezuela, divided into 100 centimos.

B

Bolivia currency: boliviano (BOP), divided into 100 centavos.

boliviano The standard currency unit of Bolivia, divided into 100 centavos.

bona fide Latin for in good faith. It usually appears in reference to contracts, especially contracts of insurance. All parties to a contract are expected to reveal all information relevant to the contract in hand, i.e. they are expected to contract in good faith. The term is also used simply to mean honest or trustworthy.

bona vacantia Describing any property that has no known legal owner and no obvious claimant, such as property that remains in the hands of a liquidator after creditors have been paid.

bond 1. A promise to pay in the event of a specified situation happening. For example, a buyer may insist on a *performance bond* to ensure that a contractor performs a contract properly, in which case it will normally be issued by a bank or an insurance company to guarantee compensation in the event of failure. It helps the contractor's cashflow because it will normally be better off paying a small percentage as a fee for the bond than incurring a very heavy overdraft or lose potential investment interest at least. 2. If goods are imported (or need to be stored during maturity, such as whisky) and import duty is not paid immediately, the goods are placed in a bonded warehouse (i.e. they are held in bond) until all customs formalities are completed. 3. A security issued at a fixed rate by central government, local authorities or occasionally private companies. In this case it is essentially a contract to repay money borrowed, and as such represents a debt. Normally bonds are issued in series with the same conditions of repayment and denominations. It is also known as a fixed-interest security.

bond discount The amount by which the face value of a bond exceeds its market price. Outstanding bonds with fixed coupons go to discounts when market interest rates rise. Discounts are also caused when supply exceeds demand and when a bond's credit rating is reduced. When opposite conditions exist and market price is higher than face value, the difference is termed a bond premium.

bonded Held in *bond*.

bonded stores Stores to be used on board ship and held in bond (with no duty paid on them).

bonded warehouse A warehouse for goods on which excise duty need not be paid until the goods are removed.

B

bond equivalent yield The discounted yield on a bond reformulated as the equivalent it would receive as interest. In the UK it is worked out as

$$\frac{\text{Discount}}{\text{Purchase price}} \quad x \quad \frac{365}{\text{No. of days to maturity}}$$

See also **money market yield.**

bond insurance policy (BIP) ECGD cover for all bonds that exporters are required to provide in connection with an export contract, except for tender bonds (which can be covered separately).

bond note A document indicating that imported goods held in bond may be released, because all import formalities have been completed.

bond option An option to purchase or sell a bond.

bond premium The amount by which the market price of a bond exceeds its face value. A premium may also arise when a bond is redeemed before maturity and the holder is compensated for any lost interest.

bonus An additional payment.

boodle An informal term for money obtained through illegal dealings, often in the form of a **bribe.**

book In business the books most frequently referred to are the books of *account* in which business transactions are recorded. Books of account are normally held to be legal documents.

book debt A debt recorded in an account book.

booking centre A US term for a financial organization with headquarters overseas. Transactions recorded there can take advantage of any lower tax rates.

book-keeping The practice of keeping records of financial transactions, and analysing them if required. It may be done manually or with the aid of a computer program.

book loss A loss that has not yet been realized, i.e. the underlying security(ies) has not yet been sold.

book profit A profit that has not yet been realized, i.e. the underlying security(ies) has not yet been sold.

book runner A bank or other financial institution that is responsible for the documentation and management of an issue of a security or syndicated loan.

B

book value The monetary value of a balance sheet asset or group of assets.

boom A long pole for carrying.

boom fork-lift truck A fork-lift truck that is appropriate for carrying rolls of goods, such as carpets, paper, etc. using a boom in the centre of the roll.

BOOT Abbreviation of *build-own-operate-transfer* scheme.

BOP (ISO) code Bolivia – currency: boliviano.

borrower's option An option that fixes the maximum interest rate payable.

borrowing A term most widely used in the sense of accepting money that is not one's own on the understanding that it will be repaid, usually with interest, at a later date.

borrowing against bill pledging The acceptance of securities by a bank or other financial institution for a limited period with the depositor, or third party, agreeing to repurchase them after a stipulated period. Also, more specifically, a type of closing finance practised by banks in some countries as window dressing to keep within required liquidity ratios.

borrowing power of securities The relative worth of different types of securities to be used as *collateral* in lending.

BOT Abbreviation for bought or *balance of trade*.

BOTB Abbreviation of *British Overseas Trade Board*.

Botswana currency: pula (BWP), divided into 100 thebe.

bottom Generally referring to the lowest point of something. In shipping, however, the term refers to a ship and bottomry is anything to do with shipping.

bottom line The last line of an account, showing either profit or loss. In this sense the phrase has come to mean the "brutal truth" in general usage.

bottoming out An informal term for a very sudden and serious fall in market prices.

bottomry bond A bond used to raise money by the master of a ship, who uses the ship and its cargo as security.

B

bought ledger An account book in which a business records purchases and is, by extension, the credit-control department of an organization.

bounce 1. When a cheque is not honoured by the paying banker it is said to bounce because it is passed back to the collecting banker. This may happen for several reasons, but the most common is that there are not enough funds in the account to cover the cheque. A cheque that bounces may be popularly called a rubber cheque. 2. A sudden sharp rise in the value of a market item that has previously been performing badly.

boundary condition A stipulation of the maximum or minimum price or some other limit to the price of an option.

bounty A government *subsidy* given to aid particular industries. It may be in the form of tax concessions or a cash handout.

box A package customarily with six flat, not necessarily equal rectangular sides and of firm material such as wood or cardboard. A wooden box may also be called a crate. It is appropriate for holding solid goods, but is now less often used because of increasing cost. Box is also a popular name for any container.

box spread A combination of a time call spread and a time put spread. Both spreads have identical maturity dates on their long and short positions. For time constraints *see also* **calendar spread; time spread**.

boycott A refusal to trade with a certain company or nation or in certain goods.

B/P Abbreviation of *bills payable*.

B/R Abbreviation of *bills receivable*.

branch A part of a business, such as a bank or a shop, that functions apart from, but under the overall control of, the central organization.

branch clearing A system in which cheque collection from branch banks is organized by a department in the bank's head office.

branch credit Funds deposited for a customer of another branch of the same bank.

brand To put a name (the brand name) on something or to design and package a product so that it is easily recognizable by a consumer. A brand name can be protected by law against misuse by competitors hoping to benefit from the reputation associated with a particular branded product.

branded goods Goods that are packaged by the manufacturer with the brand name clearly visible. Branded goods may often be sold at a higher

B

price than others because of the selling power of the name.

brand leader A brand of a certain type of goods that has the largest share of the market. A brand leader may often be seen as a company's most valuable asset.

brand loyalty A marketing concept by which consumers continually purchase certain goods which they identify by brand name (and associate with quality and value for money).

brand value A monetary value assigned to a company's brand name, classified as an intangible asset.

Brazil currency: real (BRC), divided into centavos.

BRC (ISO) code Brazil – currency: real.

breach of contract The failure of one party to a contract to act according to its terms, for which the other party may sue.

breach of government undertakings insurance Insurance cover is provided by many export credit agencies, including the ECGD, against breach of undertakings (generally of a political or administrative rather than commercial nature) given by host national, local and provincial governments to overseas enterprises or investors. This, like the ECGD's cover, is usually provided on a case-by-case basis.

breach of warranty of authority The action of an agent who exceeds his or her authority and is thereby liable (and not the principal).

breadth of the market A measure of a commodity's share of/turnover in a specific market.

break When prices have been rising steadily over a period, a break is a sudden and substantial drop in prices.

breakage Although breakage is ordinarily included in cargo insurance it is normally excluded if the commodity is very fragile, such as china or glass.

break-bulk cargo A cargo stowed loose in a ship's hold and not in a container(s).

break even To cover one's costs, making neither a profit or loss.

break-even chart A graph showing the relationship between total fixed costs, variable costs and revenues for various volumes of output.

break-even point The point at which fixed and variable costs are exactly covered by sales revenue. At greater volumes of output an operation would normally expect to make a profit.

break-forward On the currency market a combination of a currency option contract and a forward-exchange contract that can be broken at a pre-set fixed rate of exchange if exchange rates move in favour of the buyer.

breaking an account Closing an account and transferring the balance to another one.

breakout What happens when a commodity price breaks a previously fixed, or at least stable, pattern.

break-up value The value of any stocks of goods or other assets if sold off individually rather than dealt with collectively.

Bretton Woods Agreement An international agreement between the USA, Canada and the UK formulated at a conference held at Bretton Woods, New Hampshire, in 1944. It defined a new system of international monetary control that resulted in the setting up of the International Monetary Fund (IMF) and the International Bank for Reconstruction and Development. The exchange rate of the US dollar was fixed in terms of gold, with all other currencies being fixed in terms of the US dollar.

bribe An illicit payment made by one person to another in order to gain rights or privileges that the recipient would not normally be entitled to. Often offering or accepting a bribe is a criminal offence.

bridge financing Any form of short-term funding in anticipation of the arrival of funds, such as to cover seasonal sales peaks or the period between seeding and harvesting for farmers etc.

bridging loan Also called bridging advance, *see bridge financing*.

British Export Houses Association An organization formed by export houses in the UK for the provision of free advice to exporters seeking such services.

British Overseas Trade Board (BOTB) An organization that arranges trade missions, fairs, guides and interpreters, export intelligence, some subsidies, etc. for British exporters.

British Venture Capital Association (BVCA) A trade association of companies that deal in venture capital.

broken date A non-standard date in a forward contracts or option transaction, e.g. 23 days.

B

broken stowage Wasted space of a container or of a ship's hold resulting from not being able to fit awkwardly shaped cargo in snugly.

broker An independent intermediary between a buyer and a seller for a commission.

brokerage A payment made to a *broker* for services rendered. It is also known as a broker's *commission*.

broker-dealer A firm that acts in the dual capacity of commodity dealer for its clientele and as dealer for its own account.

broker's cover note A *cover note* issued by an insurance agent specializing in cargo/marine insurance.

broker-trader On the London International Financial Futures Exchange a firm that acts as both broker and trader for its own account. It is similar to a *broker-dealer*.

Brunei currency: Brunei dollar (BND), divided into 100 cents.

BSD (ISO) code Bahamas – currency: Bahamian dollar.

bubble An industry or trend with no substance in it. A bubble usually bursts with more or less disastrous consequences for those involved.

bubble company A company formed with no real business to undertake.

bucket shop In finance, a popular phrase describing brokers of any commodity who are not recognized as members of any exchange.

budget A plan that details expected future income and outgoings, normally over a time span of a year. It is also the sum of money set aside for a given activity or project.

buffer stock 1. In manufacturing industries, a stock of raw materials held as an insurance against shortages or sudden price rises. 2. On the commodity markets, buffer stocks are held for release at certain strategic times in order to stabilize prices and markets.

building society An institution in the UK that accepts deposits upon which it pays varying rates of interest and lends money, originally only in the form of a mortgage.

build-own-operate-transfer (BOOT) scheme. A more specific form of project financing supported by the ECGD where the financing is expected to be repaid from tolls, or other such charges, imposed upon subsequent users. *See also* **turnkey project**.

B

built-in Something that is planned or accounted for at the outset.

BUK (ISO) code Myanmar (formerly Burma) – currency: kyat.

Bulgaria currency: Bulgarian lev (BGL), divided into 100 stotinki.

bulge A sharply rapid price advance.

bulk cargo Cargo that is not bagged or crated (termed unbound cargo) before being loaded aboard ship. It can be measured only in terms of volume or weight.

bulk licence An export licence issued to bulk suppliers when only a specified maximum is allowed over a given period.

bulk unitization The ability to consolidate or group multiple units into a single load for transportation.

bull An exchange dealer or analyst who believes that prices or investment values will increase. On this conviction the dealer buys now and profits by selling later at a higher price.

bull call spread An options market tactic to arrange a combination of calls and puts at different strike prices in order to benefit as the price of a security or commodity rises. It involves the purchase of a call option with a low strike price and the sale of one with a high strike price. *See also bear call spread* .

bullet 1. The final payment of a loan consisting of the whole of the principal (previous payments being of interest only). 2. A security that pays a guaranteed (fixed) interest at a specific date.

bullet loan A loan in which all early payments are of interest only; the final payment (bullet) includes the principal.

bullish Describing a market or person with the qualities of a *bull*.

bull market A market in which rises in commodity prices over several months or more have been accompanied by high levels of business.

bull position The position of an investor whose purchases exceed his or her sales and therefore who stands to gain in a rising or *bull market*.

bull put spread An options market tactic to arrange a combination of calls and puts at different strike prices in order to benefit as the price of a security or commodity rises. It involves the sale of a put option with a high strike price and the purchase of one with a low strike price. *See also bear put spread* .

B

bull spread A type of options trade which takes a view that prices are likely to rise.

bunching The practice of combining many small transactions at the same time in an exchange. This can save a little of the cost for the individual clientele.

bunker adjustment factor (BAF) A surcharge imposed by a shipowner to cover rising fuel costs. It is alternatively known as *fuel surcharge adjustment factor*.

buoy dues Dues claimed by Trinity House from shipowners when using ports where there are buoys.

bureau An office that specializes in a certain form of business, e.g. advice or advertising for a *commission*.

bureau de change An office at which currencies may be exchanged on payment of a *commission*. Some bureaux offer additional services, such as the encashment of travellers' cheques.

burgernomics The *Economist's* Big Mac index as to whether currencies are at their correct levels on a purchasing-power parity basis. The Big Mac PPP is the exchange rate at which hamburgers would cost the same in the USA as in other countries. Intended light-heartedly, it is taken more seriously in some circles as having some genuine guidance value.

Burkino Faso (formerly Upper Volta) – currency: CFA franc (HVF); there is no subdivision.

Burundi currency: Burundi franc (BIF), divided into 100 centimes.

business account A bank account opened in the name of a business.

business adviser A professional person who provides business customers with advice and information about financial services.

business credit card A credit card whose payments are charged to the account of a company, not of a private individual.

business cycle The repetitive economic periods of expansion or recovery and contraction or recession. It can affect cashflow and profitability. Fluctuations in inflation can, in turn, affect investments.

business day The times between which most businesses operate (e.g. 9.00 am to 5.00 pm); weekends and official national holidays are not counted.

B

business development loan A loan made for buying fixed assets such as plant and premises.

business information report A detailed report on a specified business by a credit agency for the benefit of its client.

business segment Either a separate part of commerce or any provider of goods and services forming a significant section of an industry.

bust Informal term for bankrupt.

busted bond A bond whose issuer has defaulted on the loan raised to finance the issue. Valueless except as collectors' items, busted bonds are also called old bonds.

bust-up take-over A US term for *asset stripping*.

butterfly spread A combination of a bull and bear spread, either put or call, used as a anti-volatility strategy. The idea is that it should prove profitable provided no dramatic price movements happen in the market(s).

buy To obtain goods in return for money. It can be synonymous with a bargain.

buy American restrictions (BARs) Various restrictions on US companies purchasing foreign goods and services, arising from the Buy American Acts of 1933 and 1988.

buy-back An agreement to purchase products that will eventually be produced by the capital equipment supplied under an export sales agreement. For example, it could be an agreement to buy cars from a factory that the exporter has constructed, thereby assuring the buyer an initial order.

buyer credit (BC) Situation in which a bank lends money directly to an importer so that he can pay the exporter on cash terms (occasionally, alternatively, with recourse) and then repay the bank in instalments. The importer is expected to pay an initial amount of up to 20% of the price and the remaining bank loan is guaranteed by the Export Credits Guarantee Department (ECGD) or any other competitive credit insurance agency.

buyer risk Also known as *purchaser risk*. Serious buyer risks for which the ECGD provides cover to exporters include the insolvency of their buyers, and of any surety, where applicable; and their buyers' (and surety's, again where applicable) failure to pay within six months of the

B

due date; and also the buyers' failure to meet their contractual obligations.

buyer's market A market in which there are too many sellers and not enough buyers, so that buyers are in a position to influence prices or conditions of purchase.

buyers over On the Stock Exchange, a condition in which there are more buyers than sellers. The opposite is sellers over.

buy forward To buy for delivery at a later date. In essence buying forward is a gamble on the current price in the hope that cost of the the item in question rises in the future and can then be sold at a profit. *See also selling short.*

buy in 1. On the options market it is a hedge whereby the writer of the option buys a matching option (the only difference being in the premiums). The second thereby offsets the first, and the profit or loss is restricted to the difference between the premiums. 2. On the Stock Exchange any transaction in which a trader is unable to deliver the shares on time and so has to seek them from another source.

buying price The price at which a market maker is prepared to buy (e.g. a currency).

buy on close Practice of buying contracts on a financial futures market at a price within the closing range. *See also **buy on opening**.*

buy on opening Practice of buying contracts on a financial futures market at a price within the opening range. *See also **buy on close**.*

buy on the bad news Policy of buying a currency or security after hearing any bad news about it in the expectation that its price will fall as a result. Such a technique can indeed be quite profitable if the bad news proves to be only temporary.

buy order An order to buy a specified security at market or another stipulated price.

buyout The purchase of an entire company.

BVCA Abbreviation of *British Venture Capital Association*.

BWP (ISO) code Botswana – currency: pula.

by transfer The transfer of money without using cash. Cashless transactions are becoming increasingly common, particularly in retailing and tourism.

BZD (ISO) code Belize – currency: dollar.

C

CABAF Abbreviation of *currency and bunker adjustment factor*.

cable Dealers' slang for the sterling/US dollar spot rate.

cabotage The reservation of internal or coastal traffic to national flag carriers. In such circumstances a foreign road traffic haulier may be allowed to pick up goods only for a foreign destination, and not be allowed to carry any internal traffic.

CACM Abbreviation of *Central American Common Market*.

CAD (ISO) code Canada – currency: Canadian dollar.

CAD Abbreviation for *cash against documents*.

CAF Abbreviation of *currency adjustment factor*.

calendar spread The buying and selling of similar options having the same strike prices but maturing at different times to try to make a profit should the market price rise. Also known as a horizontal spread or time spread.

call An option to buy.

callability Feature of a bond that allows the issuer to pay it off before it matures.

callable bond A bond that may be called for payment before its *maturity date*.

callable fixture A short-term (3-week to 3-month) loan made by a bank to a discount house. The bank thus has a secure deposit that earns interest and the discount house has the use of funds for buying short-term bills or bonds. The loan is repayable on demand. *See* **call money**.

call date When buying a bond, it is important to know if and when it has a call date. Where this has been authorized in the original issue the bond can be redeemed before its maturity, at par or at a small premium to par, and hence thereafter might no longer earn any further interest.

called-up capital A sum of money that has been paid to a company by its shareholders.

call loans Credits, usually given to brokers, dealers or investment bankers repayable on demand.

C

call money A type of loan made by a bank that must be repaid on demand. It is also known as money at call.

call option An option to buy. *See also* **currency option**.

call premium The money that a buyer of a call option has to pay to the seller for the right to buy at a specified price by a specified date or the amount over par that an issuer has to pay to redeem a security early.

call provision A condition attached to a **bond** by which the issuer is entitled to redeem it at a fixed price after a specified period of time.

call-up An alternative term for *call*, especially with respect to partly-paid shares.

Calvo clause A contract clause regarding foreign investment. It states that in the event of a dispute the parties agree to abide by the law of the foreign country.

Cambodia currency: riel.

Cameroon currency: CFA franc (CMF); there is no subdivision.

Canada currency: Canadian dollar (CAD), divided into 100 cents.

cancellation 1. The voiding of an agreement, either in due course (such as the discharge of a bill of exchange or the payment of a cheque) or by defacement or mutilation of a document. 2. The offsetting or nullification of an accounting entry.

C & F Obsolete abbreviation of *cost and freight*.

C & I terms Abbreviation of cost and insurance terms. It is NOT an *incoterm*, but is nevertheless used in some contracts, such as where any country with an over-zealous protectionist attitude demands that insurance must be handled by one of its own national companies. Like normal incoterms the risk still passes from the seller to the buyer once the goods have passed over the ship's rail at the port of loading.

CAP Abbreviation of *Common Agricultural Policy*.

cap An option that fixes a maximum interest rate payable for a series of interest periods, often used as a hedge. For example, it will dictate the highest level interest rate that can be paid on a floating-rate note. Thus the note might have a cap of 7%, meaning that its yield is not to exceed that 7% even if the general level of interest rates goes much higher than that. *See also* **collar; hedging**.

C

cap and collar loan A loan with fixed upper and lower limits of a variable interest rate.

capacity A measurement of a company's ability to produce goods or services.

capacity tonne-mile A costing measurement used in the carriage of goods, e.g. a 10-tonne capacity vehicle journeying 1000 miles has used 10,000 capacity tonne-miles.

capacity utilization rate The proportion of a firm's, industry's or a whole country's productive capacity actually being used. While full capacity is possible in theory, in practice the reality is likely to be quite a bit less than that, because of maintenance problems, holidays, sickness, etc. The capacity utilization rate is expressed as a percentage of the potential full capacity.

Cape Verde Islands currency: Cape Verde escudo (CVE), divided into 100 centavos.

capital A vague term that most often requires qualification. Unqualified it usually refers to the resources of an organization or person (e.g. equipment, skill, cash).

capital account A part of the *balance of payments* that refers to international movements of capital, including intergovernmental loans.

capital adequacy A legal requirement that a financial institution (such as a bank) should have enough capital to meet all its obligations and fund the services it offers.

capital allowances Amounts deducted from a company's profits before tax is calculated to take into account *depreciation* of capital assets (such as vehicles, plant and machinery, and industrial buildings).

capital asset A long-term asset/fixed asset.

capital budget The forward planning of future capital movement, involving larger sums of money and longer timescales than a *cash budget*.

capital employed The capital that a company uses to finance its assets. It is taken to be the sum of shareholders' funds, loans and deferred taxation.

capital expenditure The expenditure on capital goods, e.g. *fixed assets* such as plant or on trade investments and current assets. Capital expenditure is classed as below-the-line for accounting purposes. *See also trade investment.*

C

capital exports 1. Flows of capital from one nation to another. 2. Direct investments by multinational companies.

capital flight The movement of large sums of money from one nation to another in order to escape political and/or economic disturbances or to seek greater profits.

capital formation Savings made by creating or expanding capital or goods.

capital gain A gain made from a capital transaction, e.g. the buying and selling of assets.

capital goods Goods (such as machines) that are used for the production of other goods.

capital growth The increase in the value of an investment over a period of time.

capital increase The raising of share capital of a company by issuing more shares.

capital-intensive Describing a business in which capital is the most important and costly factor of production. Thus an industry in which the major cost is the purchase and maintenance of machinery (*fixed assets*) is capital-intensive.

capital investment An alternative term for *capital expenditure.*

capitalism An economic and political system in which people are entitled to trade for profit on their own account. It is also known as free or private enterprise.

capitalist economy An economy in which business is conducted for the profit of companies and persons engaged in it.

capitalization 1. The conversion of a company's reserves into share capital by issuing more shares. 2. The total amount of capital available to a company in the long term.

capitalization ratio The ratio of net worth to the total debt. It is useful in assessing the relative risk and capital gearing of a company.

capital/labour ratio The proportion of capital to labour used in an economy.

capital lease A lease in which the lessee gains all advantages and risks of the leased property.

capital loss The amount by which the cost of acquiring a capital asset has exceeded the proceeds obtained from its subsequent sale.

capital market A market made up of the various sources of capital for (medium- or long-term) investment in new and already existing companies. In the UK it is centred on the London Stock Exchange and the *Alternative Investment Market*.

capital outflow The exit of capital from a country. Political and economic fears may stir people to sell their assets and direct their money to other countries that are perceived as being more stable.

capital outlay The expenditure on fixed assets such as machinery. *See also* **capital**.

capital profit The profit generated by selling capital goods (*fixed assets*), rather than by trading.

capital requirement The minimum capital needed to be able to operate a business normally.

capital reserves The profits from a company's trading that represent part of the company's capital and so may not be repaid to shareholders until the company is wound up.

capital resources The net assets (capital funds) of a company, i.e. the excess of assets over liabilities.

capital saturation A situation in a company or industry in which there is such a proportion of capital to labour that any increase in capital would have no significant positive effect on output.

capital stock The value of all capital goods owned by a company, industry or nation, after *depreciation* has been taken into account.

capital transactions The long-term transactions included in determining a country's balance of payments, e.g. payments from savings to offset trade balance deficits.

capital turnover The comparison of the annual sales of a company divided by its average net worth, so as ascertain how much it has been able to expand without any further additions of capital.

capped loan A loan with a fixed upper limit to its variable interest rate.

captive agent An agent working exclusively for one company, but receiving a commission, at least in part, rather than being a salaried employee.

C

captive fund A fund for venture capital held by a large financial services group. *See* **venture capital**.

captive market A market in which there is a monopoly of production allowing the consumer no option but to buy that company's product.

CAR Abbreviation of *compound annual return*.

car Alternative term for a *futures* contract.

carboy A large globular glass bottle frequently protected by a frame, such as a metal basket. It is appropriate for holding dangerous liquids, such as acids. It is largely limited to sea transport and can be subject to leakage.

card A plastic card embossed with account details and provided with a magnetic strip, used in (usually personal) financial transactions.

cargo Goods transported on a ship or aircraft, etc.

cargo carrier A freight company; any transporter of cargo by land, sea or air.

cargo insurance Insurance that covers risks to goods being carried.

cargo manifest A list of the cargo stowed on board a ship or plane.

carnet A document valid internationally that allows the passage of dutiable goods without duty having to be paid until the goods reach their destination.

carr fwd Abbreviation of *carriage forward*.

Carriage and Insurance Paid to (…named place of destination) **(CIP)** An *incoterm*. The seller pays the freight costs to the named destination, but the risk passes to the buyer once the goods are delivered to the first carrier, whatever the mode of transport. The seller additionally must insure the goods on behalf of the buyer for all modes of transport to the place of destination.

carriage forward Statement that the carrier's freight charges have been agreed to be paid at the place of destination.

carriage paid Statement that the price charged for goods includes the delivery charges to the buyer's premises.

Carriage Paid To (…named place of destination) **(CPT)** *An incoterm.* The seller pays the freight costs to the named destination, but the risk passes to the buyer once the goods are delivered to the first carrier, whatever the mode of transport.

Caribbean Common Market (CARICOM) An organization established in 1973, with headquarters in Georgetown, Guyana, by 13 English-speaking Caribbean countries for purposes of mutual trade.

Caribbean Free Trade Association (CARIFTA) An organization that set up a free trade area in the Caribbean, superseded in 1973 by the *Caribbean Common Market*.

CARICOM Abbreviation of *Caribbean Common Market*.

CARIFTA Abbreviation of *Caribbean Free Trade Association*.

carrier A person or company engaged in carrying goods or passengers for payment.

carry Money borrowed or lent in order to finance trading in futures. The process of borrowing and lending in this way is known as carrying.

carry over To postpone payment on a bargain (deal) traded on a stock exchange from one settlement day to the next.

carry-over day The first day of each (two-weekly) new account on the London Stock Exchange, so-called because people who cannot pay for shares ordered from a stockbroker ask for payment to be carried over into the next accounting period.

carte blanche Full authorization to act, e.g. to contract on behalf of another or to fill in any of the details on a blank cheque.

cartel Any group that comes together to monopolize a market, agreeing which of them is to preside over which area of operation. As well as applying to companies it can also apply to groups of individuals, as, for example, when they act in unison to lower the price of unpaid and uncollected goods being auctioned off at a dockside. Cartels are illegal in the UK and the USA.

carton A light box or container, usually made of cardboard. It is frequently used because it is cheap and easy to handle. It is very flexible. Although it is vulnerable, it is relatively robust, particularly when packed with foam polystyrene, which in turn is useful for insulation.

CASC An abbreviation of Compania Argentina de Seguros de Credito a la Exportacion S.A., the Argentine credit insurance agency.

C

cascade tax A tax imposed at each stage of production. For example, a product may pass from one country to the next as each stage of production is carried out, and would thus attract several taxation stages, and the price of the finished product would be higher than if it had been produced in one country.

case A package or covering used to enclose or contain goods, made of wood, leather or metal-lined. It increases protection, particularly against pilfering, and is generally easy to handle.

case of need An abbreviation of referee in case of need, a local employee or agent employed by an exporter to nag an importer into paying for or, failing that, to arrange for the disposal of, goods. He is also personally liable if he endorses any accompanying bill/note.

cash Ready money, such as notes and coins, or to turn something into ready money.

cash advance A line of credit or credit card loan, where the cash advance rate is usually higher than that charged on normal purchases made with the same card.

cash against documents (CAD) A method of payment for goods for export, whereby the documentation for shipment (without the use of a sight bill of exchange) is sent to an agent or bank at the destination. This is passed to the consignee upon payment. The consignee is then free to take delivery of the shipment when it arrives.

cash and carry Popular term for a wholesale warehouse, from which retailers or sometimes individual purchasers buy their goods and carry them away.

cash at bank Funds that a person or business has on deposit at a bank. *See also cash in hand.*

cash book A book in which all receipts and payments are recorded in the first instance.

cash budget A forward plan of day-to-day income and expenditure.

cash card A plastic card that allows the holder, by using a personal identification number (PIN), to withdraw cash from a bank or other such financial institution through a *cash dispenser*. It may also allow access to such facilities as a display of the account balance and the ability to order bank statements and cheque books.

cash cow A product that continues to provide a healthy revenue after its initial launch with relatively little extra investment.

cash deal   An arrangement or transaction concluded with a cash payment. On the Stock Exchange, it is a deal to be completed on the next trading day.

cash dealing   Describing the practice of making Stock Exchange deals that must be settled on the following settlement day. Such bargains are said to be for cash settlement rather than account settlement.

cash discount   A reduction in the price of goods in return for payment in cash.

cash dispenser   A machine that issues cash to customers of a bank or other such financial institution, usually by inserting a *cash card* and using a personal identification number (PIN). It is also called an automated teller machine (ATM).

cash dividend   A dividend paid in cash (rather than as shares).

cash earnings   Cash income less cash expenses, so items like depreciation are excluded.

cash equivalents   Financial instruments that are virtually as good as cash, e.g. acceptances, treasury bills, etc. with a maturity of three months at the very most.

cash float   In a bank, money a cashier has to cash customers' cheques or to change money from one denomination to another. In a business, it is money a cashier has to give customers change.

cashflow   The flow of money payments to or from a firm.

cashier   A person who receives and issues cash and usually keeps records of transactions. In a bank a cashier at a counter is also called a teller.

cashier's check   US term for a bank draft.

cash in advance   A method of payment in which the purchaser pays for goods or services before delivery, with all the attendant risks and cashflow problems.

cash in hand   Funds held as cash (notes and coins) as opposed to those on deposit at a bank. *See also cash at bank.*

cash investment   An investment that provides immediate or short-notice withdrawal of funds at minimum risk; the funds invested are guaranteed. They include a current account or deposit account at a bank, National Savings and various building society accounts.

cash limit   1. The maximum amount provided by a loan or overdraft.

C

2. The maximum amount that can be withdrawn from a *cash dispenser*. 3. The maximum amount stated on a cheque guarantee card. 4. The maximum amount a business can spend in a specified time.

cash management A type of bank account available to business clients, which offers services such as debt collection and cashflow services.

cash market A spot market in contrast to a futures market, in which contracts are completed at a specified time in the future.

cash on delivery (COD) Distribution system whereby the person in receipt of goods makes payment for them on the spot to the deliverer. It can be very disadvantageous to the supplier should the consignee refuse to take delivery, because he will have the delivery costs to pay and have to make alternative arrangements.

cashpoint An alternative term for *automated teller machine or cash dispenser.*

cash position The state of the finances of a person or business at a given time, particularly whether there are funds available (cash positive) or unavailable (cash negative).

cash price The price at which goods may be bought using cash. The price paid in cash is usually different from the hire-purchase price, e.g., in that the latter normally includes interest.

cash purchase A purchase that has been made in cash.

cash ratio Cash and easily marketable securities, such as bills of exchange, divided by current liabilities, and hence narrower than the liquidity ratio.

cash surrender value The amount an insurer will return to a policyholder if a policy is cancelled. The insurer may lend against the cash value of its policies, often at an advantageous rate.

cash with order (CWO) Terms of an agreement by which goods are supplied only if payment is made in cash at the time the order is placed.

CAT Abbreviation of *computer-assisted trading.*

Category 1 (under the OECD's Arrangement) is currently a GNP of above $5,445 per capita based on 1997 data. All other countries are in Category 2.

Category 2 (under the OECD's Arrangement) consists of all countries that are not already in Category 1, i.e. those that do not have a GNP of above $5,445 per capita based on 1997 data.

caveat A caution or warning.

caveat emptor Latin for "let the buyer beware". In legal terms this maxim means that a buyer of goods should use his or her own common sense and that the law is not prepared to aid someone who buys goods foolishly.

caveat subscriptor Latin for "let the signer beware", meaning that anyone who signs a document is bound by its contents.

CB Abbreviation of *container base*, alternatively known as a container freight station.

CBD Abbreviation of cash before delivery.

CBI Abbreviation of *Confederation of British Industry*.

CBOE Abbreviation of *Chicago Board Options Exchange*.

CBT/CBOT Abbreviation of *Chicago Board of Trade*.

CCC Abbreviation of *customs clearance certificate*.

CD Abbreviation of *certificate of deposit*.

C/D Abbreviation of *cash against documents*.

CEDEL Abbreviation of *Centrale de Livraison de Valeurs Mobilières*.

cedi The standard currency unit of Ghana, divided into 100 pesewa.

CeFA A professional qualification awarded to financial advisers who pass examinations set by the Institute of Financial Services (*ifs*).

CEFTA Abbreviation of *Central Europe Free Trade Association*.

cent A subdivision (1/100) of a euro, dollar or other decimal currency unit. It is the most common of all subdivisions.

centavo A subdivision (1/100) of the legacy currencies of Spain, Portugal, Mozambique and some Latin American countries.

centesimo A subdivision (1/100) of the Chilean peso and the peso Uruguayo.

centime A subdivision (1/100) of a franc or various other currencies with a decimal currency unit, such as Belgium, France, Switzerland, etc.

centimo A subdivision (1/100) of the Costa Rican colon and Venezuelan bolivar.

Central African Customs and Economic Union (UDEAC) Union Douanière et Economique de l'Afrique Centrale, an organization

C

established in 1966 to found a Central African common market with a common tariff. Its terms were revised in 1974.

Central African Republic currency: CFA franc (CFA); there is no subdivision.

Central American Common Market (CACM) Common market established in 1960 among Central American countries. It was revised beginning in 1973.

Centrale de Livraison de Valeurs Mobilières (CEDEL) An organization of international banks, established in Luxembourg in 1970 as a settlement system for trading in Eurobonds. It acts as an agency for the collection of dividends and as a clearing house.

Central Europe Free Trade Association (CEFTA) An organization, similar to the European Free Trade Association (EFTA), formed by the Czech Republic, Hungary, Poland and Slovakia.

Central Moneymarkets Office (CMO) A method of electronic book-keeping, established in 1990, for transactions in negotiable instruments such as cheques and banker's drafts. Each member has a unique number and password, and is on-line to the CMO from his or her own premises.

central operating unit A unit created to coordinate a consortium's operations.

certificate of analysis A verification certificate used in shipping drugs.

certificate of bonds A document issued to a registered bond holder confirming that the bonds are registered in his or her name.

certificate of damage A document, issued by a dock company, certifying that goods it has received were damaged on arrival.

certificate of deposit (CD) A negotiable certificate issued by a bank against a deposit. The certificate entitles the bearer to interest plus the principal at the maturity date.

certificate of inspection A certificate issued by a trusted neutral organization confirming that goods have been inspected prior to shipment.

certificate of manufacture A requirement of a documentary letter of credit, where a certificated confirmation of a producer that the goods have actually been produced by him in his factory is needed.

certificate of origin A certificate (issued by a local Chamber of Commerce) evidencing where an item for export was produced.

certification of transfer The act of signing a transfer deed in order to transfer stocks from one owner to another. The transfer is further made official by reporting it to the registrar.

CESCE Abbreviation of Compania Espanola de Seguros de Credito a la Exportacion S.A, the Spanish credit insurance agency.

cesser clause In a charter agreement, a clause that absolves the charterer from responsibility for a cargo once it has been landed at its destination. *Cesser* is Latin for "to stop".

CET Abbreviation of *common external tariff*.

CFA (ISO) code Central African Republic – currency: CFA franc.

CFA Abbreviation of Communaute Financière Africaine – belongs to the French franc zone.

CFP Abbreviation of Colonies Françaises du Pacifique – belongs to the French franc zone.

CFR Abbreviation of *cost and freight*.

CFS Abbreviation of container freight station, alternatively known as a *container base*.

CFTC Abbreviation of *Commodity Futures Trading Commission*.

CGF (ISO) code Congo – currency: CFA franc.

Chad currency: CFA franc (TDF); there is no subdivision.

chamber of commerce A UK voluntary organization that promotes and represents the interests of those involved in commerce in a particular geographical area. Chambers of commerce in other countries may be state-aided. *See also chamber of trade*.

chamber of shipping An organization similar to a *chamber of commerce* that represents the interests of shipowners and shippers.

chamber of trade An organization of retailers in a particular area that promotes their interests, particularly to local government. It is more limited in composition and purpose than a *chamber of commerce*.

CHAPS Abbreviation of *Clearing House Automated Payment System*.

Chaps & Town Clearing Company Limited A company established in

C

1985 to operate the UK's twice-daily same-day clearance system under the auspices of CHAPS (*Clearing House Automated Payment System*).

charges forward When goods are to be delivered, a notice that all carriage charges must be paid at the time the goods are actually delivered.

chart analysis A graphical analysis to predict market movements.

chartered agent A broker who finds space aboard ship for a particular cargo.

chartered company A UK company that is incorporated by Royal Charter, originally for purposes of international trade. Unlike an ordinary company, it is treated in law as an individual person. Famous chartered companies of the past include the East India Company and the Hudson's Bay Company.

charter party A contract according to which an owner leases a vessel to a charterer for a specified period of time or for a certain voyage(s).

charter party bill of lading A bill of lading covering a *charter party*. Banks are not responsible for scrutinizing them because they are non-standardized.

chartism The activities of a *chartist*.

chartist A stock market or economic analyst who believes that trends (e.g. in price movements and so on) follow recognizable patterns and so predicts future trends with the aid of charts.

chaser A reminder from a remitting bank requesting an update from the collecting bank on the latest situation relating to a collection.

chattels Moveable property, as opposed to fixtures (property that cannot be moved).

cheapest to deliver The bond or gilt issue matching the deliverable criteria of a futures contract that costs least to purchase in the cash market.

cheap money Also called easy money, money borrowed at a low rate of interest, usually consisting of funds made available by authorities wishing to encourage economic activity.

check sample A sample taken from a consignment of goods and examined to determine whether or not the consignment is acceptable.

Cheque and Credit Clearing Company Limited A London-based organization established in 1985, part of the Association for Payment

Clearing Services (APACS), which clears interbank cheques and paper credits in England and Wales (Scotland and Northern Ireland have their own clearing arrangements).

chest A large strong box appropriate for goods such as beverages, especially when lined to make them airtight and more resistant to extreme changes in temperature.

CHF (ISO) code Switzerland – currency: Swiss franc.

Chicago Board of Trade (CBOT) The world's largest futures exchange, established in 1848, which today deals mainly in financial futures.

Chicago Board Options Exchange (CBOE) A major world market in options, established in 1973.

Chicago Mercantile Exchange (CME) A major world market in cash and futures, established in 1919, which today deals particularly commodities.

CHIEF Abbreviation of *Customs Handling of Import and Export Freight*.

Chile currency: Chilean peso (CLP), divided into 100 centesimos.

China currency: yuan (CNY).

CHIPS Abbreviation of *Clearing House Interbank Payments System*.

choice price An identical bid and offer price when comparing different market makers' bid-offer spreads on a futures market.

chon A subdivision (1/100) of the South Korean won.

chose-in-action A legal term for a right that cannot be enforced by physical possession, such as a copyright or debt. *See also* **chose-in-possession**.

chose-in-possession A legal tern for an asset that can be secured by physical possession, such as a book. *See also* **chose-in-action**.

CI Abbreviation of *consular invoice*.

CIA Abbreviation of current insured amount.

CIF (ISO) code Ivory coast (Côte d'Ivoire) – currency: CFA franc.

CIF Abbreviation of *cost, insurance and freight*.

CIM Abbreviation of *Convention on International Merchandise* by rail (in full Convention international concernant le transport des merchandise par chemin de fer).

C

CIP Abbreviation of *Carriage and Insurance Paid to*.

circular letter of credit A letter of credit from a bank instructing other banks to pay the holder the sum stated on the production of satisfactory proof of identity.

CIRRs Abbreviation of *Commercial Interest Reference Rates* (the OECD's Arrangement rates), also known as the *consensus rates*.

CISS Abbreviation of *comprehensive import supervision scheme*.

City, The The financial district of London, situated in the City of London. It covers an area of roughly one square mile and for this reason is also sometimes known as the Square Mile.

CIV Abbreviation of *Convention Internationale de Voyageurs*.

civil commotion insurance A special **SR & CC** clause inserted in marine insurance for an extra premium to cover the risks of civil commotions.

CKD Abbreviation of *completely knocked down*.

class of options All call or put options for the same asset.

claused bill of lading If a shipper receives any goods that have been inadequately packed, are damaged, or for which some of the contents are obviously missing etc., he marks the bill of lading as such. This is a claused bill of lading. Obviously it is usually unacceptable to a bank either because it differs from a documentary letter of credit's strict stipulations or because it is inadequate as a security and is therefore rejected.

Clayton Act An antitrust law passed in the USA in 1914 to maintain competition mainly by banning price discrimination among the buyers and sellers of commodities.

clean bill of lading A bill of lading that does not contain any clause or annotation expressly stating that the condition of the goods and/or their packaging is defective.

clean collection The presenting of a bill/draft without presentation of the shipping documents.

clean float A floating exchange rate in response to normal pressures of supply and demand, with little or no central bank intervention.

clean letter of credit A letter of credit not requiring the presentation of shipping documents, such as a standby letter of credit.

C

clean on board A note on a bill of lading recording that the cargo really has been loaded onto the named ship.

clean price The price of a fixed-income security excluding accrued interest. The "dirty" price includes accrued interest.

clean remittance An alternative term for *clean collection*.

clean report of findings Where a pre-shipment certificate is required by an importer and/or the importing country, the inspecting agent will be expected to report to its principal as to whether or not the goods have passed inspection. If satisfactory, it will issue a clean report of findings.

clear days For the term of a contract, days that exclude the days on which the contract starts and ends.

cleared without examination Confirmation that customs has decided not to inspect imported goods before accepting them for clearance. It otherwise has a right to inspect any non-EU goods being imported into the UK completely at random.

clearing The practice of organizing the payment of financial instruments (such as cheques). In the UK, commercial banks are usually members of the Banker's Clearing House, which settles their daily balance.

clearing agent An agent acting on behalf of a shipper to clear goods through customs and other formalities on arrival.

clearing firm/member Not all members of a financial exchange are members of the clearing house as well. Non-clearing members' transactions must be registered with and ultimately settled through a clearing member.

clearing house An organization that runs and regulates a financial market.

Clearing House Automated Payments System (CHAPS) An organization established in 1985 as part of the Association for Payment Clearing Services (APACS), that provides a guaranteed same-day electronic transfer of sterling funds within the UK.

Clearing House Interbank Payments System (CHIPS) A US organization established in 1970 that provides on-line electronic transfer of funds in US dollars, mainly for international transactions.

close The end period of a trading day on a financial exchange.

closed indent A situation in which an overseas customer has given an order to an export house and the overseas customer designates the supplier.

close out A procedure used by banks when a customer does not deliver currency he has sold forward, or take up currency he has bought forward. The customer is deemed to have bought or sold currency at the spot rate to fulfil the forward contract. The customer's account is credited or debited with any profit or loss.

closing date The last date on which a port will accept goods through its transit shed for a specific ship. It refers neither to cargo carried on the deck and delivered directly over the quay, nor to cargo delivered over the side by a lighter.

closing price The price at which a transaction is made at the close on a given trading day of a financial exchange. It also more frequently refers to the prices of a range of transactions and is likely to be recorded in the financial press.

closing purchase transaction The purchase of an option identical in strike price and expiration date to an option originally sold to settle an open option position.

closing range The high and low prices at which transactions took place at the *close*.

closing rate The rate at the close of business for the day for the foreign exchange of spot money.

closing sale On an options market, a transaction in which an option is sold in order to close a position.

CLP (ISO) code Chile – currency: Chilean peso.

CME Abbreviation of Chicago Mercantile Exchange.

CMF (ISO) code Cameroon – currency: CFA franc.

CMO Abbreviation of *Central Moneymarkets Office*.

CMR Abbreviation of Convention on Merchandise carried by road hauliers (in full *Convention relative au contrat de transport international de merchandise par route*).

CMR consignment note A contract of carriage by road, but not a document of title (i.e. proof of ownership), unlike a bill of lading. Many countries have made it compulsory for road hauliers to follow this convention which standardizes the international laws relating to road haulage.

C/N Abbreviation of *consignment note*.

CNAR Abbreviation of *compound net annual rate*.

CNY (ISO) code China – currency: yuan.

Co Abbreviation of "and company", words sometimes added to a crossed cheque.

C/O Abbreviation of *certificate of origin*.

COD Abbreviation of *cash on delivery*.

code of conduct Also called code of practice, the norm of behaviour expected from the members of a group, organization or business community.

coemption A legal term for *cornering the market*.

COFACE Abbreviation of Compagnie Française d'Assurance pour le Commerce Exterieur, the French credit insurance agency.

co-financing The provision of finance for projects in developing countries from a commercial bank and a major international institution such as the World Bank.

collar The simultaneous purchase of a *cap* and sale of a *floor*.

collateral An alternative term for security put up for a loan.

collateral agreement A contract or agreement running in parallel with an existing one.

collateral security A second security for a loan, in addition to the borrower's personal security.

collecting bank The bank that is responsible for obtaining an importer's acceptance on a bill of exchange (where this is applicable) and which collects the payment of a collection, in accordance with the principal's instructions received from the remitting bank.

collection The handling and delivery by banks of financial and/or commercial documents, in accordance with the instructions they are given. They also have to obtain acceptance and/or payment of any accompanying bill of exchange or promissory note.

collection order The complete and precise instructions given by an exporter to his bank and which the collecting bank and any other bank involved in the collection must follow.

collections A payment method in which an importer and exporter agree to employ the exporter's bank to handle payment for goods.

Colombia currency: Colombian peso (COP), divided into 100 centavos.

C

colon The standard currency unit of Costa Rica, divided into 100 centimos.

combination A position created either by buying a put and a call or by writing a put and a call on the same item, but with different strike prices and/or expiry dates.

combined bill of lading A bill of lading covering several modes of transport.

combined transport Describing a consignment sent by means of various modes of transport.

combined transport operator A freight carrier who uses multi-modal transport for international freight. It is accountable for the whole of the journey. The shipper thus will seek compensation for any goods that have been lost or damaged from the combined transport operator who in turn is expected to sort the trouble out with the individual carrier responsible. This therefore considerably simplifies the legal and practical problems for the shipper.

COMECOM Abbreviation of *Council for Mutual Economic Assistance*.

COMEX Abbreviation of *Commodity Exchange of New York*.

commercial bill A bill of exchange that is not a Treasury bill.

commercial documents Invoices; transport and insurance documents; certificates of origin, health, inspection, and quality etc. involved in trade.

commercial interest reference rate (CIRR) currencies The Australian dollar, Canadian dollar, Czech koruna, Danish kroner, euro, Korean won, New Zealand dollar, Norwegian kroner, Swedish krona, sterling, Swiss franc, US dollar and Japanese yen.

Commercial Interest Reference Rates (CIRRs) Minimum interest rates that may benefit from *official support* by the participants have been established for 14 currencies, the majority of which are based on either the 5-year Government bond yields or on 3-, 5- and 7-year bond yields, according to the length of the repayment period. Member countries can select the basis for their own CIRR. CIRRs are adjusted monthly to reflect commercial rates. They are also known as the *consensus rates*.

commercial invoice A document that contains the seller's description and prices of the goods and may also include contract terms and signed statements etc. Where a commercial invoice is submitted under a letter of credit its description of the goods must agree with the description in the letter of credit.

commercial paper   A short-term corporate debt in a tradeable form (e.g. a promissory note). In the USA it can mean the non-bank market in which firms lend money to each other without the intervention of a financial intermediary.

commingling   The practice of combining in the same shipment, in such a way that they cannot easily be separated, articles that attract different rates of customs duty. Unless the shipper or his agent separates them, the highest rate of duty applicable to any one item will be applied to the whole consignment.

commission   A fee by the parties in a transaction to an agent or broker for arranging it.

commission broker   A trader on the floor of a financial exchange who transacts for *off-the-floor* clientele.

commitment fee   1. A bank fee for keeping loan facilities available to a customer (even if they are not used). 2. A charge made by a forfaiter for undertaking to forfait a transaction and to hold a discount rate for a specified period of time.

commodity   1. A raw material or food that can be traded (hence commodity markets for cotton, coffee, etc.). 2. In economics and finance it can be any form of tangible good that is traded (including a financial asset, such as a share, for instance).

commodity broker   A broker who deals in any *commodity*, usually in a commodity market.

commodity exchange   A commodity market on which *actuals* and *futures* are traded.

Commodity Exchange of New York (COMEX)   A commodity market in metals established in 1870 which, together with the London Metal Exchange, has a leading role in the world. It deals mainly in futures contracts and in 1994 merged with the *New York Mercantile Exchange*.

commodity fund   An investment trust that mainly invests in commodity bills, such as for coffee etc.

Commodity Futures Trading Commission (CFTC)   The US federal agency that regulates the USA's futures markets.

C

commodity market A market on which *commodities* are traded.

commodity pool A syndicated investment agreement by which the total amount of the funds is invested on behalf of the members jointly to buy and sell futures. A large cash reserve is usually set aside to meet day-to-day obligations, such as margin calls.

commodity pool operator The manager of a *commodity pool*.

commodity trading adviser A specialist who offers advice about futures trading.

Common Agricultural Policy (CAP) A policy that aims to stabilize agricultural supplies and prices within the European Union. But because that has involved imposing duties on non-EU goods and providing subsidies to EU farmers, the *World Trade Organization* (WTO) has been working to reduce/eliminate these.

Common Budget Funds available to the European Commission, mainly to intervene to support the Common Agricultural Policy (CAP).

common carrier A public carrier legally liable for everything except acts of God, acts of the Queen's enemies, inherent vice, fraud of the consignor and fault of the consignor (consequently many carriers opt out of this liability when making any contract) .

common external tariff (CET) An import tariff charged by all members of a trading community (such as the EU) on goods being imported from non-member states.

common market Any market organization among countries that have a common external tariff (unlike a free-trade area). The EU is a modern example.

comparative advantage The economic state of being more efficient in one activity than in another, relative to a different country. For example, a country is able to produce cars twice as efficiently as another, but produces aircraft ten times more efficiently. In a free market, this country should export aircraft and import cars, and it is said that, in the production of aircraft, it has a comparative advantage over the other country.

compensation In international trade, a single agreement under which an exporter agrees to supply goods and services in exchange for goods and services of an equivalent value supplied by the importer, which the exporter must then sell to finance his original sale. It is frequently used in *countertrade*.

competitive market An open market in which goods and services are freely offered for sale by any number of sellers to anybody willing to buy, at prices agreed between them.

competitive pricing The setting of a price on goods and services based on what competitors charge for the same or similar products. Sellers in a strong market position (perhaps because of a well-known brand name) can force others to sell at a discount in order to make significant sales. In a market where buyers perceive all products to be similar, no seller dare set a price higher than the competition.

completely knocked down (CKD) Describing goods that are unassembled or disassembled for shipment or storage.

complex cover (EXIP) (ECGD) Insurance cover that supports termination or arbitration moneys to be advanced from an ECGD-supported loan. This supplementary credit insurance can be covered under the ECGD's export insurance policy in respect of any elements such as those that are not financed directly under the loan.

composite currency peg A type of exchange-rate system in which a country pegs its currencies to a basket of currencies of its main trading partners.

compound annual return (CAR) The total return on a sum invested or lent over a period of a year, including the return on interest previously accrued.

compound interest A rate of interest calculated by adding interest previously paid to the capital sum plus previous interest payment. After n years a sum S invested at x per cent compound interest is worth $S[100 + n)/100]^n$. *See also* **simple interest**.

compound net annual rate (CNAR) The return, after deduction of tax at the basic rate, of interest from a deposit or investment that includes the return on interest previously accrued.

compound option An option to buy an option at a pre-agreed price and date.

comprehensive import supervision scheme (CISS) Scheme set up by a number of developing countries to ensure that they will get value for the money they have spent, usually backed up by their insisting on a pre-shipment certificate from an independent inspection agency to prove it.

computer-assisted trading (CAT) A method of trading in which brokers and traders use computers on, e.g., a foreign exchange market or a stock exchange.

C

concentration risk A risk in dealing in securities if they are concentrated in any one market sector or if mostly only one type of security is held.

concession An allowance made to somebody who otherwise would have to pay; or the right to use somebody else's property as part of a business.

concessional financing Tied aid with *official support* (under the OECD's Arrangement) that enables the financing of capital infrastructure projects to the benefit of the recipient country and by promoting exports of the donor country. It is prohibited for countries that are not eligible for 17- to 20-year loans from the World Bank (currently those with a GNP per capita income in excess of $3,125 based on 1997 data) and for "commercially viable" projects (excepting for LLDCs), i.e. projects that generate cashflow sufficient to cover the operating costs and to service the capital employed.

concessionality levels for transactions which incorporate tied aid (under the OECD's Arrangement) A minimum of 50% for the poorest "Least Developed Countries" (LLDCs) as classified by the UN, and 35% concessionality level for all other developing countries.

conditional bill of sale A bill of sale by which the owner of the goods transferred retains the right to repossess them.

conditional bond A bond that is conditional upon the buyer proving that the exporter has defaulted. Payment is usually limited to the lower of the buyer's loss or the amount of the bond.

conditional endorsement An endorsement on a bill of sale on which the endorser has added a condition, which has to be fulfilled before the endorser receives the proceeds of the bill. The condition does not affect the paying banker, who can ignore it.

conditional sale agreement An agreement by which goods are paid for in instalments and, although the buyer may have possession of the goods, the legal property in them remains with the seller until payment is complete.

conditions of carriage The conditions laid down by a carrier for carrying goods and/or passengers.

Confederation of British Industry (CBI) An organization established in 1965 by the combining of the British Employers Confederation, the Federation of British Industry and the National Association of British Manufacturers. With some 250,000 members, it promotes British industry and represents it in discussion with the government.

c

conference A group of shipowners who agree sailing times, ports of departure and destination, and a structure of tariffs between themselves. Usually they also offer extra inducements to shippers who use them exclusively.

confirmed Denoting a letter of credit for which the advising bank enters into a commitment to pay that is independent of, and in addition to, the issuing bank's commitment. The confirming bank undertakes to honour its commitment regardless of whether or not the issuing bank is in a position to reimburse it.

confirmed irrevocable credit A letter of credit that has been sent by the issuing bank to its branch/correspondent bank in the beneficiary's (exporter's) country with a request that the branch/correspondent bank confirm it. The confirming bank, should it agree to do so, consequently also becomes a party to the letter of credit and must pay any legitimate claim from the beneficiary whether or not it itself is likely to be reimbursed by the issuing bank. The exporter, provided he has complied properly with every requirement, is accordingly covered against transfer and political risks in addition to credit risks.

confirming bank An *advising bank*, normally an exporter's bank in his or her own country, that has been authorized by the *issuing bank* to add its own confirmation to a letter of credit. By confirming the letter of credit it is committed independently of and in addition to the issuing bank's commitment and so must honour it whether or not the issuing bank does. It is such a serious commitment that it obviously has the right to refuse to confirm it. On the other hand, if it does add its confirmation the *beneficiary* will be paid earlier (i.e. not have to wait until the confirming bank is reimbursed by the issuing bank) and for large amounts this considerably helps his or her cashflow.

confirming house A company that buys goods for foreign businesses by confirming that the order is from a respectable customer and guaranteeing that the exporter will be paid immediately.

Congo currency: CFA franc (CGF); there is no subdivision.

Consensus The common name for the *International Agreement for Guidelines on Officially Supported Export Credit*.

consensus rates Minimum interest rates that may benefit from *official support* by the participants have been established for 14 currencies, the majority of which are based on either the 5-year Government bond yields or on 3-, 5- and 7-year bond yields, according to the length of the repayment period. Member countries can select the basis for their own

C

consensus rates. Consensus rates are adjusted monthly to reflect commercial rates. They are also known as the *Commercial Interest Reference Rates*.

consideration In most forms of contract, the agreement is made binding by the promise or payment of a sum of money or other favour from one party to the other. Such a payment or favour is known as a consideration. The term is also used informally for any kind of payment.

consignee The receiver of goods.

consignment A batch of goods sent by a public carrier.

consignment note A contract of carriage by rail, but not a document of title (i.e. proof of ownership), unlike a bill of lading. It is a document covering the contract for the carriage of goods by rail that is covered by the CIM convention and thereby makes the rail company liable for any loss, damage or delay (from which it might otherwise have tried to exclude itself).

consignment stocks Stocks (of goods) held in the importer's country by a commission agent to ensure a regular sales flow.

consignment trading A situation in which an exporter remains the owner of a consignment, but the goods are sold by an overseas agent who submits an *account sales*.

consignor The sender of goods.

consolidation The combining of single units of goods into a whole load (an air cargo term).

consortium An association of several commercial enterprises.

constant prices The practice of expressing prices in terms of a base year so that figures can be compared without being affected by inflation.

constructive possession The possession of the documents of title to goods, rather than actual possession of the goods themselves.

consular invoice An invoice (usually on a special form) with a certification by the consulate of an importing country that it conforms with its rules, as to origin and price etc. It is used only in a few countries.

container A large boxlike receptacle of standard design for the transport of goods, particularly from one mode of transport to another.

container base An area within or close to a seaport or airport, generally managed by a consortium of freight forwarders or other transport owners devoted to the speedy and efficient clearance of containers. It is also known as a container freight station.

container freight station   *See container base.*

container port   A port specializing in handling goods that have been stored and carried in containers.

container ship   A ship designed to carry goods that have been stored and carried in containers.

containerization   A system of transporting goods in large boxlike receptacles of standard design.

containerize   To pack in, or adapt to transport by, container, or to transport by container.

contango   A stock exchange term for a delayed settlement of a bargain from one account to the next. A *premium* is payable. The term is also used more frequently in futures trading to mean the opposite of *backwardation*.

contingent   Describing something that depends on an uncertain event taking place, such as a bank agreeing to grant a loan only providing that a particular contract is formalized.

contingent liability   A potential liability that a business has to take into account (particularly as a note to its balance sheet), e.g. the calling of a bond or the non-payment of a bill of exchange etc.

contra proferentem rule   A legal interpretive rule that contractual clauses exempting a party from liability will be interpreted strictly against the party that includes them.

contract   A legally binding agreement between two or more people or companies, by which one party supplies goods or services to the other party in return for payment or some other compensation.

contract bond   An alternative term for *performance bond.*

contract commercial interest reference rate (CIRR)   Under the OECD consensus rates (the Agreement) it is a rate committed no earlier than the date of the contract.

contract in writing   A written contract, legally required for various purposes such as bills of exchange, transfers of shares and credit sale or hire-purchase agreements.

contract month   The month in which futures contracts may be made or delivered.

C

contract of affreightment A contract between a shipowner and a shipper relating to carriage of cargo by sea.

contract of novation A new contract that replaces an existing one, usually retaining the same rights and liabilities, as when one partner in a partnership is replaced by another.

Convention international concernant le transport des merchandise par chemin de fer (CIM) The International convention on the carriage of goods by rail.

Convention Internationale de Voyageurs (CIV) The international convention on the carriage of passengers and their luggage by rail.

Convention on International Merchandise (CIM) The international convention covering the carriage of goods by rail.

Convention on International Merchandise by road (CMR) The international convention on the carriage of goods by road.

Convention relative au contrat de transport international des merchandise par route (CMR) The international convention on the carriage of goods by road.

convergence The tendency for the gap between spot and future prices to close towards equality as the delivery date approaches.

conversion factor A factor used to determine the amount to be paid at delivery for a cash bond delivered against a futures contract. It is also known as the price factor.

convertible currency A currency that can be freely exchanged for other currencies or by non-residents for other currencies without permission being required from the central bank of the currency's country. Full convertibility means that there are no controls for residents either.

convertibles Loan stock, bonds and debentures that can easily be converted into ordinary shares. In the USA they are known as converts.

cooperation agreement between export credit agencies A "one stop shop" export credit service agreement provided by a group of export credit agencies to exporters when they bid together for major projects in other countries.

COP (ISO) code Colombia – currency: Colombian peso.

cornering the market To build a virtual monopoly in particular goods or services, so that the monopolist is able to dictate price.

Corn Exchange A London commodity exchange that deals in such commodities as cereals and animal foodstuffs.

corporate bond A bond issued by a company or corporation, which most frequently occurs in the USA.

corporate finance Funding for a business or large corporation, usually from a bank.

Corporation of Lloyd's The market for cargo/marine insurance. Most of the insurance is syndicated.

correspondent bank A foreign bank with which a UK bank has formally and mutually agreed to work on behalf of each other.

corridor The simultaneous purchase of a cap at one strike price and sale of a cap at a higher strike price.

COSEC Abbreviation of Companhia de Seguro de Creditos E.P., the Portuguese credit insurance agency.

cost and freight An *incoterm*. The seller must pay the costs and the freight to the port of destination, but the risk passes to the buyer as soon as the goods have crossed over the ship's rail in the port of shipment. Because insurance costs are not included, the buyer must pay for these if he or she wants to insure the goods.

cost of carry The cost in holding a financial asset that consists of interest lost on tying up the funds.

cost per freight tonne-mile Cost of transport calculated as follows:

$$\frac{\text{Cost of operating a vehicle}}{\text{Number of freight tonne-miles carried}}$$

cost, insurance and freight (CIF) An *incoterm*. The seller must pay the costs and the freight to the port of destination and in addition must provide marine insurance for the buyer during the carriage of the freight. However, the risk passes to the buyer as soon as the goods have crossed over the ship's rail in the port of shipment.

Costa Rica currency: colon (CRC), divided into 100 centimos.

COT Abbreviation of customer's own transport, when used to deliver goods to or collect them from a carrier.

Côte d'Ivoire (formerly Ivory Coast) currency: CFA franc (CIF); there is no subdivision.

COU Abbreviation of *central operating unit*.

C

Council for Mutual Economic Assistance (COMEA or **COMECOM)** A group of Communist bloc countries that combined in 1949 with the aim of producing a self-sufficient economic bloc that could be coordinated from a central point (and to consolidate Soviet influence in the area). Its members were: Bulgaria, Cuba, Czechoslovakia, East Germany, Hungary, Mongolia, Poland, Romania, USSR and Vietnam. In 1991 is was superseded by the Organization for International Economic Cooperation (OIEC).

counter-indemnity The irrevocable commitment from an exporter that he will repay the bank should he fail in any commitment, e.g. in the event of a bond being called.

counterparty The parties on each side of a transaction.

counterpurchase Two separate agreements under which a buyer agrees to purchase and pay for goods and a seller agrees to purchase and pay for goods of a (usually) equivalent value.

countertrade 1. An umbrella term referring to a growing number of trading and financing techniques in which payment is made either wholly or partly in the form of goods. 2. Foreign trade based on barter or similar arrangements, rather than payments in foreign exchange.

countervailing (or **counter) credit** Generally treated as an term for a *back-to-back credit*, but some banks distinguish it as applying only when both credits have been issued by their own bank.

coupon The interest rate paid on a fixed or floating-rate bond issue.

courier A special messenger.

cover 1. To take out forward contracts to gain protection against losses from adverse exchange rate movements between the date of the contract and the due payment date. 2. In dealing, to lay off.

cover note A broker's statement that cargo insurance has or will be effected. Little reliability can be placed on it, because it is neither evidence of a insurance contract, nor of its terms.

C/P Abbreviation of *charter party*.

CPT Abbreviation of *Carriage Paid To* (…named place of destination).

cranage A port authority's charge for using its crane facilitries.

crane jib fork-lift truck A fork-lift truck used for lifting and carrying goods, such as bins, buckets, and canisters.

crate A large lightweight case made of thin narrow overlapping pieces of wood, plastic or metal. It is appropriate for larger fragile goods, such as machinery and consignments of fruit.

CRC (ISO) code Costa Rica – currency: colon.

credit 1. A loan of money. 2. To add a sum to an account. 3. In book-keeping, a balance that shows a profit. 4. The financial standing of a person or company.

credit freeze An alternative term for *credit squeeze*.

Credit Guarantee Insurance Corporation of Africa, Ltd The South African credit insurance agency.

credit insurance Insurance to cover an exporter in the event of his buyer(s) not paying him.

credit line A fixed amount or limit of credit set up for a borrower. It is the amount of outstanding credit that may not be exceeded at any time. Such lines are usually set up for companies or countries.

credit management The management of the amount and repayment time of credit allowed to debtors to ensure a satisfactory cashflow for an exporter.

creditor A person who is owed money by a debtor.

credit rating An evaluation of a borrower's suitability to receive commercial credit or the act of so doing.

credit reference agency Organization that provides records, ratings and reports on other organizations and individuals who borrow money or order goods on credit. Any borrower in the UK who is not allowed credit as a result of an adverse report can now legally challenge such a report and have it amended if it is wrong.

credit risk The risk that a counterparty will default on a transaction.

credit squeeze Action by the government and/or banks and other financial institutions to restrict the credit granted to borrowers.

credit status An evaluation of a borrower's suitability to receive commercial credit.

credit status report A report from a credit reference agency estimating a borrower's suitability to receive commercial credit.

creditworthy Describing an institution or individual whose risk of defaulting on a debt is considered to be low.

creeping expropriation An indirect method of expropriation of property or an investment by depriving the owner or investor of all or most of it. The ECGD's overseas investment insurance scheme will provide cover for overseas investments that have been subject to it for a period of at least a year.

CRF Abbreviation of *clean report of findings*.

CRN Abbreviation of *customs registered number*.

Croatia (Hrvatska) currency: kuna.

Croner's Consulates Guide A guide to consulates' requirements regarding consular invoices, import requirements, hours of business etc.

Croner's Reference Book for Exporters A secialized handbook covering general developments and also the detailed requirements for all the countries of the world. It is updated monthly.

Croner's Reference Book for Importers A specialized handbook covering general developments and also the detailed requirements for all the countries of the world. It is updated monthly.

crore 1 crore = 10 million Indian rupees.

cross-border Describing any transaction that is literally enacted across a border between two countries and also used to distinguish specific transactions that are controlled from abroad. For example, a credit agreement can either by cross-border and the lender deals directly with the foreign borrower or it may be more domestically arranged whereby, although the credit agreement is arranged cross-border between two or more financial institutions, the local financial institution in the borrowers' country is responsible for collecting the amounts due.

cross hedging The hedging of a different, but related, cash instrument with a futures contract.

cross rate 1. The exchange rate between two foreign currencies in a third country, e.g. the cross rate between US$ and euros in London. When a dealer in London sells (or buys) euros in exchange for dollars, he uses a cross rate. 2. An exchange rate that does not involve the US dollar.

cruzeiro real The standard currency unit of Brazil (also called simply the real), divided into 100 centavos.

CSK (ISO) code Czech Republic – currency: koruna.

CT Abbreviation of *combined transport*.

C term The category of *incoterm* in which the seller has to arrange the carriage of the goods at his own expense.

CTD Abbreviation of *combined transport document*.

CTO Abbreviation of a *combined transport operator*.

Cuba currency: Cuban peso (CUP), divided into 100 centavos.

CUP (ISO) code Cuba – currency: Cuban peso.

currency adjustment factor (CAF) A surcharge imposed by a shipowner to cover the adverse fluctuations of a floating currency.

currency and bunker adjustment factor (CABAF) A combined surcharge made to cover both the currency and the bunker adjustment factors under the same fee.

currency clause A clause in an export contract that specifies that the sum payable in the buyer's currency (say, Saudi Arabian riyals) should vary in line with the market exchange rate against the seller's payment. In this way, the exporter is not exposed to exchange risk from movements in exchange rates (e.g. Saudi Arabian riyals against sterling) and the exchange risk is borne entirely by the buyer, even though he is invoiced in his own currency.

currency option (pure option) Different from a forward exchange option contract, it gives the holder the right, but not the obligation, to buy or sell a specified quantity of a foreign currency at a specified rate of exchange, either on or before the expiry date of the contract. The person or institution granting the option is called the option writer. The price of an option is known as the premium.

currency swap An exchange of interest flows and principal amounts in different currencies.

current delivery Describing a futures contract that becomes deliverable during the current month.

current transactions The short-term transactions included in determining a country's balance of payments, e.g. exports, imports, tourism, etc.

custody bill of lading A bill of lading used by US warehouses.

customs A national authority charged with collecting duty levied on exports and imports. The term is also used to describe the area in which customs officials can examine goods entering or leaving a country. *See also* next entry.

Customs and Excise In full Her Majesty's Customs and Excise, the UK government department charged with levying indirect taxes, including value added tax (VAT) and customs duty on goods imported into the UK or produced in the UK for home consumption (*excise duty*).

customs bond A bond used for temporary imports, such as in entrepot trade and samples for a trade fair. Should anything occur to prevent the re-export of such goods, such as theft, the bond will be called.

customs clearance The process of clearing exported/imported goods through a customs and excise examination.

customs clearance certificate A certificate that goods have been cleared through customs.

customs duty A duty levied on imports, either as a protectionist measure or simply to raise revenue.

Customs Handling of Import and Export Freight (CHIEF) The UK customs' computerized system for clearing imports and exports.

customs invoice A few importing countries require an invoice made out on a form specified by their customs authorities.

customs registered number A reference number given to an exporter or his or her agent by HM Customs when the simplified customs procedure is used.

customs tariff A list of dutiable goods.

customs union An agreement between two or more nations to remove or standardize restrictions on mutual trade, and apply common duties, tariffs or quotas to countries outside the union.

CVE (ISO) code Cape Verde Islands – currency: Cape Verde escudo.

CWE Abbreviation of *cleared without examination*.

CWO Abbreviation of *cash with order*.

cycle 1. In economics and finance, a recurrent round or period of circumstances or the time needed for such. 2. A set of expiration dates applicable to different classes of option, or of delivery months applicable to futures.

CYP (ISO) code Cyprus – currency: Cypriot pound.

Cyprus currency: Cypriot pound (CYP), divided into 100 cents.

Czech Republic currency: koruna (CSK), divided into 100 haleru

C

D

DA Abbreviation of *deposit account* or *discretionary account*.

D/A Abbreviation of *documents against acceptance* (or alternatively, sometimes, deposit account).

D/A draft Method whereby a collecting bank is allowed to release the documents to an importer only against a draft (bill of exchange), representing the exporter's only security once the shipping documents have been released. Consequently the exporter should have a greater confidence in the buyer's integrity and creditworthiness.

DAF Abbreviation of *Delivered at Frontier* (… named place).

daily price limits The maximum and minimum prices at which a futures contract can be transacted. These are determined by the futures exchange clearing house and expressed in relation to the previous day's settlement price.

daily settlement The settlement in a futures market in which the daily price changes are paid by those incurring losses to those making profits.

dalasi The standard currency unit of Gambia.

damages A civil court award of monetary compensation for loss or injury.

D & B rating The credit agency Dunn & Bradstreet rate businesses according to their financial strength and the level of risk (including "early warning" signs).

dangerous goods Goods that could pose a risk to the health and safety of people or property, therefore requiring special care in handling and storage.

dangerous goods note (DGN) Document that contains all the particulars of dangerous goods, including any special instructions as to how to deal with them in the case of an emergency.

data Items of information, particularly in computer applications.

database Data organized to allow easy access to the most up-to-date information and its collation with older data. The term is generally applied to computers that can store, organize and search for data more rapidly than was hitherto possible.

D

data privacy A business requirement to maintain the privacy of personal information relating customers or staff. *See also* **Data Protection Act**.

data processing The sorting and organization of data in order to produce the desired information, generally according to standard procedures and generally using a computer.

Data Protection Act 1984 UK legislation that is designed to protect people whose personal details are held in a computer system. Businesses that hold such data have to register with the Data Protection Registrar.

data security The protection of data from electronic criminals. It generally entails the production of programs intended to deny unauthorized persons access to a database by means of passwords and other identification procedures. Maximum security is obtained by encryption, in which information is held in a coded form.

date The day, month and year. In the UK these are usually recorded numerically in that order (e.g. 1:10:01 is 1 October 2001). However in continental Europe and the USA they are recorded in the order month, day, year (e.g. 1:10:01. is 10 January 2001). The potential for confusion is vast.

dated security A security, such as a bill of exchange or a bond, that has a stated date for repayment (redemption date) of its nominal value. It may be described as short-dated or long-dated.

dated stock Stock that has a fixed maturity date, as opposed to undated stock.

date of shipment In letters of credit this can be crucial, because goods shipped too late, or even too early, can nullify the contract. Unless otherwise prohibited by the letter of credit phrases such as "loading on board", "date of pick-up" or "taking in charge" etc. on the relevant transport document are all acceptable. *See also* **on or about**.

day book A ledger in which transactions are listed on a daily basis prior to transfer to ledgers that deal with transactions on a subject basis. It is usual to keep separate purchase and sales day books.

daylight overdraft A situation that occurs when a bank allows a customer's account to go into the red, on the understanding that the debt will he repaid by the end of the day.

day order An order that is placed to be dealt with, if possible, during only one trading session. If the order cannot he exercised that day, it is automatically cancelled.

days of grace An additional number of days' interest charged by a forfaiter to reflect the number of days' delay normally experienced in the transmission of payments from the debtor country. Adding, normally three, days of grace to the payment of a bill of exchange is virtually obsolete these days. (The practice was that if a bill was due on the 4th, for instance, it would actually fall due for payment three business days later.)

day-to-day loan An alternative term for an overnight loan or day-to-day money, borrowed particularly by a financial institution that is temporarily illiquid. The money is lent to companies wishing to be paid interest on money earned in the previous day's trading. Interest rates on day-to-day loans are high and variable.

day-to-day money Type of loan made by a that must be repaid on demand. It is also known as money at call.

day trading The creation and liquidation of the same futures position or positions within one day's trading.

DCF Abbreviation of *discounted cash flow*.

DCR Abbreviation of *domestic content requirements*.

DDP Abbreviation of *delivered duty paid*.

DDU Abbreviation of *delivered duty unpaid*.

DDU cleared A situation in which a seller pays all the delivery costs including, unlike the pure DDU *incoterm*, the customs clearance of the goods as well. The payment of the import duty will, of course, still be the buyer's responsibility.

dead-cat bounce A brief rise in the stock index of a falling market. The term refers to the supposed ability of a cat always to land on its feet: if a falling cat bounces, it must be dead.

dead freight Where a charterer has agreed to load a full cargo, but has not done so, dead freight is an allowance given for the resulting reduced loading costs. The main claim would be by the carrier (i.e. the shipowner) against the shipper.

dead security Security backed by an exhaustible industry (such as mining), which is thus a poor risk for a long-term loan.

dead-in-the-water Describing a project that has failed completely, often before it is properly underway.

D

deadweight debt A debt that is not covered by or incurred in exchange for real assets. For example, part of the National Debt taken on to pay for war is a deadweight debt.

deadweight tonnage The total load-carrying capacity of a ship measured in tones weight. It is calculated by subtracting the ship's unladen displacement weight from its displacement weight when it is down to its *loadline*. The difference also includes bunkers, water and stores, as well as its *payload*.

deal An agreement or transaction; in particular, any bargain made on the foreign exchange market.

dealer A merchant who operates on his or her own in a market at his or her own risk and hence is a speculator. This includes anyone who is engaged in trading on a financial market.

dealing The activity of dealers.

dealing for the account Speculative financial market trading in which shares are bought and sold in the very short term. Because accounts do not have to be settled until *account* day, it is possible for a dealer to buy thousands of pounds worth of stock without having to pay for it. If the stock is then sold before account day, the dealer can keep any profit resulting from price fluctuations while the stock was held. Conversely, the dealer may sell stock that he does not actually possess in the belief that he will be able to buy back the stock at a lower price as the market falls. This practice is known as selling short.

dear money Money is said to be dear when it is difficult to find investment or loans and the interest rate for borrowing is consequently high.

death-valley curve The period of time during which a start-up company uses venture capital at an extremely fast rate, to the point where it is using equity capital to fund overheads, an unhealthy state of affairs.

death-valley days A colloquial term for the "dry" days on the financial markets – days on which little trading takes place.

debenture A long-term loan to a company made at a fixed rate of interest and usually with a specified *maturity date*, generally between 10 and 40 years. Debenture holders are numbered with the company's creditors, and in the event of liquidation have preferential claims on the firm. Debentures may be treated as tradeable securities.

debenture capital That part of a company's capital that is issued in the form of *debentures*.

debenture issue An issue of *debentures*, whether secured or unsecured, by a company wishing to raise loan capital. The debenture holders become the company's principal *creditors* and have the right to preferential repayment of their loans in the event that the firm encounters financial difficulties.

debenture stock *Debentures* may be divided into units and traded on an exchange. These securities are known as debenture stocks.

debit A sum owed by or a charge made on a person.

debit balance In accounting, a balance that shows a debit.

debit card A plastic card issued by a bank to its customers that may be used in place of a cheque book. By accessing the bank's electronic records, the debit card makes *direct debit* of an account possible.

debit entry An item of debit recorded in a ledger for accounting purposes.

debit note In accounting, a notification sent to a customer that the supplier is about to debit the client's account with a certain sum. Debit notes are normally issued in unusual situations, e.g. when a client has been charged too little for goods received.

debit side In accounting, the side of a ledger on which debits are listed. Hence, in informal use, it denotes the negative points in an argument.

debt A sum of money, or value of goods or services, owed by one person, group or company to another. Debt arises because the seller allows the purchaser *credit*. Assignable debts may be transferred in whole from one person to another. In commerce, the term is also used to describe the whole of a company's borrowings.

debt bomb Financial repercussions envisaged if a major international debtor were to default.

debt buy-back In international trading, an arrangement whereby a debtor nation buys back its debt at a discount for cash.

debt capacity The ability of debtor to repay his or her loans. Creditors assess applicants' repayment ability on what they own or earn. Any outstanding loans are offset against this capacity. It is also called repayment ability.

debt collection agency A firm that charges a commission for collecting its clients' outstanding debts.

debt collecting The business of a company or organization that collects debts on behalf of other companies or individuals. *See also factoring.*

debt discounting The purchasing a debt at a discount, usually from a trader such as an exporter.

debt factoring The purchasing of a company's debts (at a discount) by a factor. *See* **debt discounting; factoring**.

debt-for-equity The substitution of an equity stake for a debt that is proving difficult to recover, despite the good prospects of the borrower.

debt forgiveness In international finance, writing off part of a nation's debt, or selling the debt to a third party for a large discount.

debt instrument A written promise to pay a debt; or a medium for obtaining a (usually short-term) loan.

debt market A market (such as the New York Bonds Exchange) in which debt securities are bought and sold.

debtnocrat A bank official who specializes in high-level lending, often to developing nations.

debt-to-equity ratio A company may finance itself through borrowing or through shareholder investment, depending on current interest rates. The proportion of each is known as debt-to-equity ratio, or *gearing*.

debtor (Dr) A person or company that owes money, goods or services to another.

debtor days Average time customers who buy goods or services on credit take to pay for them.

debt rescheduling When a debtor has difficulties making repayments, a method by which the lender defers interest or repayments, extends the loan period, or agrees to a completely new loan.

debt service ratio In international finance, a nation's annual repayments on its foreign debt divided by the value of its exports (in hard currency).

debt servicing The payment of interest on a debt.

decentralization The distribution of the constituent parts of a company or government to a variety of geographical locations.

deck cargo A cargo that is stored on the deck of a ship (as opposed to being stowed as belly cargo).

declaration of solvency A formal statement by a company's directors that it is seeking voluntary liquidation but that it expects to pay its creditors within at least 12 months.

decontrol An alternative term for *deregulation*.

de-diversification The shedding of interests and companies acquired by a corporation in the process of *diversification*, so as to reduce the variety of business in which the company engages.

deductive value The value of imported goods deduced by customs, based on their resale price (less certain expenses).

deed A document that records a transaction and may bear the seals of the parties concerned to testify to its validity.

deed of partnership An agreement that forms the basis and terms of a partnership between two or more people.

deed of transfer A legal document that gives authority to registrars of securities to transfer them from the seller to the buyer.

deep discount stock Also called zero coupon stock, loan stock issued at a greater discount than other stock of the issuer, providing lower (or zero) interest.

deep market A financial market where many transactions can occur without affecting the price of the underlying financial instrument.

deep pocket A description of a company or person who seems to have plenty of money. A deep-pocket view of some subsidiaries is that they may have access to more funds than an independent company of a similar size. A subsidiary may thus be able to call upon the greater resources of its parent company to engage in competition with independents in its sector.

de facto By virtue of existence, rather than any legal right. For example, the de facto owner of a property may be the person in occupation, whether or not he or she has legal title to the land.

default Failure to comply with the terms set out in a *contract*. Legal proceedings generally follow if the matter cannot be settled amicably.

default bond A bond that is conditional upon a buyer proving that an exporter has defaulted. Payment is usually limited to the lower of the buyer's loss or the amount of the bond.

default notice A notice issued by a lender to a borrower who is in default on a loan (in the UK it is subject to the Consumer Credit Act 1974). If the notice is not complied with, the lender can seek an enforcement order.

defeasance A condition built into the wording of a deed that renders the deed void if the condition is complied with. The term is also used for any annulment or act that renders something null and void.

defective documents Documents that do not meet with the strict requirements of a letter of credit, such as a *dirty bill of lading*, or a *port of departure* or *flag* may not be in agreement with the letter of credit, or incorrect insurance provided, or signatures missing etc.

defensive stock Shares in companies that are not affected by economic cycles because they produce necessities (such as food).

defensive tactics The strategy used when a "player" feels threatened by aggression. Thus the subject of a hostile take-over bid sometimes arranges defensive tactics with the aim of making the take-over more difficult, e.g. by pushing up its own share price.

deferment Postponement, e.g. of a payment.

deferral The spreading of befits accruing from an asset over the whole life of the asset, rather than accounting for them in the financial year of its acquisition.

deferred asset An expense incurred that does not match the income it will provide in the same accounting period. It is also termed a deferred debit.

deferred coupon note A bond on which interest is not paid until after a specified date. It is known in the USA as a deferred interest bond or extended bond.

deferred credit Income received before it is earned in a given accounting period, such as a government grant. It is also termed a deferred liability.

deferred futures Futures contracts that are farthest away from *maturity*. *See also* *nearby futures*.

deferred interest bond US term for a *deferred coupon note*.

deferred liability A liability that does not fall due until after a period of a year.

deferred ordinary shares A category of shares, usually issued to a company's founders, entitling them to special dividend rights.

deferred payment A letter of credit may contain a liability by the issuing bank to make a payment on a date later than when the beneficiary presents the documents. This type of payment is used instead of acceptance terms for countries that impose hefty taxes on bills of exchange.

deferred rebate A loyalty rebate paid by an individual or group of shipping lines for using them exclusively or mostly.

deferred taxation A tax for which a person or company is liable, but which has not yet been considered or demanded.

deficit The excess of expenditure over income, or liabilities over assets.

deflation A persistent decrease in prices, generally caused by a fall in the level of economic activity within a country. Deflation should not he confused with *disinflation*.

defray To settle an account or to lay out money in payment for goods or services.

defunct Describing a company or organization that no longer functions as such.

degearing A reduction of risk or leverage. Examples include cutting borrowing and reducing exposure to forces that a company or dealer cannot control. *See also* **hedging**.

delayed payment surcharge An extra payment (in addition to interest) that is charged while a debt is outstanding.

del credere Italian for "of belief" or "of trust". It is the commission a selling agent receives if he agrees to carry the risk of any bad debts. Obviously the agent is likely to undertake such an obligation only if the debtor is believed/trusted to be reliable in the first place.

del credere agent A selling agent specializing in carrying the risk of any bad debts and accordingly charging a greater amount of commission for so doing.

delegation 1. A body of accredited representatives to a gathering (e.g. a conference). 2. To cede responsibility to other, usually junior, members of staff.

delegatus non potest delegare Latin for a "delagate cannot delegate", a principle that prevents a contractor from subcontracting part of the work.

Delivered at Frontier (DAF) An *incoterm*. The seller bears all of the costs and all of the risks until the goods have arrived at the named frontier, but *before* they pass through customs. The buyer clears the goods and pays the duty, bearing the risks thereafter.

D

Delivered Duty Paid (... named place of destination) (DDP) An *incoterm*. It involves the maximum responsibility for the seller, but the buyer must help the seller to obtain any requisite import licence and/or dealing with any other official import requirements, such as customs formalities should the seller ask. Further, the buyer must pay for any pre-shipment inspection costs, unless the exporter's country has already required the seller to do so.

Delivered Duty Unpaid (... named place of destination) (DDU) An *incoterm*. Similar to *DDP*, but the buyer is additionally responsible for obtaining any import licence and/or dealing with any other official export requirements, such as customs formalities.

Delivered Ex Quay (... named port of destination) (DEQ) An *incoterm*. The seller bears all the costs and risks until the goods are on the quay at the destination, inclusive of customs duty payable on entry to the importer's country. The buyer bears the risks of unloading and thereafter.

Delivered Ex Ship (... named port of destination) (DES) An *incoterm*. The seller bears all the costs and risks of taking the goods to the port of destination, whence from the unloading onwards they are transferred to the buyer.

delivered pricing The practice of calculating a price of goods for sale that includes the cost of delivery.

delivery charge A charge for carrying goods, including the interest, storage, and insurance costs.

delivery Handing over of property or monetary assets. In the City the term has two more specific meanings. It describes a transfer of securities, or it is the receipt of the financial instrument or cash payment specified in a financial futures contract. *See also* **cash on delivery; delivery note**.

delivery month The month when delivery against a futures contract can be made.

delivery note Broadly, a note advising a recipient of the intended delivery of goods. In the securities market, however, a delivery note requests the delivery of a security.

delivery of bill The transfer of possession of a bill (or a cheque) from one person to another or his or her agent.

D

delivery order An order to deliver specified packages out of a combined consignment included in one single bill of lading.

delivery price The price at which deliveries on futures contracts are invoiced. It is fixed by the exchange's clearing house.

delivery verification certificate (DVC) A document used in the USA to record the movement of imported goods from an importer to a manufacturer, used to substantiate any claim for manufacturing *drawback*.

delta The rate of change of an option premium with respect to the underlying financial instrument. It is also a Stock Exchange classification of shares that are traded on the *alternative investment market*, generally relatively inactive and stable shares in small companies. *See also **alpha**; **gamma**.*

DEM (ISO) code Germany – currency: deutschemark. The 1999 legacy conversion rate was 1.95583 to the euro. It will fully change to the euro/cent from 2002.

demand 1. The desire for possession of a particular good or service at a specific price expressed by those able and willing to purchase it. 2. A request, such as a request for payment of a debt.

demand bill A bill of exchange to be paid on demand, also called a demand draft. It is also a cheque and a draft drawn by a bank on itself or its head office.

demand curve The relationship between demand and price, in the form of a graph that plots the likely demand for a product at various prices.

demand deposit A deposit of a sum of money with a bank, building society or other financial institution that may be withdrawn at a moment's notice. It is also called a sight deposit.

demand draft *See demand bill.*

demand-pull inflation Economic theory that demand is caused by excess of demand over supply, thus pulling prices up.

dematerialize To convert into electronic form information that was once recorded on paper.

demerger The splitting up of a large company or group of companies into smaller independent ones, or the selling off of a group's subsidiaries. It is usually done to improve the value of the company's shares.

demonetization 1. The process of removing a particular coin or note from circulation and declaring it to be illegal tender. In the UK, the farthing, halfpenny, three-penny and six-penny coins, and the pound note, have all been demonetized. 2. The abandonment of the use of a precious metal (gold or silver) as a monetary standard.

D

demurrage An additional charge that has to be paid if a ship is not loaded or unloaded within the time permitted.

denar The standard currency unit of Macedonia.

denationalization. The privatization of a previously nationalized industry by floating the company involved on the stock exchange and selling shares to members of the public or to institutions.

Denmark currency: Danish krøne (DKK) divided into 100 øre.

denomination The face value of something, e.g. the unitary classification of coinage, or the nominal value of **bills** and **bonds**.

Department of Trade and Industry (DTI) UK Government department that advises on and controls business and finance.

depauperization The relief of poverty (generally through economic growth).

deposit Goods or money placed with a bank or other financial institution, or an initial payment made on an item to reserve it, or an initial payment for something being bought on hire purchase or by means of a credit sale agreement.

deposit account A bank account that pays interest, but sometimes notice has to be given before funds may be withdrawn.

depositor A person who makes a deposit.

depository A secure place where money or goods are stored (deposited). Depositories may be distinguished from banks in that they do not transact other financial business and do not necessarily offer ready access to the assets stored. *See also* **deposit**.

depository receipt Also termed warehouse receipt, a document that records the delivery of goods to a warehouse.

deposit protection scheme A scheme that protects personal deposits (but not company deposits) in banks and building societies.

deposit rate The interest rate paid by a bank on a deposit account.

deposit receipt *See deposit slip*.

deposit rundown Larger than normal withdrawal of funds from a bank or other financial institution, usually in the belief that extra funds are going to be needed for some forthcoming crisis.

D

deposit slip A document that records the time and place of a deposit and its value. It is also termed a deposit receipt.

depreciation (accounting) A progressive decline in real value of an asset because of use or obsolescence. The concept of depreciation is widely used in accounting for the process of writing off the cost of an asset against profit over an extended period, irrespective of the real value of the asset.

depreciation (foreign exchange) The loss in value of a currency against one or more other currencies, especially if this happens in response to natural supply rather than by an official devaluation.

depreciation rate The rate at which *depreciation* occurs or is applied for accounting purposes.

depression A major and persistent downswing of a trade cycle, characterized by high unemployment and the underutilization of other factors of production. A less severe downswing is known as a slump or recession.

DEQ Abbreviation of *Delivered Ex Quay* (...named port of destination).

deregulation The removal of controls and abandonment of state supervision of private enterprise.

derivative A transferrable high-risk security such as a future or an option.

derivative-based funds A type of unit trust linked to the performance of derivatives (futures and options), and therefore high-risk investments.

DES Abbreviation of *Delivered Ex Ship* (...named port of destination).

designated investment exchange (DIE) A foreign investment exchange that has equivalent operating standards to home exchanges, as acknowledged by the Securities and Investment Board (SIB).

designated market maker A market maker who undertakes to be present on the trading floor of the stock exchange and to maintain up-to-date two-way prices in return for certain concessions.

despatch The bonus awarded to a charterer for completing his loading and/or unloading in less than the specified time. It is usually assessed at half the normal rate of *demurrage*.

destocking The deliberate reduction in the stock (inventory) held by a company, achieved by cutting production or by buying less stock. It reduces the amount of capital locked up in stock (or the need for borrowing to pay for it).

detention A fee charged for keeping a container or a trailer at the shipper's premises for longer than was originally contracted.

detinue A legal term for action to recover something that has been detained.

deutschemark The standard legacy currency unit of Germany, divided into 100 pfennig.

devaluation A reduction in the relative value of a currency. The devaluation may be relative to an absolute value (e.g. the *gold standard*) or to other relative values (e.g. other currencies). The pound sterling was devalued against the US dollar in 1949 and again in 1967.

develop To begin to realize the potential of, e.g., a product or company.

developing country A country that is beginning to industrialize, but which is still too poor to do so without foreign aid. Developing countries are characterized by improving standards of health, wealth (standard of living), education, capital investment and productivity, and by a broadening of the economic base.

development aid Financial and material aid to a *developing country*.

development area An economically depressed area suitable for reindustrialization. Development areas are designated by the state and incentives are provided to help to attract new businesses to the area, to encourage the relocation of existing businesses, and to enhance the prospects for employment.

development capital Funds made available (to *venture capital* companies and other specialists) through investment in equities and loan capital.

development credits Interest-free loans provided by the International Development Association, the World Bank affiliate that provides for economies with low per-capita incomes.

development expenditure Money spent by a company on research and development (R & D). It may be tax deductible.

deviation The diversion of any form of transport, such as a ship, aeroplane or lorry, to call at any other places than the original destinations. Contracts of carriage usually have clauses allowing this, because it is not legally permissible otherwise.

DGN Abbreviation of *dangerous goods note*.

diagonal spread A combination of *vertical spread* and *calendar spread*.

diarising The keping a written or computerized record of actions to be taken in the future. For example, a bank keeps a diary of customers' direct debits and standing orders.

DIE Abbreviation of *designated investment exchange*.

dies non A day that is not counted for some purpose. For example, Saturday and Sunday are not counted as days of the working week. *See also **non-business days**.*

differential The difference between two values, e.g. prices or salaries.

dilution 1. The reduction in the skill of a workforce overall, as comparatively unskilled workers are recruited in response to a rise in demand. 2. A deliberate increase in the number of shares on the market, which has the effect of reducing the price of each individual share.

dilution of equity A reduction of individual stakes in a company by the issue of further shares.

dime The popular term for a US coin worth 10 cents ($^1/_{10}$ of a dollar).

diminishing Describing something that is declining or falling.

diminishing balance (method) Method of calculating depreciation by writing off a fixed proportion of the total residual value of an asset each year.

diminishing marginal product An alternative term for *diminishing returns*.

diminishing returns A concept that suggests that as additional units of one factor of production are added, the relative increase in output will eventually begin to decline. For example, a factory can increase its output by employing more labour, but unless the other factors of production (e.g. machinery) are also increased each additional employee will be working with a smaller proportion of the other, fixed, resources available.

dinar The standard currency unit of Algeria (where it is divided into 100 centimes); Bahrain, Iraq, Jordan, Kuwait and Yemen (where it equals 1000 fils); Tunisia (where it equals 1000 millimes); Bosnia-Herzegovina and Yugoslavia (where it equals 100 paras); Libya (where it equals 100 dirhans); and Sudan (where it equals 100 piastres). It is also a subdivision (1/100) of the Irani real.

direct Immediate or unobstructed.

direct action An attempt to take control of a company by purchasing a controlling interest of shares, rather than by negotiation with the company itself.

direct arbitrage Foreign exchange dealings that are restricted to one centre.

direct costs Costs of materials, items or activities that are directly involved in the production of goods, and without which those goods could not be produced in the short run.

direct debit The practice of debiting a bank account with the sum owed on the authorization of the account holder, but without his or her direct involvement (e.g. in issuing a cheque or making a cash transfer) at the time. The essence is that it is a claim made by a creditor as opposed to a payment made by a debtor. It is a type of banker's order, although the amount to be debited is not specified.

direct expenses Expenses that may be attributed to one or another factor of production. *See also* **indirect expenses**.

direct exporting A transaction between an exporter and an importer that does not involve a third party (such as an agent).

directive A piece of European Union (EU) legislation that states what has to be done within a given timescale, without defining how it is to be done.

direct labour Members of a company's workforce who are directly involved in the production of goods or services. For example, a welder is part of the direct labour force, whereas an estimator is not.

direct mail A form of advertising and selling. Individual potential customers receive promotional material and information through the post, and order goods that are delivered by post or courier.

direct marketing Selling activity aimed directly at potential customers, such as door-to-door selling and direct mail.

direct offset A condition imposed by a buyer whereby a seller must also supply him with technology or goods directly related to the sale.

direct placement The selling of shares directly to the public without using an underwriter.

direct production A system of production that does not use machinery or division of labour. In a true system of direct production, each person makes the things that he or she requires, rather than making them to sell for profit.

D

direct quotation A quotation of a currency exchange rate in terms of one unit of the home currency, e.g. £1 = 1.5 euros.

direct rate A variable amount of home currency against a fixed amount of foreign currency. Usually, the foreign currency is quoted in units of 100.

direct response marketing A method of marketing that aims to get customers to contact a suppler (often the manufacturer) directly.

direct sale A sale made directly to the end-user (usually by a manufacturer or wholesaler), without the intervention of a retail outlet.

direct selling A system in which an exporter uses his or her own home firm to contact and deal with overseas customers directly.

direct taxation A system of taxation whereby companies and individuals pay tax on income directly to the Inland Revenue (or through an employer), as opposed to *indirect taxation*, in which tax is added to the price of goods and services.

director One of the principals of a company, in a *public limited company* (plc) appointed by its shareholders. Most companies have a group of directors (the board of directors) who act collectively as the senior management of the company, being responsible to the shareholders for its efficient running and future development. The duties and legal responsibilities of a director are defined in the Companies Acts. They include the compilation of an *annual report* and the recommendation of an annual dividend on shares.

directorate An alternative term for board of directors.

directors' interests Interests in a company's debentures, shares and share options held by the directors of the company, which must by law be disclosed.

directors' valuation In accounting, the right of a board of directors to estimate the value of a firms shareholding in an unquoted company. The directors' valuation is called for only if the value of the shares concerned has changed since they were purchased. *See also unlisted company.*

dirham The standard currency unit of Morocco (where it is divided into 100 centimes) and the United Arab Emirates (where it is divided into 10 dinars).

dirty bill of lading Carriers protect themselves by adding a protective

D

clause absolving themselves from any liability for obvious damage or other defect caused before the goods have been taken into their custody (e.g. "10 drums of oil, one leaking"). This will patently not only affect the insurance cover, but the consignment will not comply, should it be shipped under a letter of credit, unless otherwise agreed.

dirty cargo Unclean cargo shipped in bulk or in containers with a disposable lining, possibly posing a fire or health risk.

dirty float A partly-managed floating exchange rate, in which the central bank continues to intervene in the market for its own currency.

dirty money Money obtained illegally, generally through unlawful international business activities.

dis. Abbreviation of *discount*.

disagio The difference between the nominal/par value and the underlying value.

1. The discount charged for exchanging a depreciated foreign currency.

2. The loss sustained below the market price by countertrading goods instead of selling them for cash. It is the opposite of *agio*.

disaster recovery plan A comprehensive statement of consistent actions to be taken before, during and after a disaster. The plan is designed to provide for the continuity of operations and the availability of critical resources should a disaster occur.

disbursement A payment made on behalf of a client by a banker, solicitor, or other professional person. It is ultimately charged to the client's account.

discharge 1. To dismiss a member of staff from one's employment. 2. To pay a debt such as a bill of exchange.

discharged bankrupt A person discharged from bankruptcy (*see discharged in bankruptcy*). The debts of the person concerned are considered to be settled and, if solvent, he or she can begin again.

discharged bill A bill of exchange that has been paid by the drawer or drawee, or is being held by an *acceptor*. If a holder renounces rights to the debt against an acceptor, the bill is also deemed to be discharged.

discharged in bankruptcy Situation that occurs when a bankrupt is released from bankruptcy by the court after his or her debts have been paid, or it has been seen that all reasonable efforts have been made to do so.

D

discharge of contract The end of a contract, either because it has been fulfilled or because it is impossible to fulfil.

disclaimer A clause in a contract that states that one of the parties does not take responsibility for some occurrence. E.g. the owners of many car parks advise drivers that they disclaim any responsibility for loss or damage to cars or anything contained in them.

disclosure The revealing of relevant information. There are a wide variety of uses ranging from requirements that a limited company must disclose its financial dealings and position, to politicians having to declare their interests, to the requirement that parties to any contract should disclose relevant information, e.g. a person holding a life assurance policy must notify the assurers of his or her medical history.

discount In commerce, term with five specialized meanings:

1. The amount by which a new share issue stands below its par value. *See parity*.
2. The price of a share whose price/earnings ratio is below the market average.
3. The amount by which a currency is below par on the foreign exchanges.
4. To make a reduction in the face value of an article (or the price being charged for it), generally in order to make a purchase more attractive to a customer.
5. On financial markets, the charge made for cashing an immature bill of exchange, the discount being proportional to the unexpired portion of the bill.

discount broker A broker who acts as an intermediary between those who want to buy and sell bills of exchange.

discount house A company whose main activity is the discounting of bills of exchange.

discounting back A method of estimating the present value of a future sum, carried out by finding what sum earning x per cent compound interest over the time in question will equal the future sum. The interest rate x is the one in use when the calculation is made.

discount market That part of the London money markets that involves the buying and selling of short-term debt between the commercial banks, the *discount houses* and the Bank of England, which acts as the lender of the last resort.

D

discount rate 1. The rate at which a bill of exchange is discounted. *See discounting*. 2. The percentage interest rate used to calculate the present value of a future cash flow.

discount window A method by which a bank gets short-term funds from a central bank, either by securing a loan or by issuing Treasury bills.

discounted cash flow (DCF) A method of assessing a company's investments according to when they are due to yield their expected returns, in order to indicate the present worth of the future sum. In this way it is possible to determine preference for one of a number of alternative investments.

discounted value If a share price falls below its par value, the lower price is known as its discounted value.

discounting The act of making a discount. More specifically, it is the practice of selling a debt at a discount to an institution.

discounting bank A bank that specializes in discounting bills of exchange.

discrepancy In letters of credit, any difference, inconsistency or other failure to correspond exactly between the documents and/or stipulated conduct of the parties and the terms of the letter of credit.

discretionary Describing something that is not compulsory, but is left to the discretion of the person or authority involved, such as a *discretionary grant*. It is the opposite of mandatory.

discretionary account A futures account that is controlled by anybody other than the person in whose name it is in.

discretionary funds Money left with a stockbroker, to be invested at his or her discretion.

discretionary grant A grant that is not automatically paid (unlike a mandatory grant), but is made at the discretion of the authority concerned.

discriminating monopoly A monopoly in which the monopolist sells its goods or services at two different prices to two or more different sectors. For example, the electricity industry may sell electricity at a cheaper rate to industrial users than to domestic users, in an attempt to prevent the larger industrial users from changing to cheaper forms of power.

D

disguised unemployment Also known as concealed unemployment,

unemployment of those who are not earning and not searching for work. For example, during times of high unemployment, a housewife may wish to work but decides it is not worth trying to find a suitable job. This form of unemployment can be "disguised" by the method of calculating unemployment figures.

dishonour To refuse to accept or discharge a bill of exchange when it falls due for payment. Cheques are sometimes dishonoured ("bounced") by a bank if there are insufficient funds in the drawer's account to make the payment. *See also* ***acceptance for honour***.

dishonoured cheque A cheque that a bank refuses to pay, usually because the account on which it is drawn contains insufficient funds or because payment would make the account overdrawn beyond any overdraft limit.

disinflation The curbing of ***inflation*** by the adoption of mild economic measures such as the restriction of expenditure. Other measures include increasing ***interest rates*** and the deliberate creation of a budget surplus. Disinflation is a mild form of ***deflation***, which by contrast indicates an uncontrolled fall in prices.

disintermediation The withdrawal of a financial intermediary from a negotiation. The term may also be applied to the flow of funds from lenders to borrowers "off the balance sheet" without the intervention of an intermediary (e.g. a mortgage broker).

disinvestment The withdrawal or sale of an investment. Governments and companies sometimes decide to disinvest from nations whose economic or political complexion offends them.

dismissal A notice of redundancy served on an employee.

dispensation notice An instruction to a bank from the holders of a joint account to send just one statement (rather than one to each of the account holders).

disposable income That part of a person's income that he or she may dispose of in any way, i.e. what is left after such necessities as accommodation and food have been paid for.

disposables Non-durable goods; those that are consumed during their use. Food, drink, and fuel are all disposables.

dissaving A preference for spending rather than saving.

dissident shareholder One of a group of shareholders who have expressed their discontent with present management performance, and are determined to replace current managers.

dissolution The winding up of a company, usually by the legal process of liquidation. In the case of a partnership, dissolution may be occasioned by the death or retirement of one or more partners, by **bankruptcy** or by the expiry of a specified time period, without recourse to law.

distraint The legally-authorized seizure of *assets* to compel a debtor to pay a debt. If the debt remains outstanding, goods obtained by distraint may be sold in order that a *creditor* may obtain satisfaction.

distribution The transport, allocation and placement of raw materials or goods to and from a factory to warehouses and shops; or payments made by a company from its profits (i.e. dividends); or the apportioning of a scrip issue or rights issue of shares.

distribution channel The route followed by a product from its producer to its ultimate purchaser.

distributive trade That part of industry that sells goods and services direct to the consumer. Retailers are the main contributors to the distributive trade.

distributor A wholesaler; a person or company that acts as an agent in the distribution of goods to retail outlets.

diversification The enlargement of the range of goods and services offered into new areas, either material or geographical.

dividend A share in the profits of a limited company, usually paid annually. Dividends are generally expressed as a percentage of the nominal value of a single ordinary share. Thus a payment of 10p on each £1 share (or 10c on each $1 share) would be termed a dividend of 10%. They may also be expressed in terms of the dividend yield, which is the dividend expressed as a percentage of the share value.

dividend protection A situation in which the strike price of an over-the-counter option is reduced by the amount of any dividend paid on the underlying financial instrument.

dividend yield The ratio of a dividend to the price of the underlying financial instrument.

DJF (ISO) code Djibouti Republic – currency: Djibouti franc.

Djibouti Republic currency: Djibouti franc (DJF); there is no subdivision.

DKK (ISO) code Denmark – currency: Danish krøne.

DMD (ISO) code Dominica – currency: East Caribbean dollar.

D/N Abbreviation of *debit note*.

D/O Abbreviation of *delivery order*.

dobra The standard currency unit of São Tomé and Principe.

doc credit An abbreviation of *documentary letter of credit* (as distinct from a standby letter of credit).

dock dues A charge levied on vessels entering or leaving dock.

dock receipt A receipt issued by a warehouse supervisor or port officer certifying that a cargo has been received by the shipping company.

dock warrant A document that establishes the ownership of goods stored in a warehouse at the docks.

documentary bill of exchange A bill of exchange, or draft, issued with supporting papers or documents attached.

documentary credit In the export of goods, credit facilities made available at a home bank by a foreign importer. An exporter can then use this credit to discount bills drawn upon the importer.

documentary draft A draft issued with supporting papers or documents attached.

documentary letter of credit A letter of credit guaranteed by the bank issuing it and accompanied by shipping documents and also possibly a bill/draft when presented for payment.

documentary remittance The forwarding of bills of exchange and/or other documents.

documents against acceptance (D/A) An instruction on a draft used in exporting in connection with a collection against documents or a documentary credit indicating that the documents may be surrendered to the drawee against acceptance. In other words the buyer does not have to pay immediately, but has only to sign liability to pay at a future date.

documents against payment (D/P) An instruction on a draft used in exporting in connection with a collection against documents or a documentary credit indicating that the documents may be handed over to the importer only against payment.

D

dollar The standard currency unit of the USA, divided into 100 cents. It is also the name of the standard currency units of Anguilla, Antigua and Barbuda, Australia, the Bahamas, Barbados, Belau, Belize, Bermuda, the British Virgin Islands, Brunei, Canada, the Caymen Islands, the Cook Islands, Dominica, Fiji, Grenada, Guam, Guyana, Hong Kong, Jamaica, Kiribati, Liberia, Malaysia, the Marshall Islands, Micronesia, Montserrat, Namibia, Nauru, New Zealand, Puerto Rico, Saint Kitts and Nevis, Saint Lucia, Saint Vincent and the Grenadines, Singapore, the Solomon Islands, Taiwan, Trinidad and Tobago, Tuvalu, the Virgin Islands, the West Indies, and Zimbabwe. These currencies are referred to as Australian dollars, Hong Kong dollars, and so on if there is a risk of confusion with US dollars. All are divided into 100 cents. *See also* **eurodollar**.

dollar premium An extra charge, above the official exchange rate, sometimes demanded for the purchase of US dollars.

dollar rate The exchange rate of a foreign currency quoted against one unit of the US dollar, regardless of where the dealer is located or in what currency he is requesting a quote. The exception is the sterling/ US dollar rate (commonly called "cable"), which is quoted as units of the US dollar to sterling.

domestic content requirements (DCR) A condition imposed by some countries that imported goods should contain a certain amount of components made within that country using domestic labour and materials.

domiciled acceptance For a bill of exchange, the place of the acceptance is usually the drawee's address, as stated on the bill, but a different place (usually a bank) may be nominated on the bill for it to paid upon maturity, and this instruction must be compiled with.

Dominica currency: East Caribbean dollar (DMD), divided into 100 cents.

Dominican Republic currency: Dominican Republic peso (DOP), divided into 100 centavos.

dong The standard currency unit of Vietnam, divided into 100 xu.

DOP (ISO) code Dominican Republic – currency: Dominican Republic peso.

dot com stocks A colloquial description of shares in a company that relies in some way on the Internet to market its products or services.

D

double auction The normal type of outcry for trading in commodity markets, in which both bids and offers are made in competition with each other.

double bottom In the analysis of share market trends, describing a price that hits a low point equal to the last low point. The prediction is that once two similar low points have been reached, the price will tend to go up.

double option An option either to buy or sell but once either of the options has been exercised it nullifies the other, so if the right to buy is used it voids the right to sell and vice versa.

double top In the analysis of share market trends, describing a price that rises twice to similar high points. The prediction is that after the double top, the price will tend to fall.

doubtful debts Money that is owed but thought unlikely to be paid. Provision can be made for such sums in a company's accounts until they become *bad debts*.

down-and-in call/put option An option that becomes valid only when the price of the underlying security falls below a pre-set price.

down-and-out call/put option An option that becomes invalid when the price of the underlying security falls below a pre-set price.

downside The amount a person stands to lose when taking a risk.

downstream dumping The sale by a foreign producer to another producer in the home market at below cost price. The second producer then further processes the goods and exports them.

downtick Describing a transaction concluded at a lower price than a similar previous transaction. It is also a term for a small and temporary fall in the price of a share.

D/P Abbreviation of *documents against payment*.

D/P draft A documentary draft drawn up on documents against payment terms.

drachma Standard unit of Greek legacy currency, divided into 100 lepta.

draft A signed, written order by which one party (drawer) instructs another party (drawee) to pay a specified sum to a third party (payee). Payee and drawer are usually the same person. In foreign transactions, a draft is usually considered synonymous with a bill of exchange, but

D

some authorities draw a distinction that, in their view, it is not usually called a bill of exchange until it has been accepted. When prepared without supporting papers, it is a clean draft. With papers or documents attached, it is a documentary draft. A sight draft is payable on demand. A time draft is payable either on a definite date or at a fixed time after sight or demand.

dram The standard currency unit of Armenia.

dragon bond A colloquial term for a bond issued in the markets of a far Eastern country (usually Hong Kong or Singapore).

draw To write a bill of exchange, cheque or promissory note. The person who does so is the drawer, and the person or institution it is addressed to is the drawee.

drawback The repayment of customs and excise duty on certain goods to an exporter who has already paid duty on imported raw materials to make them.

drawdown A sum of money borrowed, usually referring to the staged drawing of funds from a credit facility.

drawee The person upon whom a bill of exchange is drawn.

drawer The person who draws up (i.e. writes out) a bill of exchange. Until the drawee accepts the bill of exchange, the drawer is the sole person liable on it.

drawing The presentation of documents for acceptance/payment under a documentary letter of credit.

drawing rights A method by means of which members of the International Monetary Fund (IMF) that have balance of payments difficulties get financial help. Each member has a quota, up to 25% of which can be drawn on demand. *See also* **special drawing rights**.

drawings Payments (or goods in kind) made to a partner or sole proprietor.

drop lock A loan stock issued when a specific interest rate is reached. The purpose is to convert short-term borrowings into long-term loans.

drop ship A specification that the price of a shipment by an exporter directly to an importer includes all shipping expenses.

drum A cylindrical container that may be made from various materials, including metal and plastic. It is appropriate for liquid or fatty/oily goods such as beer, lard, petroleum, etc. and even acid in suitably protective drums. Drums are subject to leakage and rust, if made of ferrous metal.

dry container A specialized container for carrying solid dry goods or for the bulk carrying of cereals and various kinds of powdered goods.

D term The category of *incoterm* in which the seller is responsible for the arrival of the goods at the agreed destination. In other words, whether or not he insures the goods he will have to replace them or be financially responsible for them in the event of any loss, damage, or non-arrival.

DTI Abbreviation of *Department of Trade and Industry*.

dti Abbreviation of direct trader input.

Dubai United Arab Emirates currency: dirham (AXD), divided into 100 fils.

dual capacity A stock exchange system that makes no distinction between the functions of stockbrokers and jobbers. One person (called a market maker) may therefore both buy and sell stocks and shares on the exchange.

due date The date on which a drawing under a deferred payment credit becomes due for payment.

dumping The sale of surplus goods and/or services to other countries at below cost so as to penetrate the other market with a view either to obtain foreign currency at any price and/or to stifle competition.

Dun and Bradstreet One of the world's best known and most influential *credit reference* agencies.

dunnage Various materials with many different uses for stowage (such as securing or separating other things, etc.). It can comprise any odd items from mats and tarpaulins to straw and old tyres, etc.

duopoly A market in which there are only two competing companies. Because competition between duopolists is particularly fierce and destructive, there tends to be some form of implicit or even explicit agreement to share the market (e.g. on a regional basis).

duopsony A market in which there are only two purchasers of a type of goods or services, but a number of competing suppliers.

duplicate documents Documents that were sent in the past in case the originals were lost or mislaid, but the practice is rather anachronistic and very rare now.

durable goods Goods that are not consumed by their use but which endure for a reasonable period of time. Some manufacturers of durables incorporate some form of obsolescence to ensure a continuity of demand.

duration The weighted average time of receiving cash flows from a fixed-income security. Used to measure interest-rate sensitivity.

Dutch auction A type of auction in which the seller begins by proposing a high price and gradually lowers it until somebody agrees to buy.

dutiable cargo A cargo on which duty, such as excise duty or VAT, has to be paid.

duty Broadly, any tax levied by a public authority, particularly that imposed on imports, exports and manufactured goods. *See also* **excise duty**.

duty-free Describing goods on which no *duty* has to be paid. The practice of allowing people entering or leaving a country to purchase duty-free goods at ports and airports ended in the EU in June 1999.

duty-paid An authenticated statement attached to goods on which duty has been paid, to facilitate their passage through customs.

duty-paid contract A type of ex ship contract in which import duty is paid by the seller.

duty-paid foreign goods Imported goods on which all duty and taxes have been paid and which have been cleared by customs.

DVC Abbreviation of delivery verification certificate.

DWT Abbreviation of *deadweight tonnage*.

DZD (ISO) code Algeria – currency: Algerian dinar.

D

E

E & OE Abbreviation of *errors and omissions excepted.*

EAPE Abbreviation of *exchange as per endorsement.*

early bargain A deal struck on the stock exchange after the exchange has closed and considered to be among the first transactions of the following day. Early bargains are also known as after-hours dealings.

early exercise The use of an option before its expiry date.

early withdrawal penalty A penalty charged for withdrawal of funds from a fixed-term investment before the maturity date.

earnest money A part payment (a deposit) made on goods or services, demonstrating that the buyer is serious about buying; or the margin on a futures market.

EASDAQ Abbreviation of *European Association of Security Dealers Automated Quotation System.*

easy market A market in which there are few buyers; prices are therefore low.

easy money Money borrowed at a low rate of interest, usually consisting of funds made available by authorities wishing to encourage economic activity. It is also known as cheap money.

EBRD Abbreviation of the *European Bank for Reconstruction and Development.*

EC Abbreviation of *European Commission* and of European Community, now replaced by the *European Union.*

ECA Abbreviation of *export credit agency.*

ECGC Abbreviation of Export Credit and Guarantee Corporation, the Indian credit insurance agency.

ECGD Abbreviation of **Export Credit Guarantee Department**, the British agency that provides government-backed insurance on longer-term exports.

ECGD export insurance policy (EXIP) The ECGD provides insurance against such buyer and political risks as a buyer going bankrupt, war breaking out in the buyer's country, or the buyer's country running out

E

of foreign exchange. The insurance policy is suitable for capital goods transactions, major services and construction projects and includes cover for costs incurred before delivery of goods to the buyer or otherwise establishing a right to payment (e.g. buying raw materials, manufacturing parts, or hiring staff – including overheads). Exporters wanting insurance for the sale of consumer goods or commodities on short payment terms are expected to seek private insurance.

ECGD insurance for finance packages. Through its export insurance policy (EXIP) the ECGD provides supplementary cover to support such situations as when the exporter has not yet been able to obtain finance, but is already exposed to loss, such as during the design, manufacture or shipment stages, etc. Also it may possibly even cover certain foreign goods and progress payments, etc. The type of supplementary cover offered depends on the particular type of ECGD finance facility granted.

ECGD-supported line of credit A facility that offers non-recourse finance to exporters of capital and project goods or services with contracts worth at least US$ 25,000 and offers several years of credit to their buyers. A UK bank provides the loan to the overseas buyer, which is guaranteed by the ECGD.

ECHO Abbreviation of *Exchange Clearing House*.

ECI Abbreviation of *export credit insurance*.

ECIC Abbreviation of *Export Credit Insurance Committee*.

ECICS Abbreviation of Export Credit Insurance Corporation of Singapore Ltd, the Singapore credit insurance agency.

ECIS Abbreviation of Export Credit Insurance Service (Ministry of Commerce & Industry), the Cypriot credit insurance agency.

e-commerce Commerce carried out electronically, particularly over the Internet.

Economic and Monetary Union A plan to bring together the currencies and monetary policies of the EU member states, as laid down by the Maastricht Treaty. There would thus be a single currency (the *euro*) and a single central bank. The plan was implemented in January 1999, but not all member states (including the UK) initially took part.

economic exposure The foreign exchange risk of a company in such areas as overseas investment and raw material costs.

economic sanction An alternative term for an embargo on trade with another country, almost always for political reasons.

economic risk The long-term risk to a company's competitive position from movements in exchange rates, or similar external factors.

economic union An agreement between two or more countries to do away with trade barriers with each other and to apply common tariffs on imports from non-union members.

ECP Abbreviation of *euro-commercial paper*.

ECS (ISO) code Ecuador – to currency: sucre.

ECSI Abbreviation of *export cargo shipping instruction*.

ECU Abbreviation of *European Currency Unit*, the legacy currency unit of European Union. It is still used in the valuation of the European Monetary Cooperative Fund.

Ecuador currency: sucre (ECS), divided into 100 centavos.

EDC Abbreviation of Export Development Corporation, the Canadian credit insurance agency.

EDF Abbreviation of *European Development Fund*.

EDI Abbreviation of *electronic data interchange*.

EDIFACT Abbreviation of Electronic Data Interchange for Administration, Commerce and Transportation, an international syntax for standard e-messages (e.g. *electronic data interchange (EDI)* for administration, commerce and transport).

EDISHIP An international syntax for exchanging data electronically between carriers and shippers.

EDP Abbreviation of electronic data processing.

EEA Abbreviation of *European Economic Area*. It is a wider tariff-free area than the EU and includes countries that belonged to the *European Free Trade Area*, to which the UK once belonged before it (like a number of other countries) left to join the EU.

EEC Abbreviation of *European Economic Community*.

effective exchange rate A weighted average of a country's exchange rate and that of its significant trading partners.

efficient market A market in which prices take into account all the information available.

EFIC Abbreviation of Export Finance & Insurance Corporation, the Australian credit insurance agency.

E

EFT Abbreviation of *electronic funds transfer*.

EFTA Abbreviation of *European Free Trade Association*.

EGM Abbreviation of *extraordinary general meeting*.

EGP (ISO) code Egypt – currency: Egyptian pound.

Egypt currency: Egyptian pound (EGP), divided into 100 piastres.

EHA Abbreviation of *equipment handover agreement*.

EIBK Abbreviation of The Export-Import Bank of Korea, the Korean credit insurance agency.

EID/MITI Abbreviation of Export Insurance Division Ministry of International Trade and Industry, the Japanese credit insurance agency.

EIR Abbreviation of *equipment interchange receipt*.

EIS Abbreviation of *Export Intelligence Service*.

EKN Abbreviation of Exportkreditnamnden, the Swedish credit insurance agency.

EKR Abbreviation of Eksportkreditradet, the Danish credit insurance agency.

elastic currency The US principle that home currency should meet the needs of trade and commerce, with the expansion of credit keeping pace with the expansion of business.

elasticity The variability in either demand or supply that companies a change in price.

ElecTra A *SITPRO* system that allows international traders to complete, save and send their documentation by electronic data interchange (EDI).

electronic data interchange (EDI) The passing of data by a computer link, especially in connection with superseding the need to send documents physically.

electronic funds transfer (EFT) The transfer of funds by computer.

electronic purse card A plastic card that operates in a similar way to telephone pay-as-you-go cards, the customer pre-purchasing a card for a specific amount. It is more secure than having to carry cash and payment can be made in more than one specified foreign currency.

E

eligible bank A UK bank that is entitled to discount acceptances at the Bank of England.

eligible bill In the UK, a bank bill that is issued by a bank entitled to discount acceptances at the Bank of England (an eligible bank); it may be rediscounted at the Bank of England. In the USA, another term for *eligible paper*.

eligible paper In the USA, a banker's acceptance that may be rediscounted at the Federal Reserve Bank.

EMA Abbreviation of *European Monetary Agreement*.

EMI Abbreviation of *European Monetary Institute*.

emalangeni (singular lilangeni) The standard currency unit of Swaziland, divided into 100 cents.

embargo A prohibition on the export or import of specified goods to or from a particular country or bloc, generally for political reasons.

EMS Abbreviation of *European Monetary System*.

EMU Abbreviation of *European Monetary Union*.

endorsement A written declaration on a document made out to order (such as a bill of exchange, bill of lading, or insurance policy/certificate), usually written on the back, with which the endorser (i.e. the owner) assigns his or her rights to the endorsee (i.e. the person named in the endorsement).

endorser A person who endorses a bill of exchange and thus accepts liability on it to honour it on the due date.

English/Scots law clause Where possible an exporter should arrange contracts (especially in the case of bonds) to be subject to the jurisdiction of English or Scottish courts, because foreign laws can vary considerably and in some cases adversely affect the exporter's interests.

enroute expenses A US term for travelling expenses incurred in the course of doing business overseas.

enterprise zone A geographical area in which economic activity is promoted by the government. Small businesses are encouraged, and the relocation of companies and industries to enterprise zones is helped by the provision of various incentives.

entrepot port A commercial centre for importing and exporting, and for collection and distribution.

entrepot store A warehouse used for the temporary storage of goods in transit.

E

entrepot trade International trade in which goods are imported and immediately re-exported.

entry documents Documents that an importer needs when goods are being cleared through customs.

entry summary documentation Documents prepared by customs after inspecting imported goods and estimating the duty to be paid.

equipment handover agreement (EHA) A method used whenever any of a carrier's equipment is hired or lent to another party, in which the latter signs an acceptance as to the state of the equipment on the handover. It thereby helps to resolve any possible subsequent disputes about any damage arising during such use.

equipment interchange receipt (EIR) A receipt used for containers as they are moved from one operator to another.

equity The risk capital of a company.

ERG Abbreviation of Geschaftsstelle fur die Exportrisikogarantie, the Swiss credit insurance agency.

Eritrea currency: birr (ETB), divided into 100 cents.

ERM Abbreviation of *Exchange Rate Mechanism*.

errors and omissions excepted (E & OE) The denial of responsibility for clerical errors and omissions, often included on invoices as a safeguard.

escalation clause Also called an escalator clause, a condition in a long-term contract that sets out the agreement concerning rising costs (of, e.g., raw materials or labour).

escape clause A clause in a contract that allows one or other party to withdraw from the contract should certain events take place. For example, in a lease, it is possible to have a clause that allows the lessee to withdraw should the lessor increase the rent.

escrow account A bank account set up in hard currency in the joint names of the buyer and seller and in which the various monies involved in any export sale in general and in a countertrade agreement in particular (usually a forward purchase) are held in trust.

escudo The standard legacy currency unit of Portugal and Cape Verde, divided into 100 centavos.

ESP (ISO) code Spain – currency: peseta. The 1999 legacy conversion rate was 166.386 to the euro. It will fully change to the euro/cent from 2002.

E

Estonia currency: kroon, divided into 100 kopecks.

ETA Abbreviation of estimated time of arrival.

ETB (ISO) code Ethiopia – currency: birr.

ETD Abbreviation of estimated time of departure.

E term The category of *incoterm* in which the seller's obligations are minimal.

Ethiopia currency: birr (ETB), divided into 100 cents.

EUR (ISO) code European Union – currency: euro.

EU Abbreviation of *European Union*.

euro The standard currency unit of the European Monetary Union, introduced at the beginning of 1999 (but not adopted then by Denmark, Greece, Sweden and the UK; Greece joined in 2001). Currently only non-cash payments may be made in euros. *See also European Currency Unit (ECU)*.

Eurobond A negotiable debt security issued outside the country of its currency and intended for international distribution.

euro commercial interest reference rate Since 15 January 1999 the replacement for the national **CIRRs** of all the participating *Euroland* countries.

euro-commercial paper (ECP) Commercial paper issued in a eurocurrency, in a market (chiefly centred on London) that was established in 1985.

eurocurrency A deposit account in any major currency outside the country of that currency.

Eurodollar A dollar deposited with a bank outside the USA.

Eurogiro A pan-European electronic payment system operated by European girobanks.

Euroland Theoretical political association comprising EU countries that have adopted the euro.

euro legacy currency conversion rates

Austrian schilling	13.7603	to euro	(1999)
Belgian franc	40.3399	to euro	(1999)
Dutch guilder	2.20371	to euro	(1999)

E

Finnish markka	5.94573	to euro	(1999)
French franc	6.55957	to euro	(1999)
German mark	1.95583	to euro	(1999)
Greek drachma	340.750	to euro	(2001)
Irish punt	0.787564	to euro	(1999)
Italian lira	1936.27	to euro	(1999)
Luxembourg franc	40.3399	to euro	(1999)
Portuguese escudo	200.482	to euro	(1999)
Spanish peseta	166.386	to euro	(1999)

euromarket The market in which eurocurrency is traded.

European Association of Securities Dealers Automated Quotation System (EASDAQ) A Europe-wide stock market, established in Brussels in 1966, based on the US National Association of Security Dealers Automated Quotation System (NASDAQ) and catering mainly for high-growth companies.

European Bank for Reconstruction and Development (EBRD) An organization whose aims are to foster the transition towards open-market economies and their integration into the international economy as a whole.

European Commission (EC) A major institution of the EU, established in 1967, responsible for implementing the Treaty of Rome. It introduces EU legislation and reconciles disagreements between members.

European Committee for Banking Standards An organization that sets and monitors acceptable standards for international banking practice for both commercial and savings banks.

European Community (EC) Short form of the European Economic Community (EEC), now called the *European Union*.

European Currency Unit (ECU) The unit of account dating in use by the European Economic Union (EEC) from 1979 and now by the European Union (EU). The value of the ECU is calculated by taking a weighted avergae of the current value of EU member-states' own currencies. It exists on paper, and is used to settle intra-Union debts and in the calculation of Union budgets. Because it is an inherently stable currency, the ECU is increasingly favoured in the international money markets as a medium for international trade. *See also **euro**.*

E

European Development Fund (EDF) A fund established in 1976 by the

European Community (now EU) to provide financial aid on advantageous terms to certain developing countries.

European Economic Area (EEA) A European free trade area, established in 1994 by agreement between the European Union (EU) and the European Free Trade Association (EFTA).

European Free Trade Association (EFTA) A trade association, established in 1960 between several west European countries, some of whom left when they joined the European Union (EU).

European Monetary Agreement (EMA) An agreement that allows currencies of European member states to be traded without restriction. It was made in 1958 by the then Organization for European Economic Cooperation (now the Organization for Economic Cooperation and Development, OECD).

European Monetary Institute (EMI) An organization created in 1991 under the Maastricht Treaty to manage currency reserves of EU central banks, with a view towards a single monetary policy and the Europe-wide use of the European currency unit (ECU).

European Monetary System (EMS) A system established in 1979 for stabilizing exchange rates between EU member states. It was seen as a step towards a European Central Bank and a single currency as part of European Monetary Union.

European Monetary Union (EMU) One of the aims of the Maastricht Treaty that would result in all EU member states having a common currency (the European currency unit, ECU). It was originally termed Economic and Monetary Union.

euronote The standard currency unit of the European Union, divided into 100 cents.

European Union (EU) An association of European nations formerly known as the European Economic Community (EEC) or European Community (EC), and before that the Common Market. It is intended that in the long run all the factors of production may be moved within the community at will, and remaining customs barriers are expected to be removed in the near future. The EU operates a protectionist policy by maintaining common tariffs on imports, and generates a substantial part of its income from import duties and value-added tax. In finance, its committed aims include a European Monetary System (EMS), and all that it entails.

Eurotunnel An undersea rail tunnel (the Channel Tunnel) that links

E

England and France, which has had an enormous impact on British transport links with the rest of Europe.

European Monetary Cooperative Fund currency: ecu (XEU), divided into 100 cents.

European Monetary Union (EMU) The ultimate aim to standardize the currency of the EU, the euro. Another objective is to create a deep and liquid capital market in Europe, reducing the cost for issuers and increasing the choice for investors.

European option A currency option that can be exercised only on the expiry date. It originated in Europe and its use is not restricted in anyway geographically. *See also* **American option**.

European Union currency: euro (EUR), divided into 100 cents.

EUROPRO The trade facilitation organization of the EU and EFTA countries.

euro rates Interest rates payable on currency deposits outside the country in whose currency the deposit is denominated.

event of default A clause in a loan agreement that, if breached, requires repayment of the loan immediately.

evergreen clause In a letter of credit, a clause that specifies a regular expiry date with automatic extension.

evidence account A record of all imports and exports by the parties involved in a countertrade agreement that over a fixed period of time a specific ratio of sales to purchases must be achieved.

exchange A physical location for trading, e.g. the Chicago Mercantile Exchange.

exchange as per endorsement A specialized type of discounting whereby the amount and collection charges and interest for a bill of exchange are converted into the importer's currency to take advantage of a lower rate of interest and the opportunity to pay in the importer's own currency. The bank covers itself by selling forward to cover the exchange risk. Currently out of vogue, it is useful when interest rate differentials are very large.

exchange clause On a bill of exchange, the clause that determines the exact amount to be paid.

Exchange Clearing House (ECHO) A clearing house for foreign exchange derivatives, founded by an association of Barclays Bank (UK), Banque National de Paris (France), Commerzbank (Germany) and Rabobank.

exchange control Regulations restricting or forbidding certain types of foreign currency transactions by residents of the country enforcing the regulations.

exchange exposure The extent of the risk that results from quoting assets or liabilities in a foreign currency, because variations in the exchange rate can affect the values.

exchange gain The profit made by an importer if there is a favourable change in the exchange rate.

exchange rate The price of one currency expressed in terms of another currency.

exchange loss The loss made by an importer if there is an unfavourable change in the exchange rate.

Exchange Rate Mechanism (ERM) An EU regulation that restricts variations in the exchange rates of its member states to within closely defined limits. It is a vital feature of the European Monetary System (EMS). Britain and Italy left the ERM in 1992.

exchange rate risk The potential loss that could be incurred from a movement in exchange rates.

exchange risk guarantee scheme A UK government scheme to cover any exchange risk (for an annual service charge) on loans in foreign currencies from the European Coal and Steel Community or the European Investment Bank.

exchange traded options Options that can be bought in "parcels" for standard amounts on future/option exchanges.

excise duty Duty levied on home-produced goods, either to control consumption and thus influence spending, or to raise revenue (goods that currently attract excise duty in the UK include alcohol, petrol and tobacco). In the USA, a similar levy is known as excise tax.

exclusionary clause Any contractual clause excluding one party's liability for any breach or failure etc.

ex-coupon Describing stock that does not give the purchaser the right to the next interest payment due to be paid on it.

ex-dividend Often shortened to ex div, describing stock that does not give

E

the purchaser the right to the next dividend payment, or to any dividend payment due within a specified period, generally the next calendar month. However, he or she does have the right to receive subsequent dividends.

exemption clause A clause in a sales contract that excludes the seller from liability for breach of a condition or warranty.

exercise To make use of a right or option.

exercise notice A notice issued when the holder of an option wishes to take up his or her right to buy or sell the security for which the option has been agreed.

exercise price The price at which an option may be exercised (also known as the strike price).

EXGO Abbreviation of Export Guarantee Office, the New Zealand credit insurance agency.

EXIMBANK Abbreviation of Export-Import Bank of the United States, the American credit insurance agency.

EXIP Abbreviation of the *ECGD export insurance policy*.

expense budget A financial plan that details expected future outgoings, normally over a time span of a year.

expiry The end of the acceptability or specified length of time allowed. See *expiry date*.

expiry date The final date on which an option can be exercised.

export To sell goods or services outside their country of origin; or the goods or services themselves.

export broker A person or company that brings together buyers and sellers (for a commission) but does not take part in sales transactions.

export cargo shipping instruction (ECSI) The shipping instructions that a shipper gives to a carrier.

export controls Government restrictions on goods leaving the country (exports).

export credit Financial facilities or delayed payment terms made available to foreign buyers.

export credit agency (ECA) An official organization that provides export credit insurance and loans.

E

Export Credit Guarantee Department (ECGD) A UK government departmental agency established in 1919. It provides government-backed insurance on longer-term exports (of two years or more duration). In 1991 its short-term business was sold to the Dutch credit insurance company *Nederlandshe Credietverzekering Maatschappij*.

export credit insurance (ECI) A type of insurance that covers the substantial risk to exporters of non-payment due to buyer failure or foreign government intervention.

Export Credit Insurance Committee (ECIC) An organization that mantains sound principles and discipline for all the member countries of the *Berne Union* (of which the ECGD is a founder member).

export declaration A statement provided to the Customs and Excise detailing the cost, price, destination and nature of goods leaving the country.

export duty A tax levied on exports. Export duties tend to discourage exports and adversely affect the balance of payment, and for these reasons they are seldom used.

export group An organization in which, like other joint selling schemes, the firms retain their own proprietorships but share marketing, transport, advertising and costs etc. which they organize from a central distribution point.

export house Generally a firm that acts both generally as an *export merchant* and as a *confirming house*.

export incentives Government incentives designed to encourage exports. They include direct-tax incentives, subsidies, favourable terms for insurance and the provision of cheap credit.

Export Intelligence Service (EIS) A market information service provided by the *British Overseas Trade Board*.

export licence A document issued by a government authorizing a restricted item to be exported.

export leasing Practice of selling goods for export to a leasing company in the country of origin, which ships them overseas and leases then to foreign customers.

export licensing Licences may be granted to an overseas company to manufacture and sell goods on a royalty basis either under a British manufacturer's own brand name or its own name. *See also national export licence* for licences issued as a national control.

E

Exportmaster Specialized computer software for export management and documentation.

export merchant A person who is responsible for buying goods on his own account, or as an agent on behalf of a client, or acting for an overseas buyer.

exposure A company (or individual) has exposure in a currency: 1. When its assets and liabilities in that currency are not equal, so that it has an "open" position (whether long or short) in that currency; or 2. When the maturity dates of its assets and liabilities differ (i.e. the maturity dates of forward contracts to buy and sell differ).

expropriation insurance Insurance that covers losses arising from nationalization or confiscation of property. *See also* **creeping expropriation**.

extended guarantee Foreign buyers often require that the fixed expiry date of a bond or guarantee can be "extended or paid". The exporter should try and resist such claims, but in practice may have difficulty in resisting local pressures. Nevertheless acceptance of this practice could jeopardize any insurance claim for the unfair calling of the bond or guarantee.

extension fork-lift truck A fork-lift truck fitted with extended forks to handle goods of a greater than average length.

extraordinary general meeting (EGM) A company shareholders' meeting other than the *annual general meeting*.

EXW Abbreviation of *Ex Works*.

ex warehouse (EXW) A term that is synonymous with *Ex Works*.

EXW loaded Although the loading of the goods in an ex-works contract is the buyer's responsibility, this term describes the situation in which the seller agrees to do so instead if this preferred.

Ex Works (...named place) (EXW) An *incoterm*. It represents the minimum responsibility for the seller. Unless otherwise agreed, he has only to provide suitable packing and to pay for any necessary checking such as counting, weighing, or quality checking, etc. and/or to help the buyer with obtaining any documentation or arranging insurance details. The buyer has to deal with everything else.

E

F

face vet A quick initial check by a customs entry clerk so that he or she can reject entries with obvious defects.

facilitating intermediary A US term for any person or organization that arranges for shipments to be sent to overseas destinations.

facility A general term for any kind of loan, usually from a bank.

facility guarantee A guarantee used as a security for a bank to lend to a subsidiary of a foreign company.

factor A person or company that undertakes *factoring*.

factoring In international trade, a type of *non-recourse/without recourse* finance. It originates from the buying of the exporter's debts, thereby guaranteeing him cash payment and relieving him of the credit risk. The factoring company can offer additionally to administer the exporter's sales ledger, and collect the buyers' payments once the goods have been shipped. It can thereby also relieve the exporter of a lot of the administrative costs. An advance can also be given to the exporter to cover the shipment and even some of the post-shipment finance, thus considerably helping his cashflow. This additional service is normally referred to as *invoice discounting*. Where it is offered on its own without any supporting cash payment or guarantee it is occasionally referred to by some modern factoring companies as *recourse/with recourse* factoring, which on the face of it is a contradiction of terms. Factoring has become more popular with the increase in *open account* trading, which is very popular in the European Union and can also support *collections*.

factoring company In international trade, a company that administers on behalf of an exporter its sales ledger, and collects payments for the exporter once the goods have been shipped. See *factoring*.

faculative endorsement An endorsement to a bill of exchange that absolves the endorser of certain duties (such as waiving the need for a notice of dishonour).

fair value The value of an asset that could be obtained in an arm's-length transaction between a willing seller and a willing buyer, each acting in his or her own self-interest.

F

FAK Abbreviation of *freight of all kinds*.

Faroe Islands currency: Danish krøne (DKK), divided into 100 øre.

FAS Abbreviation of *Free Alongside Ship* (…named port of shipment).

fate The decision whether or not to pay a cheque or other negotiable instrument when it is presented for payment.

fate enquiry A reminder from a remitting bank requesting an update from a collecting bank on the latest situation relating to a collection.

FBL Abbreviation of *forwarder's bill of lading*.

FC & S Abbreviation of *free of capture and seizure*.

FCA Abbreviation of *Free Carrier* (…named place).

FCIA Abbreviation of The Foreign Credit Insurance Association, an American private credit insurance company.

FCL Abbreviation of full container load.

FCR Abbreviation of *forwarder's certificate of receipt*.

FCT Abbreviation of *forwarder's certificate of transport*.

FDI Abbreviation of *foreign direct investment*.

FECDBA Abbreviation of *Foreign Exchange and Currency Deposit Brokers' Association*.

FEDERAL Abbreviated name of The Federal Insurance Company Limited, a private company dealing with Swiss credit insurance.

feeder vessel A smaller ship used to bring containers and other cargoes to and from large ocean-going ships.

FES Abbreviation of *forward exchange supplement*.

ffi Abbreviation of for further instructions.

FIATA Abbreviation of Federation Internationale des Associations de Transitaires et Assimiles – the International Association of Freight Forwarders.

fictitious value The imaginary or assumed value of goods, which cannot be used for customs purposes in the USA.

fidelity guarantee A guarantee by one person for the fidelity or integrity of another, usually for employment purposes.

fiduciary A person or body acting in trust. Anybody holding, say, cash in trust for another is said to be acting in a fiduciary capacity.

fiduciary deposit A bank deposit that the bank lends to somebody else at the depositor's risk (although the depositor earns a fairly high rate of interest). It is a system used by some Swiss banks.

Fiji currency: Fijian dollars (FJD), divided into 100 cents.

filler A subdivision (1/00) of the Hungarian forint.

fill or kill On a futures market, an order to trade that must be either fulfilled immediately or cancelled.

fils A subdivision (1/100) of the United Arab Emirates dirham, and a subdivision (1/1000) of the dinar in Bahrein, Iraq, Jordan, Kuwait and the Republic of Yemen.

FIM (ISO) code Finland – currency: markka. The 1999 legacy conversion rate was 5.94573 to the euro. It will fully change to the euro/cent from 2002.

final response A full commitment by all the contributing export credit agencies in a cooperation agreement to provide the necessary reinsurance to the lead agency in any given transaction.

finance house A company that provides funding (credit), e.g. for hire-purchase agreements. The finance house pays a trader in full, and charges interest to the purchaser of goods provided by the trader.

finance house base rate The rate of interest charged to borrowers by UK finance houses. It is set monthly by averaging the three-weekly average of the three-month LIBOR (London Inter-bank Offer Rate), rounded up to the nearest ½%.

finance house deposit A deposit placed with a finance house by a large lender such as a bank.

Finance Houses Association An organization established in 1945, originally by six large UK finance houses. It ensures that the houses have a consistent policy on deposits, interest rates and hire-purchase finance.

financial documents Bills of exchange, promissory notes, cheques, payment receipts or other similar instruments for obtaining the payment of money.

financial future A contract for the delivery of a financial instrument (i.e. a currency) on a future date. Financial futures are used to hedge against the rise and fall of interest and exchange rates.

F

financial instrument Any method of financing, such as a bond, certificate of deposit (CD) or treasury bill.

Finland currency: markka (FIM), divided into 100 pennia. The 1999 legacy conversion rate was 5.94573 to the euro. It will fully change to the euro/cent from 2002.

fine bank bill A bill of exchange accepted by or drawn on an eligible bank. It is also termed a prime bank bill.

fine bill A bill of exchange for which the backer is extremely creditworthy and so there is little or no risk.

fine price The price of a security on a market in which the difference between the buying and selling prices is very small.

fine rate The best rate of interest that can be obtained in a given situation.

fine trade bill A trade bill with reputable drawer and drawee, which commands a fine rate of discount.

fio Abbreviation of free in and out. See *free in clause* and *free out clause*.

FIO and stowed Term commonly used in the chartering of aircraft and ships to cover the loading, discharge and stowing costs. It is alternatively known as *FIO and trimmed*.

FIO and trimmed Term commonly used in the chartering of aircraft and ships to cover the loading, discharge and *trimming* costs. Alternatively known as *FIO and stowed*.

firm bid Also called a firm offer, a bid (or offer) that has no conditions.

firm market A market in which prices are steady.

firm order An order to buy or sell a security that can be carried out without further confirmation.

firm price A guaranteed price, usually offered if the cost of providing goods and services can be assessed extremely accurately.

first bill of exchange Where sets of bills of exchange are used, the first or chief copy is the one that has to be presented and honoured. Once this has been effected the other copies are voided. This practice ensures that there is only one obligation, but at the same time allows for anything going wrong (like the first copy going astray in transit). It is a legacy of times subject to the vicissitudes of the post, but is becoming increasingly obsolete due to the increased application of electronic data interchange (EDI).

F

first-class paper Bills issued by financial institutions of high standing (such as the Treasury).

first notice day On a futures contract, the first day on which notice can be given of intended (or expected) actual delivery.

fiscal charges (on road vehicles) Some countries, such as Switzerland, impose taxes on foreign haulage operators carrying goods through their country, although in many cases there are reciprocal bilateral agreements to waive these.

fiscal measure In international trade, the imposition of a tax to discourage imports.

fix To settle a price in the commodity markets by trading.

fixed asset Also known as capital asset, an asset that are used in furtherance of a company's business, such as machinery or property. *See capital asset.*

fixed exchange rate An official exchange rate set by monetary authorities (government or a similar authority) for one or more currencies. In most instances, even fixed exchange rates are allowed to fluctuate between definite upper and lower intervention points.

fixed-interest security A security for which the income is fixed and does not vary. Such securities include bonds, debentures and gilt-edged securities.

fixed rate Describing a charge or interest rate that does not change (unlike a floating rate). It offers a borrower the benefit of knowing in advance what his or her liabilities will be throughout the life of a loan.

fixed rate export finance (FREF) (ECGD) Although the buyer in a buyer credit pays a fixed rate, the bank usually has to fund it through the shorter-term money markets. The cost to the bank can consequently fluctuate over the life of the loan. The ECGD's fixed rate export finance (FREF) scheme covers the bank's own variable funding costs. It uses an interest equalization formula known as *interest make up*.

FJD (ISO) code Fiji – currency: Fijian dollars.

flag The country in which a ship is registered is represented by a flag, flown at the stern. Not all countries have the same stringent requirements regarding the seaworthiness and staffing etc. of their vessels, so the flag can be a very important issue, particularly for meeting letter of credit requirements etc.

F

flag of convenience A flag flown by a merchant vessel registered in a country whose manning, taxation and safety requirements are less stringent than elsewhere, to the advantage of the shipowner.

flat container A specialized container for carrying large and/or heavy single items, such as large machinery parts, metal pipes, rock, etc. There are various types ranging from those with collapsible ends to cater for goods of excess length and for situations where there is any restriction regarding height. It is also known as a half-height container.

flat yield Also known as running yield, the interest rate expressed as a percentage of the price paid for a fixed-interest security.

flight capital Capital that is hurredly removed from one country that seems to be politically (or economically) unstable, and taken to a more stable environment.

flip-flop bond A bond that an investor can easily convert into another kind of debt instrument, and then just as easily convert back.

floater A security owned by the bearer, the person who holds it. More formally it is termed a bearer security.

floating asset An alternative name for *current asset*.

floating currency A currency whose value varies up and down according to its supply and demand.

floating exchange rates A system in which exchange rates are determined by supply and demand in the foreign exchange markets.

floating policy A cargo insurance policy covering a series of consignments.

floating-rate buyer credit Because some buyers prefer a floating rate, the ECGD's guarantee method works exactly like a fixed-rate buyer credit except that there are no interest make-up arrangements, and it does not pay a margin to the bank.

floating-rate loan A loan on which the interest rate is reset at periodic intervals.

floating-rate note A security whose rate of interest is not fixed, but is adjusted, usually quarterly, based on the base rate or other money market changes.

floor 1. An option that fixes the minimum interest rate receivable on a deposit for a series of interest periods. 2. The trading area of an exchange.

floor broker A member of a commodity market who is authorized to deal on the trading floor. In the USA, a floor broker is a member an exchange who deals in securities, on behalf of clients, on the trading floor. *See also floor trader.*

floor trader A member an exchange who deals in securities on the trading floor on his or her own behalf. *See also floor broker.*

flotsam Goods or part of a shipwreck found floating on the surface of the sea.

flowchart In trade, a distribution chart that indicates the physical movement of goods from their place of production to the place of consumption. It locates the main places of cost concern and thereby suggests opportunities for cheaper alternatives.

fluctuating foreign exchange rate agreement An exporter and a buyer may agree that the price charged by the exporter can move in response to changes in the rate of exchange (which might possibly be of mutual benefit, because the price could go down as well as up). In other words, the exporter receives a guaranteed amount (say, acceptable at the rate of exchange ruling at the time of the contract). This obviously merely transfers the risk to the buyer, if the latter is prepared to accept it.

fluctuation A movement of prices up or down on a market. Downward fluctuation is also known as slippage.

FMV Abbreviation of *foreign market value.*

FOB Abbreviation of *Free On Board* (...named port of shipment).

FOMEX Abbreviation of Fondo para el Fomento de las Exportaciones de Productos Manufacturados, Banco de Mexico S.A., the Mexican credit insurance agency.

forced sale (by auction) Exported goods that have not been taken up by the importer are frequently disposed of this way to mitigate the exporter's loss and/or to pay for unpaid duties/storage and any other outstanding charges. Also port authorities frequently dispose of unclaimed goods this way.

force majeure Any unforeseeable event excusing the fulfilment of a contract.

foreign bank From the point of view of somebody in the UK, a bank with headquarters abroad that is authorized to open offices in the UK. Substitute any other country for "UK" and the definition still stands.

foreign bill A bill of exchange drawn in a foreign country, i.e. that is not an

F

inland bill (in the UK an inland bill is designated by the Bills of Exchange Act 1882 as a bill drawn and payable in Britain or drawn in Britain on a British resident).

foreign bond A bond denominated in a currency other than that of the issuer and sold in the domestic market of that currency (such as a Japanese yen bond issued by a German company and sold in Japan). Such bonds are known as bulldog bonds in the UK and yankee bonds in the USA.

foreign currency account Also called a nostro account, an account held by a home bank in a foreign country. The term may also describe a home bank account whose funds are in a foreign currency.

foreign currency borrowing Foreign currency can be borrowed from a bank to be repaid from the proceeds of the export receivables, thus providing a cheap efficient form of finance.

foreign currency swap A deal in which currency of one country is traded for the currency of another on the understanding that the deal will be reversed at a later date.

foreign direct investment (FDI) Investment in assets overseas or in the overseas operations of a company.

foreign draft A bill of exchange that is payable abroad; or a bank draft drawn on a foreign branch, usually in the foreign currency.

Foreign Exchange and Currency Deposit Brokers' Association (FECDBA) A UK professional organization for brokers who deal in foreign exchange or deposits in foreign currencies.

foreign exchange broker A broker who deals in foreign exchange, usually on the foreign exchange market (FOREX).

foreign exchange dealer A person in a bank authorized to deal in (i.e. buy and sell) foreign currency.

foreign exchange exposure A company has foreign exchange exposure if it either: 1. Risks losses from adverse exchange rate movements; or 2. Hopes to profit from favourable exchange rate movements.

foreign exchange market A market in which foreign currencies are traded. In most developed, capitalist countries there is no physical marketplace; the foreign exchange market is made up of the major banks.

foreign exchange risk The risk taken in buying or selling foreign currency (because the exchange rate could change unfavourably between buying and selling).

foreign laws Many contracts, such as bonds and guarantees to take notable examples, are made subject to the local laws and regulations ruling in an importer's own country. This can entail great difficulties for an exporter (and in the case of bonds and guarantees for the guarantor as well).

foreign market value (FMV) The price at which goods are sold (or offered for sale) in the main markets of the exporting country.

FOREX Abbreviation of foreign exchange market.

forfaiting A specialist banking service by which a bank buys foreign debts at a discount *without recourse* thus removing the risk to the seller of non-payment. Frequently, although not necessarily, it is supported by an (or a series of) avalised bill(s)/note(s) (*see* **aval**).

forfeiture The compulsory surrender of property for failure to comply with a contract or with the law.

forgery The fraudulent imitation of a document or the writing or signature of a signatory in order to pass it off as written by another.

forint The standard currency unit of Hungary, divided into 100 filler.

fork-lift truck A vehicle for lifting and carrying loads that has a horizontal fork in front. There is a large variety of types to cater for special circumstances, such as those that can handle barrels and drums. Fork-lift trucks can also be augmented with various devices to deal with special circumstances, such as those having side shift mechanisms or squeeze clamps, etc.

Formfill Computer software provided by Formecon Services Ltd for completing export documentation and storing information, including every country's export requirements, etc.

forward To send something on to somebody (e.g. to a new address); or describing something (e.g. a futures contact) to be completed some time in the future.

forward book A book that records various net exposures a dealer has for forward contract maturities (e.g. an excess of assets over liabilities maturing on a specific date).

forward contract A contract for the delivery of a certain amount of foreign currency in the future, at a price determined when the contract

F

is made. Under a fixed forward contract, the foreign currency must be delivered at the date specified in the contact. If the forward deal is on an option basis, the currency can be delivered at any time within a specified period; the customer decides when exactly he wants to deal. Note that a forward deal on an option basis is not the same thing as a currency option. It is also termed a forward deal.

forward deal An alternative term for *forward contract.*

forwarder's bill of lading (FBL) A bill of lading issued by a forwarding agent. The International Association of Freight Forwarders (FIATA) has a standard forwarding agents' bill of lading using standard conditions of carriage.

forwarder's certificate of receipt (FCR) A non-negotiable transport document for forwarders carrying goods over land or inland waterways etc., where an FIATA *forwarding agent's bill of lading* would not be appropriate.

forwarder's certificate of shipment A certificate from a freight forwarder that the goods have been shipped on a named ship.

forwarders' certificate of transport (FCT) A transport document used where a transfer of title (i.e. ownership) is required for multi-modal transport, but where a carrier's transport document is otherwise not essential.

forwarder's delivery order A document issued by a freight forwarder authorizing the party to whom it is addressed to deliver the specified goods to a party different to the consignee named in the consignment note.

forwarder's receipt A receipt issued by a forwarding agent for goods received.

forward exchange supplement (FES) Insurance cover provided by the ECGD for the exchange risk involved in an exporter who is tendering for contracts quoted in foreign currencies entering into either a forward exchange contract with, or buying a currency option from, his or her bank. Banks normally provide foreign exchange cover only once the commercial contract has been signed.

forward/forward The simultaneous buying and selling of the same currency in the forward market, but for different maturity dates (e.g. with the forward contract to buy maturing before the forward contract to sell).

F

forward-forward An agreement to lend or take on deposit a specific amount of money for a specific period, starting on a specific future date.

forwarding agent A person who loads, or charters and loads, any form of transport or a person whose business is to receive and forward freight, often sent in a container and likely to emply multi-modal transport.

forwarding agents' bill of lading A bill of lading used by members of FIATA incorporating its standard conditions of carriage. *See forwarder's bill of lading.*

forward margins The discounts or premiums between spot rates and the forward rates for a currency.

forward points The interest rate differential between two currencies. The forward points are added to or subtracted from the spot rate to give the forward rate.

forward purchase A compensation agreement under which a buyer's goods are delivered to an exporter in advance to enable him to raise the foreign exchange to pay for his own sale. It is also known as advance compensation or junctim.

forward rate The rate at which a foreign exchange contract is struck today for settlement at a specified future date.

forward rate agreement (FRA) An agreement that fixes the interest rate payable or receivable on a given notional amount for a specified future period.

forward rates The discounts or premiums between spot rates and the forward rates for a currency.

foul bill of lading Also known as a dirty bill of lading, a carrier's receipt for goods (bill of lading) that states that the goods were damaged when received.

FPA Abbreviation of the strictly obsolete term (yet one still occasionally seen) free from particular average. It is now referred to as *Institute cargo clause* A.

FRA Abbreviation of *forward rate agreement.*

framework agreement An outline of the general terms and arrangements of a *countertrade* deal.

franc The standard currency unit of Belgium, Benin, Burkina-Faso, Burundi, Cameroon, Central African Republic, Chad, Comoros,

F

Congo, Cote d'Ivoire, Djibouti, Equatorial Guinea, France and its dependencies, Gabon, Guinea, Liechtenstein, Luxembourg, Madagascar, Mali, Monaco, Niger, Senegal, Switzerland, Togo and Rwanda. In all cases it is divided into 100 centimes. The countries of the French African Community (CFA) all use the CFA franc, which is pegged to the French franc; territories and ex-territories in the Pacific area use the CFP franc. Others are distinguished by their country, such as Belgian franc and Swiss franc.

France currency: French franc (FRF), divided into 100 centimes. The 1999 legacy conversion rate was 6.55957 to the euro. It will fully change to the euro/cent from 2002.

franchise A licence granted to an individual or group by a company to sell its goods or services in a particular specified way.

franchisee A person or group to whom a *franchise* is granted; in international trade this will be the importer.

franchising A system under which a licence is granted to manufacture or market a product or service for which the equipment or supplies are manufactured and furnished by the *franchisor*.

franchisor The company granting a *franchise;* in international trade this will be the exporter.

franco Abbreviation of the strictly obsolete term (yet one still occasionally seen) franco domicile (free from duties, transportation charges and other levies). The current expression is Delivered Duty Paid (DDP).

fraud The illegal practice of obtaining money from people under false pretences. For example, fraud is committed if facts pertaining to a contract are purposefully misrepresented. Fraudulently diverting one's company's or employer's money for one's own use is embezzlement.

FRCD Abbreviation of floating-rate certificate of deposit.

Free Alongside Ship (...named port of shipment) (FAS) An *incoterm.* The seller's responsibilities end once the goods have been placed alongside the ship on the quayside or in a lighter. The buyer bears all the costs and risks from there on. This even includes the responsibility of clearing the goods for export.

Free Carrier (...named place) (FCA) An *incoterm.* Its meaning is similar to *Ex Works*, except that the seller is additionally responsible for obtaining any export licence and/or dealing with any other official export requirements, such as customs formalities. He must also notify

F

the buyer in time whether or not the carrier has picked up the goods.

free competition A situation in which rival companies are allowed to compete freely with each other for a share of the market. In a free competition or free market economy, the laws of supply and demand regulate prices.

free contract Alternative term for *rondu*.

free exchange rate An exchange rate in a foreign market that is determined only by supply and demand, with no government intervention (as opposed to a fixed exchange rate).

free from particular average An obsolete term (yet one still occasionally seen). It is now referred to as *Institute cargo clause* **A**.

free in Describing goods whose price includes the costs of loading.

free in and out (FIO) Describing goods whose price includes the costs of loading and unloading.

free in clause A clause in a bill of lading stating that the loading charges are to be paid by the supplier.

free market A market that operates essentially by the laws of supply and demand. Or, on the stock market, a situation in which a particular security is freely available and in reasonably large quantities.

free of capture and seizure (FC&S) An insurance clause stating that the insurer is not liable for a ship or its cargo that is seized by any foreign power.

free of strikes and riots (FSR) A marine insurance clause exempting the insurer from responsibility for any strikes or riots that might arise (this is usual unless otherwise agreed).

Free On Board (...named port of shipment) (FOB) An *incoterm*. The seller is responsible as far as loading the goods on board ship at the port of departure. The risk passes as soon as the goods cross over the ship's rail.

free out clause Term meaning the same as CFR landed, i.e. the clause in a bill of lading stating that the unloading charges are to be paid by the supplier.

freeport A designated enclosed area wherein goods can be landed, stored, sorted, sifted, sampled, manufactured or repacked etc. without having to pay any customs and excise duty until they are sent into the

F

hinterland. It is similar to the bonded warehouse system, but it additionally covers the manufacture of goods and thereby encourages extra transhipment and entrepot traffic as well.

free trade The concept of international trading in which there are no tariff barriers between countries.

free trade agreement (FTA) An agreement between nations to abolish all tariffs between the two countries.

free trade area (FTA) A group of countries that permit the international trade between themselves to be left to its natural course without restriction on imports or exports.

free trade zone (FTZ) Alternative name for a *freeport*.

FREF Abbreviation of *fixed rate export finance*.

freight 1. Any transported goods, alternatively known as *cargo*. 2. A charge for transportation of goods or for the hire of a ship, aircraft, etc. for transporting goods. 3. The transportation of goods more slowly and cheaply than by express delivery.

freight account A debit note sent by a shipowner to a shipper for freight charges on his goods.

freight forward A term indicating that freight is to be paid by the consignee. The carrier has a **lien** on the goods until the freight has been paid.

freight forwarder A person who loads, or charters and loads, any form of transport or a person whose business is to receive and forward freight, often sent in a container and likely to employ multi-modal transport.

freight insurance Insurance that covers the freight, which in this sense is the payment for transporting goods or for hiring a ship.

freight note A document from a shipowner to a shipper specifying the amount of freight (i.e. freight charge) due.

freight of all kinds (FAK) A term indicating that the rate charged is assessed on all the different kinds of freight and not just for a particular type of freight.

freight tonne A bill of lading tonne. It is either 1000 kilograms or one cubic metre, whichever works out to be the greater weight/ measurement. It is alternatively called a B/L ton.

French Pacific Islands currency: CFP (French Pacific Islands) franc (PFF), divided into 100 centimes.

FRF (ISO) code France – currency: French franc. The 1999 legacy conversion rate was 6.55957 to the euro. It will fully change to the euro/cent from 2002.

front-end finance A UK bank loan to a foreign buyer for paying the UK exporter, usually covered by the Exports Credits Guarantee Department (ECGD).

front-end loading The practice of including charges such as administrative costs and commission with the first repayment of a loan or the first payment of an insurance premium, with the result that the first payment is larger than the remainder. *See also* **packing**.

front running Illegal private trading by a broker or market maker who has prior knowledge of a forthcoming large movement in prices.

frozen assets Assets that may not be converted into ready money without incurring a loss of some kind, or which may not be converted because someone has claim on them or there is an order that they may not be transferred. The latter is also called a frozen fund. *See also* **liquid assets**.

frustration The ending of a contract because of the occurrence of something preventing its fulfilment, e.g. war or a major condition suddenly being legally prohibited.

FSR Abbreviation of *free of strikes and riots*.

FTA Abbreviation of *free trade agreement* and *free trade area*.

F term The category of *incoterm* in which the seller has to deliver the goods for carriage by the buyer according to the latter's instructions.

FTZ Abbreviation of free trade zone (*see* *freeport*).

fuel surcharge adjustment factor A surcharge imposed by a shipowner to cover rising fuel costs. It is alternatively known as *bunker adjustment factor*.

full set All the original documents required in a particular dispatch of goods (all original copies of the invoices, bills of lading, and insurance documents, etc.). Originally produced in sets (often of three copies at least of each document) and sent at separate times to cover the possibility of one set being lost and causing financial loss thereby if the recipient could not claim the goods when they arrived without them, they are being used less and less frequently with the increased confidence in the use of electronic data interchange (EDI).

fund Money set aside for a specific purpose (e.g. as a contingency against

F

unforeseen events); or money lent to an institution or government. As a verb, fund means to make finance available.

fundamental terms Contractual terms that are so basic that breach of them is equated with non-performance (as opposed to conditions and warranties).

funded debt Generally, any short-term debt that has been converted into a long-term debt.

funding Substituting long-term debt for short-term liabilities.

future An agreement to buy or sell a standard quantity of a specific commodity on a future date at an agreed price.

futures Contracts that are made for the delivery of e.g. currencies or commodities on a future date. Futures markets provide an opportunity for speculation, in that contracts may be bought and sold (with no intention on the part of the traders to take delivery of the goods) before the delivery date arrives and their prices may rise and fall during that time.

Futures and Options Exchange *See London Futures and Options Exchange.*

Futures Industry Association An organization that represents dealers in the US futures market.

futures market A market that deals in futures and options on bonds, commodities, foreign currencies are shares.

G

G/A Abbreviation of *general average*.

Gabon currency: CFA franc (GAF); there is no subdivision.

GAF (ISO) code Gabon – currency: CFA franc.

Gambia currency: dalasi.

gamma The rate of change of an option premium with respect to **delta**. It is also a Stock Exchange classification of shares that are traded infrequently and in small quantitites. *See also* **alpha**.

gap A market opportunity (a gap in the market) that nobody else has yet exploited.

garnishee order A court order made on somebody who owes money to somebody else who has been judged to be a debtor, instructing him or her not to pay the debtor until that debtor has repaid others. If it is issued by a UK County Court, it is called a garnishee summons.

GATT Abbreviation of *General Agreement on Tariffs and Trade*.

GBP (ISO) code United Kingdom – currency: pound sterling.

gearing The proportion of long-term debt to equity finance on the balance sheet of a company. More specifically, it is the ratio of borrowed capital to total capital employed, expressed as a percentage (gearing ratio). It is sometimes known by the equivalent US term leverage.

GEF Abbreviation of *Global Environment Facility*.

general agent An agent with the authority to represent the principle in all matters concerning a particular activity.

General Agreement on Tariffs and Trade (GATT) An international organization, established in 1947 with headquarters in Geneva, Switzerland, and now with more than 100 member countries, whose object is to negotiate on matters of trade policy, notably the reduction of tariffs and other barriers to free trade.

general average (G/A) In marine insurance, compensation for individual losses sustained in the saving of an entire venture (e.g. jettisoning heavy cargo to keep a ship afloat).

G

general average bond A security taken from a reputable insurance organization to cover any possible loss due to *general average*.

general letter of hypothecation A bank's general right to realize the money it is owed in full or part from any of the property hypothecated (pledged) in general to it by its customer.

general purpose line of credit (GPLOC) The standard type of ECGD line of credit offered by a UK bank to an overseas bank to finance a number of different contracts.

Georgia currency: lari.

general tariff In international trade, a tariff that applies to nations that do not have most favoured nation status or other preferential treatment.

gentleman's agreement A verbal agreement between two parties who trust each other and have a strong sense of honour.

Germany currency: deutschemark (DEM), divided into 100 pfennig. The 1999 legacy conversion rate was 1.95583 to the euro. It will fully change to the euro/cent from 2002.

Ghana currency: cedi (GHC); divided into 100 pesewa.

GHC (ISO) code Ghana – currency: cedi.

Gibraltar currency: Gibraltar pound (GIP), divided into 100 pence.

GIEK Abbreviation of Garanti-Instituttet for Eksportkreditt, the Norwegian credit insurance agency.

gilt Short for *gilt-edged security*, a UK government bond.

gilt-edged market In general in the UK, the market in gilt-edged securities.

gilt-edged security A security that carries little or no risk, in particular government-issued stocks, which are known as gilts for short. In the USA, the term gilt-edged refers to bonds issued by companies with a good reputation for dividend payment and with a good profit record.

gilts Shortened term of *gilt-edged securities*.

GIP (ISO) code Gibraltar – currency: Gibraltar pound.

girobank transfers Standard transfers can be sent within most of the EU countries, Norway and Switzerland cheaply within three days (or cheaper still for less urgent ones over a 10-day period). More rapid transfers can be priced and obtained on request.

global bond A fixed-interest security issued simultaneously in Asia, Europe and the USA.

Global Environment Facility (GEF) A World Bank-supported facility for financing environmental improvement schemes.

godown A far-eastern term for a warehouse.

gold standard A monetary system in which the value of a currency is fixed in terms of gold.

gold warrant Similar to a call and put option, a financial instrument that allows the holder to buy or sell gold at a pre-set price and time (which has to be over a year).

good delivery In the context of a futures contract or option, the delivery of commodities meeting the exchange's criteria in terms of quantity and quality.

good faith *See bona fide.*

goods Physical items manufactured, sold or exchanged, from raw materials to finished products (as opposed to services, for which no physical items are transferred).

goods on consignment A method of trading in goods whereby they are sent to an agent on consignment. Although the agent has no title to the goods, he or she may sell them on to a buyer. If the goods are not sold, they are returned to the owner.

good till cancelled (GTC) Describing an order that remains in force unless it is expressly cancelled. Cancellation is usually dependent upon a satisfactory profit level being reached. It is also known as a resting order or open order.

gourde The standard currency unit of Haiti.

government bond A fixed-interest security issued by a government agent such as the Treasury. It is also known as a Treasury bond.

government broker A firm formerly nominated by the Bank of England for dealing with new issues of *gilt-edged securities*, now replaced by a number of market makers in gilts.

government securities Treasury bills, gilt-edged securities and any other government fixed-interest paper. They are sold as a means of borrowing, often to offset a budget deficit.

government stock Any bond issued by a government, most often central government stock (*gilt-edged securities* in the UK).

G

GPLOC Abbreviation of *general purpose line of credit*.

grace period The time that elapses between the granting of a loan and the first repayment is made. *See also* **days of grace**.

grading The setting of standards for type and quality for commodities (and checking them).

GRD (ISO) code Greece – currency: drachma. The 2001 legacy conversion rate was 340.750 to the euro. It will fully change to the euro/cent from 2002.

Greece currency: drachma (GRD), divided into 100 lepta.

Green Book An informal name for *Unlisted Securities Market*, published by the London Stock Exchange, setting out requirements for entry into the Unlisted Securities Market and the associated regulations.

green currency Currency of an EU country (based on the European Currency Unit, ECU) that uses an artificial rate of exchange to protect farm prices from fluctuations in the real rates of exchange.

Greenland currency: Danish krøne (DKK), divided into 100 øre.

green pound A notional unit of currency used in the administration of the Common Agricultural Policy of the EU to determine the relative prices (and hence subsidies) of farm produce from the different member countries.

grey market Any semi-legal market, usually for goods that are in short supply; it is one that keeps within the letter if not the spirit of the law.

groschen A subdivision (1/100) of the schilling, the legacy currency unit of Austria.

gross mark-up The amount by which a trader increases the purchase price of an item in order to sell it at a profit, usually expressed as a percentage of its purchase price.

gross registered tonnage (GRT) A unit that describes a ship's active capacity. It is the measurement of the completely enclosed spaces of a ship minus exempted areas, such as stairs, expressed in cubic tonnes.

gross weight The total weight of a cargo or other item, including its packing.

gross yield to redemption The yield to redemption of a bond calculated after adding back tax deducted at source.

G

groszy A subdivision (1/100) of the Polish zloty.

groupage The practice of freight forwarders to group small consignments together to fill a container or vehicle load to reduce the costs to the individual shippers. One bill of lading covers the whole grouped consignments. Contributions are acknowledged by separate *house bills of lading*.

GRT Abbreviation of *gross registered tonnage*.

GTC Abbreviation of *good till cancelled*.

guarani The standard currency unit of Paraguay.

guarantee A promise to pay the debt of somebody else in the event that the debtor defaults (compare with *indemnity*). Guarantee is also the name given to a document stating that goods or services are of good (merchandizable) quality.

guilder The standard legacy currency unit of the Netherlands and the Netherlands Antilles, divided into 100 cents.

G

H

Hague/Hague-Visby rules Reguations that apply only to exporters, where a bill of lading has been issued, and which have been superseded in a number of respects by the *Hamburg rules*, but there are different signatories to the Hamburg rules with a strong European representation. Normally these latter apply, unless otherwise agreed.

Haiti currency: gourde.

halala A subdivision (1/100) of the Saudi Arabian riyal.

haleru A subdivision (1/100) of the Czech koruna.

half-height container A specialized flat type of container, particularly used for carrying goods where there is any restriction regarding height (also known as a *flat container*).

Hamburg rules Regulations that govern the liability for loss or damage to goods carried by sea and which cover all contracts (including the shipment of live animals and deck cargo) other than charter parties, applicable to exporters and importers alike. There are different signatories to those of the *Hague/Hague-Visby* rules, with a strong African representation. They are rarely used, because the Hague-Visby rules normally apply, unless otherwise agreed.

Hammett 250 Rule A useful formula for dividing the annual sales of a business by 250 to determine the average amount of goods leaving the premises every day. It gives a good picture of the size and scope of the business. For example, £2m annual turnover seems a lot, but is roughly equivalent to only £2m/250 = £8000, or say e.g. only about eight PCs in a van, leaving the premises on any average working day!

hand pallet transporter A cheaper and smaller device than a fork-lift truck that can be operated manually and so is useful for dealing with lighter goods.

hard arbitrage Practice of borrowing a (considerable) sum of money from a bank and re-lending it profitably on a secondary market, a device disliked by central banks.

hard currency A currency whose value is expected to remain stable or to increase in terms of other currencies

haulage Cost of road transport. There may be additional charges for loading and unloading.

HAWB Abbreviation of *house air waybill*.

HAZCHEM The regulations that control the carriage of hazardous chemicals by road.

HCC Abbreviation of *high cube container*.

heavily indebted poor countries scheme (HIPCs scheme) A special ECGD scheme for orgainizations that invest in HIPCs (heavily indebted poor countries).

hedge fund An investment fund that seeks high returns, usually by taking high risks (such as investing in new financial instruments).

hedging A method of protection against price fluctuations, by limiting or reducing risk. It usually happens on futures markets, e.g. in the foreign exchange futures it can involve: 1. Buying forward a currency equivalent to the amount of a liability in that currency, in order to gain protection against a revaluation (or appreciation) of the currency, or 2. Selling forward a currency equivalent to the amount of an asset in that currency, in order to gain protection against a devaluation or depreciation of the currency.

Her Majesty's Customs and Excise Full name of the UK *Customs and Excise* department.

HERMES Short form of Hermes Kreditversicherungs A.G, the German credit insurance agency.

Herstatt risk A risk of making a loss on a currency transaction when one side of the deal has been completed but completion of the other side is delayed. It is named after a German bank that made such a loss in 1974.

hidden damage Damage incurred by goods in transit that cannot be seen by a simple external examination, especially if the goods are in crates or packages.

high cube container (HCC) A specialized container for carrying a wide variety of goods that are large in number and/or size but light in weight, such as furniture and clothing, etc.

high seas Waters that are not part of the territorial waters of any particular country.

high stowage factor An aspect of goods that are bulky in relationship to their weight, e.g. cotton.

HIPC Abbreviation of heavily indebted poor country.

hit bid A bargain in which a dealer sells immediately at a price a buyer is willing to pay, instead of waiting for a possibly better price.

HKD (ISO) code Hong Kong – currency: Hong Kong dollar.

HKECIC Abbreviation of Hong Kong Export Credit Insurance Corporation, the Hong Kong credit insurance agency.

HMC Abbreviation of Her Majesty's Customs, the Customs authority for the United Kingdom. *See **Customs and Excise**.*

hogshead A large cask. It is appropriate for liquid or dry goods and is also used as a measure of capacity of roughly 50 imperial gallons. It can be subject to leakage.

hold An area in the lower part of a ship or aircraft in which the cargo is stowed.

holder 1. The possessor of a bill of exchange 2. The purchaser of an option.

holder for value Where a *holder* cannot satisfy all the conditions necessary to be a *holder in due course,* he or she loses the advantages of negotiability, viz above all he or she cannot obtain a better title (ownership) than that from whom it was acquired, but it all the same gives him or her some limited protection.

holder in due course A holder of a bill of exchange who has taken it in good faith, for value, before it was overdue, without knowledge of any previous dishonour and without notice of any defect in the title (i.e. ownership) of the person who negotiated with him or her. Such a holder has the right to sue in his or her own name and to hold it free of any defect in the title of any previous holder. Payment can be obtained from anyone who was a party to the bill of exchange before they became a party themselves.

hold over To defer settlement of a deal on the Stock Exchange until the next settlement day.

home country The country that houses the headquarters of a company that engages in international trade or investment.

Hong Kong currency: Hong Kong dollar (HKD), divided into 100 cents.

horizontal diversification Diversification into industries or businesses at the same stage of production as the diversifying company. For example, a suit manufacturer might diversify into leisurewear, or a yacht builder into the construction of motor boats. *See also* **vertical diversification**.

horizontal integration The amalgamation of companies in the same stage of production, and which are therefore likely to possess similar skills and benefit from economies of scale.

horizontal spread The buying and selling of similar options having the same strike prices but maturing at different times to try to make a profit should the market price rise. It is also known as a *calendar spread* or *time spread*.

host country A country other than its *home country* in which an international company operates.

hot money In business, money that is moved rapidly and at short notice from one country to another to take advantage of changes in short-term interest rates or to avoid imminent devaluation of a currency. It is also an informal term for money obtained illegally (e.g., by fraud or theft).

house A firm or institution or its place of business.

house air waybill (HAWB) A document issued by an air forwarder to confirm the grouping of consignments in a *groupage* operation. It can be used at the place of destination to reclaim the goods.

house bill of lading A document issued by a freight forwarder to confirm the grouping of consignments in a *groupage* operation. It can be used at the place of destination to reclaim the goods.

hryvnia (plural hryvni) The standard currency unit of the Ukraine.

HUF (ISO) code Hungary – currency: forint.

hull insurance Insurance that covers risks to the structure a ship itself.

Hungary currency: forint (HUF), divided into 100 filler.

HVF (ISO) code Burkino Faso (formerly Upper Volta) – currency: CFA franc.

hypothecation A pledge or mortgage from Roman and Scottish law – a legal right established over property belonging to a debtor.

I

IADB Abbreviation of *Inter-American Development Bank.*

IATA Abbreviation of *International Air Transport Association.*

IBOR Abbreviation of *interbank offered rate.*

IBOS Abbreviation of *Inter-Bank On-Line System.*

IBRD Abbreviation of *International Bank for Reconstruction and Development.*

ICAO Abbreviation of *International Civil Aviation Organization.*

ICB Abbreviation of International Container Bureau.

ICC Abbreviation of *International Chamber of Commerce.*

ICD Abbreviation of *inland clearance depot.*

Iceland currency: Icelandic krona (ISK), divided into 100 aurar.

ICON Abbreviation of *indexed currency option note.*

ICSID Abbreviation of *International Centre for the Settlement of Investment Disputes.*

IDA Abbreviation of *International Development Association.*

IDB Abbreviation of *inter-dealer broker.*

IDR Abbreviation of *import duty report* and *international depository receipt.*

IDR (ISO) code Indonesia – currency: rupiah.

IEP (ISO) code Ireland – currency: Irish punt. The 1999 legacy conversion rate was 0.787564 to the euro. It will fully change to the euro/cent from 2002.

IFC Abbreviation *of International Finance Corporation.*

IFTRIC Abbreviation of the Israel Foreign Trade Risks Insurance Corporation Limited, the Israeli credit insurance agency.

ignoratia juris neminem excusat Latin for "ignorance of the law is no defence". It is a doctrine that warns that people who break the law will be punished, regardless of whether or not they are aware that they are committing a crime.

IIC Abbreviation of *Investment Insurance Committee*.

illiquidity A situation in which an asset is not easily converted into cash, or in which a person is not able to raise cash quickly and/or easily.

ILS (ISO) code Israel – currency: shekel.

IMA Abbreviation of **Interchurch Medical Assistance Inc**.

IMDG Code Abbreviation of International Maritime Dangerous Goods Code. It contains the International Maritime Organization's recommendations for the transportation of dangerous goods by sea.

IMF Abbreviation of *International Monetary Fund*.

immediate holding company A company that holds the controlling interest in another company, even though it may itself be controlled by a third company.

IMO Abbreviation of *International Maritime Organization*.

Imperial system The system of measurement used day-to-day in the UK and its former colonies and possessions, often called the customary system or standard units in the USA. It contrasts with the metric system used in Continental Europe and science (which uses the version known as SI units).

implied terms The terms of a contract that are not expressly stated, but that the law considers to be necessary to the sense of the contract and therefore implicit.

import Goods or services brought into a country for sale, from abroad, or to bring in such goods or services.

import ban Also called an embargo, a ban on specified imports, often for political rather than economic reasons.

import controls Quotas (specifying quantities of goods) or tariffs (taxes) designed to limits the amount of imports, usually to protect the home market.

import duty A government tax levied on imports.

import duty report (IDR) A document necessary for a number of importing countries to confirm that it has received or will receive the correct amount of import duty required for a particular consignment.

import licensing Licences may be granted to a British company to manufacture and sell goods on a royalty basis either under an overseas manufacturer's own brand name or its own name. *See also* **national** *import licence* for licences issued as a national control.

import penetration A measure of the home market share taken by importers.

import quota The amount of a particular good that a government allows to be imported.

import restrictions Government controls on the amount of goods that can be imported, usually because there is an adverse trade balance.

import specie point The point in the variation of exchange rates at which it becomes cheaper for a nation on the gold standard to import gold than buy foreign currency.

import substitution The promotion of home-produced goods and services to discourage imports, e.g. encouraging holidays at home instead of abroad.

import tariff *See import controls.*

IMU Abbreviation of *interest make up*.

in-and-out trader A stock-market trader who buys and rapidly sells a security on the same day.

in case of need An endorsement on a bill of exchange that identifies somebody who the holder can apply to if the bill is not honoured.

inchoate instrument A bill of exchange, cheque or promissory note that is incomplete in some way. Completion of the details may be authorized by the drawer of the financial instrument (for example, the name of the drawee on a bill of exchange may be filled in by a third party).

inconsistent documents In the interpretation of letters of credit, documents not only have to be correct but also consistent with the other related documents, particularly regarding the details of the parties involved and the description of the goods.

inconvertible Describing money that cannot be exchanged for gold of equal value. UK currency has been inconvertible since the country came off the gold standard in 1931.

incoterm Any of the international rules for the interpretation of delivery terms that are currently in use. They define the sellers' and buyers' duties and responsibilities.

indemnity Compensation for a loss suffered.

indent An order from an overseas customer to an export house or confirming house asking it to buy and send goods. *See also* **closed indent**; **open indent**.

index arbitrage The process of selling stocks at the same time as buying stock-index futures, or vice versa. It is a form of programme trading.

indexed currency option note (ICON) A document that records a debt whose value depends on the effective exchange rates between the currencies concerned. A pre-arranged rate is set between defined limits for interest payments, but changes if the limits are exceeded.

India currency: Indian rupee (INR), divided into 100 paise. Also 1 lakh = 100,000 rupees and 1 crore = 10 million rupees.

indication A suggested price or informal quotation (as before a formal foreign exchange or an insurance contract), so that the potential buyer has a rough idea of the likely cost before the seller makes a firm and binding offer.

indication-only price A price quoted by a market maker that indicates what he or she thinks a security is worth although he or she is not prepared to deal in it.

indirect expenses Also called indirect costs, the costs of items or activities, such as maintenance of buildings or machinery, that are not used in the production of goods, nor are they immediately necessary for their production. They are generally regarded as overheads, although in some methods of costing they may be allocated to cost centres.

indirect offset A condition imposed by a buyer whereby a seller must also supply him with technology or goods not directly related to the original sale.

indirect rate A fixed amount of home currency quoted against a variable amount of foreign currency.

indirect sales Sales made through agents, distributors, retailers, wholesalers and other intermediaries (as opposed to, say, door-to-door selling and other forms of direct sales).

individual licence A licence that has been issued for a particular consignment to be exported or imported.

individually validated license (IVL) Written US government approval for the export of a specified amount of items to a single (specified) customer.

Indonesia currency: rupiah (IDR), divided into 100 sen.

inelastic demand A situation in which a price increase (for goods or services) does not produce a proportionate decrease in demand. It usually occurs with necessities or goods with a very strong brand image.

inflation A persistent general increase in the level of prices. Strictly defined, it includes neither one-off increases in price (occasioned by, for example, a sudden scarcity of one product) nor any other increases caused by real factors. Its causes include an excess of demand over supply and increases in the money supply, perhaps brought about by increased government expenditure, which causes a decline in the real value of money.

inflation risk The potential for losses or reduced income arising from changes in the rate of inflation.

inherent vice Any inherent defect in goods, such as combustibility, flammability and perishability, that cannot be blamed on a carrier (e.g. overripe fruit).

initial margin The deposit paid initially by both the buyer and the seller of a futures contract or option to secure the contract.

inland bill A bill of exchange that is drawn and payable within the same country.

inland bill of lading A bill of lading used when carrying goods overland to an international carrier to be used by an exporter (usually a shipping company at a port).

inland clearance depot (ICD) A place approved by HM Customs to which goods imported in containers may be removed for entry, examination and clearance. It is also where goods intended for export may be made available for export control.

inland waterway bill of lading A contract of carriage by inland waterway, but not a document of title (i.e. proof of ownership), unlike a marine/ ocean bill of lading.

INR (ISO) code India – currency: Indian rupee.

inspection certificate A certificate issued by a trusted neutral organization confirming that goods have been inspected prior to shipment. It is otherwise known as a certificate of inspection.

Instinet A Reuters-owned electronic equity brokering service linked directly to the stock exchanges at Frankfurt, London, Paris and Stockholm.

Institute cargo clauses Clauses drawn up by the Institute of London

Underwriters (ILU) that give cover ranging from basic cargo risks to much fuller cover.

Institute cargo clauses (Air) ILU clauses that cover goods sent by air on an "all risks" basis.

Institute cargo clauses A ILU clauses that cover "all risks" including marine perils, loading and unloading, fire and theft, but excluding cover for such risks as war, terrorism, strikes, pilferage, etc., although these can be included upon payment of an additional premium.

Institute cargo clauses B ILU clauses that give cover for total or partial losses or damage accidentally caured by marine perils; they also cover *general average*.

Institute cargo clauses C ILU clauses that cover more limited risks, and do not cover total losses and *general average*.

Institute strike clause Insurance against strikes requires separate specific cover. It is not possible normally to cover these risks if there is a strike at the actual time the insurance contract is made.

Institute war clause Insurance against war requires separate specific cover. It is not possible normally to cover this risk if there is a war at the actual time the insurance contract is made.

insulated container A specialized refrigerated container for carrying fruit and other foods that must be kept cool.

insurable interest The interest that an insured person must have in whatever is being insured (i.e. he or she must be at risk).

insurance certificate (individual) Where many consignments are covered by the same general policy, an insurance certificate will be issued to cover the particular individual consignment.

insurance policy The master document that details a contract of insurance.

insurance value In a letter of credit, the minimum amount of the insurance document should be the carriage, insurance and freight (CIF) or carriage and insurance paid (CIP) value plus 10%.

intangible asset A non-monetary asset that is neither physical or current. The many examples include brand names, copyright, franchises, goodwill, leases, licences, mailing lists, patents, trademarks, etc. It is sometimes known as an invisible asset.

Inter-American Development Bank (IADB) A bank that provides development finance for Latin American countries.

interbank offered rate (IBOR) The rate of interest that banks charge to lend to other prime banks. *See also* **London Inter-Bank Offered Rate**.

Inter-Bank On-Line System (IBOS) A system that links the Royal Bank of Scotland with, among others, banks in Spain, France, Belgium, and Portugal. It is often a cheaper form of payment transfer for small transactions than the more usual *SWIFT*.

interbank sterling market A money market that involves all UK banks, allowing speedy informal trading to best use or obtain funds. Transactions are carried out through brokers.

Interchurch Medical Assistance Inc. In its capacity as a representative of the international non-governmental development organizations, it supports country-level activities in partnership with ministries of health, national task forces and local *non-governmental organizations (NGOs)*.

inter-dealer broker (IDB) A person who matches deals between anonymous buyers and sellers on behalf of two market makers.

interest 1. A charge made by a lender to a borrower in exchange for the service of lending funds (usually expressed as a percentage of the sum borrowed, but may be paid in kind), or a similar payment made by a borrower to a lender. 2. A payment made by companies to debenture holders. 3. Money invested in a company, usually in return for equity or shares, thus making the investor "interested" in the performance of the company (i.e. in anything that yields a return).

interest holiday A period during which a lender (usually a bank) postpones the requirement to pay interest on a loan (usually made to a start-up business or one in financial difficulties).

interest make up (IMU) An interest equalization formula used by the ECGD's *fixed rate export finance* scheme whereby any shortfall between the bank's cost of funds, plus a margin (the agreed rate), and the fixed rate paid by the borrower is made up. Where the borrower's fixed rate exceeds the agreed rate the difference is payable to ECGD by the bank. The margin payable to the bank varies according to the particular currency and the overall amount of the loan in accordance with a scale of charges agreed between the ECGD and the banks.

interest-only loan A type of loan for which regular interest payments are made until the loan matures, when the whole of the principal also falls due.

interest rate differential The difference between the interest rates of two currencies.

interest rate futures Financial futures purchased as a hedge against an adverse change in interest rates. If interest changes on the hedger's financial instruments produce a loss, the futures contract offsets it.

interest rate margin Also called spread, the difference rate of interest (usually the London Inter-Bank Offered Rate, LIBOR) and the rate paid on a debt security, as used for floating rate notes on the Euromarket.

interest rate risk The potential for losses or reduced income arising from changes in interest rates.

interest rate swap An exchange of interest obligations or receipts in the same currency.

interface The stage in a transport system where passengers and/or goods move from one mode of transport to another.

intermediary A person who acts between and deals with two parties who themselves make no direct contact with each other.

International Agreement for Guidelines on Officially Supported Export Credit Commonly known as Consensus, an agreement between members of the Organization for Economic Cooperation and Development (OECD) on how much they will subsidize the interest rate on loans to purchaser's of their own country's exports.

International Air Transport Association (IATA) A regulatory body consisting of individual international air operators. It issues licences for forwarding agents, and promotes safety and easier documentation etc.

International Bank for Reconstruction and Development (IBRD) An organization that provides market-based loans for World Bank projects.

International Centre for the Settlement of Investment Disputes (ICSID) An organization linked to the World Bank that provides independent arbitration of investment disputes for the many signatory countries.

International Chamber of Commerce (ICC) An organization that promotes and represents the interests of those involved in commerce throughout the world. It is particularly well known for its issuing of International Rules, which represent mercantile custom and are frequently accepted by most governments so that they are either completely or almost completely legally binding in the vast majority of countries.

International Civil Aviation Organization (ICAO) A regulatory body for civil aviation as a whole with national and United Nations representatives.

International Commodities Clearing House (ICCH) A major clearing house for the London commodity market's futures dealings, established in 1888 (as the London Produce Clearing House). It adopted its present name in 1973, and today deals mainly in soft commodities (with the exception of barley and wheat) and metals. It is also a market for options in most soft commodities.

international conventions matrix A systems tool being developed by **SITPRO** both as computer software and possibly initially for manual use as well for indexing all international trade conventions and enabling "the user to identify what impact those conventions have upon their contractual obligations, whether it be in relation to the contract of sale, transport or payment."

international courier service Any private firm that offers a world-wide speedy and secure delivery service of money, documents and other valuables.

international depository receipt (IDR) A negotiable certificate issued by a bank that proves the ownership of securities by someone outside the country of origin.

International Development Association (IDA) The World Bank affiliate that provides interest-free loans (development credits) to economies with low per capita incomes.

international direct debiting service A direct debiting service provided internationally by Barclays, and other banks, using their correspondent banks.

international economy moneymover Lloyds/TSB's cheap international money transfer system covering most northern EU countries, Spain and Norway.

International Finance Corporation (IFC) An affiliate of the world Bank that assists developing countries by encouraging private enterprise and promoting their growth (rather than supporting the public sector).

International Maritime Organization (IMO) A United Nations body for intergovernmental cooperation governing shipping and navigaton, particularly relating to safety and hence is responsible for the rules controlling the carriage of hazardous cargoes.

International Monetary Fund (IMF) An international organization established in 1944 after the Bretton Woods conference, to organize and administer the international monetary system. It was designed to help countries in financial difficulties, especially with their balance of payments. It makes loans and provides financial advisers.

international office The head international department or office of a bank with specialist sections for foreign exchange, correspondent banking, trade finance, etc.

International Securities Market Association (ISMA) An organization established in Zurich in 1969 as the Association of International Bond Dealers (AIBD). It adopted its present name in 1991, and today deals in and underwrites international bonds. There are more than 800 members from over 40 countries.

International Standards Organization (ISO) An organization that establishes international standards, particularly agreed standard sizes and weights, etc. It includes the three-letter coding for international currencies.

International Swaps and Derivatives Association (ISDA) A worldwide trade association established in 1985 to represent the privately-negotiated derivatives industry. There are more than 200 members.

International Union of Credit and Investment Insurers An international forum for discipline and consultation in export credit and investment insurance. It is perhaps better known as the *Berne Union* (because it is domiciled in Berne under the Swiss Civil Code).

Internet A message-forwarding system that interlinks computers worldwide. Its applications grow daily, and include e-mail, banking, shopping, and entertainment, as well as other types of information access and transmission. It is funded largely by the sites that receive or relay messages (not the senders), although access may not be free. Any statement about the number of users is out of date immediately, because of the rate of current growth, but at the beginning of 2000 there were an estimated 26 million users.

interpretation of technical terms Banks assume no liability or responsibility for errors in the interpretation of technical terms when using these for letters of credit and collections, etc.

interruptions of banking activities Banks obviously do not take responsibility in letters of credit for circumstances beyond their control, such as disruptions from wars and riots, etc.

intervention The action of a central bank in the foreign currency markets when it buys or sells currency in an attempt to control its exchange rate.

intervention mechanism A type of *intervention* employed by the European Monetary System (EMS) to stabilize exchange rate relationships as agreed between members. It provides short-term (75-day) finance to the central bank of a country whose exchange rate is under pressure, or grants short-term monetary support (STMS) or medium-term financial assistance (MTFA).

in-the-money Describing an option whose strike price is better than the current market price of the underlying instrument.

Intrastat The statistical return system for the EU's international administrative documentation.

intrinsic value The value of an option if it were exercised now, i.e. the difference between the strike price and underlying price.

in trust As a very great favour to a very special customer, a collecting bank may possibly release the documents of the collection to the buyer in trust. The responsibility for such a decision lies with the collecting bank alone which remains fully responsible to the remitting (supplier's) bank for their safe-keeping and recovery.

Investment Insurance Committee (IIC) An organization that maintains and develops sound principles and circulates information for all the member countries of the *Berne Union* (of which the ECGD is a founder member).

Investment Services Directive (ISD) A directive of the EU, issued in 1966, that deals with cross-border transactions by investment banks and dealers in securities.

invisible export An exported service, e.g. finance or tourism etc., and the income derived from it.

invisible import The purchase of a service from an overseas supplier.

invisible trade Trade in services rather than in tangible goods.

invoice A list of goods that have been shipped or sent, or of services rendered. It includes prices and charges. It is alternatively known as a bill.

invoice discounting A type of with recourse finance, whereby an exporter can borrow money from a finance company such as a factoring company in exchange for/on the strength of his invoiced sales to obtain working capital finance.

invoicing cycle (or billing cycle) The posting of bills/invoices or statements at regular intervals during a period of e.g. a month to even out the administrative work.

inward investment An alternative term for foreign investment.

IQD (ISO) code Iraq – currency: Iraqi dinar.

Iran currency: Iranian rial (IRR), divided into 100 dinars. Also 1 toman = 10 rials.

Iraq currency: Iraqi dinar (IQD), divided into 1000 fils.

Ireland currency: Irish punt (IEP), divided into 100 pence. The 1999 legacy conversion rate was 0.787564 to the euro. It will fully change to the euro/cent from 2002.

IRR (ISO) code Iran – currency: Iranian rial.

irrevocable credit A credit that cannot be amended or cancelled without the agreement of the issuing bank, confirming bank (if any) and the beneficiary.

IRU Abbreviation of International Road Transport Union. It promotes the development of road transport.

ISK (ISO) code Iceland – currency: Icelandic krona.

ISO Abbreviation of *Internatonal Standards Organization.*

Israel currency: shekel (ILS), divided into 100 agorot.

issuing bank The bank that opens a letter of credit on behalf of an opener/importer.

Italy currency: Italian lira (plural lire) (ITL); there is no subdivision. The 1999 legacy conversion rate was 1936.27 to the euro. It will fully change to the euro/cent from 2002.

ITL (ISO) code Italy – currency: Italian lira (plural lire).

IVL Abbreviation of *individually validated license.*

Ivory Coast (formally Côte d'Ivoire) currency: CFA franc (CIF); there is no subdivision.

I

J

jajo Abbreviation of January, April, July, October, the months in which some stock options expire.

Jamaica currency: Jamaican dollar (JMD), divided into 100 cents.

Japan currency: yen (JPY), divided into 100 sen.

jetsam Goods deliberately thrown overboard from a ship, in an emergency, to make it lighter.

jettison To deliberately throw overboard or drop goods to lighten a ship or an aircraft, etc.

jiao A subdivision (1/10) of the Chinese yuan.

JMD (ISO) code Jamaica – currency: Jamaican dollar.

jobber In the pre-Big Bang London Stock Exchange, a jobber quoted two-way prices to brokers. Today's equivalent is a market maker.

jobber's turn A profit made in a deal by a jobber.

JOD (ISO) code Jordan – currency: Jordanian dinar.

joint and several A concept by which joint debtors (e.g. two or more partners in a partnership) are responsible for the debt, both jointly and as individuals. Joint and several liability gives the lender the recourse to each of the partners in the debt in the event of default.

joint selling scheme A joint venture among firms to market products abroad and to share expenses, with government encouragement.

joint venture (corporate) An enterprise jointly undertaken by a combination of individuals or commercial enterprises sharing the risks of a commercial speculation. It is often formed solely for a specific purpose, at the end of which it is likely to be disbanded.

joint venture (informal partnership) A type of partnership in which two or more parties agree to trade together for a limited period in order to sell some particular goods.

Jordan currency: Jordanian dinar (JOD), divided into 1000 fils.

JPY (ISO) code Japan – currency: yen.

judgement debt A debt that has come before the courts and which is confirmed by the court as being repayable. The judgement creditor can then apply for repayment remedies through the court.

junctim An alternative term for *forward purchase*.

junior debt A debt that ranks after another (is subordinated), termed the senior debt, when it comes to payment in the event of default.

junk bond Also sometimes called a high-yield bond, a bond issued by a company with a low credit rating.

J

K

Kazakhstan currency: tenge.

keelage A charge levied by a port authority on ships entering it.

Kenya currency: Kenyan shilling (KES), divided into 100 cents.

kerb market The trading in securities that takes place outside an official exchange.

kerb trading The closing of a deal on a financial futures market after hours. It is so called because originally traders would emerge from the exchange after official trading stopped for the day and remain outside (on the kerb) to close any unfinished business.

kerb weight *See net weight.*

KES (ISO) code Kenya – currency: Kenyan shilling.

khoum A subdivision (1/5) of the Mauritanian ouguiya.

kickback A form of bribery of a customer who is offered a discount price then charged the original (full) price, for accounting purposes, and later reimbursed the difference.

KID (ISO) code Kiribati (formerly Gilbert Islands) – currency: Australian dollar.

kina The standard currency unit of Papua New Guinea, divided into 100 toea.

kip The standard currency unit of Laos, divided into 100 at.

Kiribati (formerly Gilbert Islands) currency: Australian dollar (KID), divided into 100 cents.

kite Another name for an *accommodation bill*. It is also UK slang for a cheque.

kite flying The raising of money by way of an *accommodation bill*.

kiting Fraudulently issuing a cheque that is not backed by funds in the account.

kobo A subdivision (1/100) of the Nigerian naira.

Korea (North) currency: North Korean won (KPW), divided into 100 zeuns.

Korea (South) currency: South Korean won (KRW), divided into 100 chon.

koruna The standard currency unit of the Czech Republic and Slovakia, divided into 100 haleru.

KPW (ISO) code Korea (North) – currency: North Korean won.

krona The standard currency unit of Iceland, divided into 100 aurar ,and of Sweden, divided into 100 ore.

krøne The standard currency unit of Denmark, the Faroe Islands, Greenland and Norway, divided into 100 øre.

kroon The standard currency unit of Estonia, divided into 100 kopecks.

KRW (ISO) code Korea (South) – currency: South Korean won.

kuna The standard currency unit of Croatia (Hrvatska).

kuru A subdivision (1/100) of the Turkish lira, divided into 100 kurus.

Kuwait currency: Kuwaiti dinar (KWD), divided into 1000 fils.

kwacha The standard currency unit of Malawi (divided into 100 tambala) and Zambia (divided into 100 ngwee).

kwanza The standard currency unit of Angola, divided into 100 lwei.

KWD (ISO) code Kuwait – currency: Kuwaiti dinar.

kyat The standard currency unit of Myanmar (formerly Burma), divided into 100 pyas.

Kyrgystan currency: som.

K

L

laari A subdivision (1/100) of the Maldives rufiya.

ladder option Also known as a step-lock option, a type of option that enables the holder to add in gains in the underlying price of the security.

laesio enormis Latin for extraordinary injury. It is a doctrine (derived from Roman law) which states that a contract price must be fair and reasonable. An unfair or unreasonable price is grounds for terminating a contract.

LAFTA Abbreviation of *Latin American Free Trade Association*.

lags The process of slowing up foreign exchange payments (and/or receipts) when a change in exchange rates is thought to be about to happen.

lakh 1 lakh = 100,000 Indian rupees.

Laos currency: kip, divided into 100 at.

larceny The act of obtaining goods by trickery (from somebody who did not want to part with them), formerly applied to any theft of personal property. If the person did intend to part with the goods but was defrauded, the offence is obtaining goods under false pretences.

lari The standard currency unit of Georgia.

LASH Abbreviation of *lighter aboard ship*.

lashing The process of securing a cargo by fastening it with a chain, cord, rope, or wire etc.

last in, first out (LIFO) 1. Accounting term for a system of stock-keeping whereby the latest items manufactured or bought are used or sold before old stock is cleared. In a period of deflation this has the effect of maximizing profit, because new goods or materials have cost less to manufacture or buy. 2. The method by which some companies make employees redundant, on the basis of length of service. Thus, the last people to be employed are the first to be laid off.

last trading day In trading in financial futures, the last day on which trading can take place before delivery.

L

late presentation Failure to present the documents of a letter of credit within the stipulated time (unless a suitable amendment has been agreed) can be used as a reason for rejection by the issuing bank.

late shipment Failure to make the shipment goods relating to a letter of credit within the stipulated time (unless a suitable amendment has been agreed) can be used as a reason for rejection by the issuing bank.

Latin American Free Trade Association (LAFTA) An organization established in 1960 to coordinate the economic activities of major South American countries (and Mexico). It was superseded by the Latin American Integration Association (LAIA) in 1981.

lats The standard currency unit of Latvia, divided into 100 santami.

Latvia currency: lats (LVR), divided into 100 santimi.

laundering A method of disguising the origin of money by moving it rapidly from one country to another. It thus becomes a complicated business to trace its origins, movements and eventual destination. Counterfeit or stolen money may be laundered, although more usually the money represents the proceeds of crime.

lay days The days allowed for a ship to load or discharge its cargo, as agreed between a charterer and a shipowner.

LBP (ISO) code Lebanon – currency: Lebanese pound.

L/C Abbreviation of *letter of credit*.

LCL Abbreviation of less than a container load, referring to any package that is too small to fill a whole container and consequently subject to *groupage/consolidation*.

LDC Abbreviation of lesser developed country.

lead agency The export credit agency that has the largest share of an export credit support deal and/or is the agent for the country of the main contractor. The whole transaction is based upon its own scheme (simplifying the procedures for the exporters and their buyers). It also coordinates the reinsurance with all the other export credit agencies involved.

leads and lags The process of accelerating (leads) or slowing up (lags) foreign exchange payments (and/or receipts) when a change in exchange rates is thought to be about to happen.

Lebanon currency: Lebanese pound (LBP), divided into 100 piastres.

L

LEC Abbreviation of *local export control*.

legacy currency A currency used as a national currency before the country's adoption of the euro, e.g. the Deutschemark in Germany.

lek The standard currency unit of Albania, divided into 100 qindars.

lender's option An option that fixes the minimum interest rate received.

lepta A subdivision (1/100) of the Greek drachma.

lesotho currency: loti (plural maluti) (LSM), divided into 100 lisente.

letter of assignment A document with which an assignor assigns his rights to a third party.

letter of credit (L/C) Any arrangement whereby a bank (the issuing bank) acting at the request and on the instructions of a customer (the applicant for the credit): 1. Makes payment to or to the order of a third party (the beneficiary), or pays or accepts bills of exchange drawn by the beneficiary; or 2. Authorizes another bank to effect such payment, or to pay, accept or negotiate such bills of exchange against stipulated documents, provided the terms and conditions of the credit are complied with.

letter of guarantee A declaration of guarantee on the part of a third bank in the case of a provisional negotiation.

letter of hypothecation A document in which a customer pledges goods or documents of title to them to his or her bank as a security for a loan. The bank usually warehouses the goods in its own name and stipulate its right to sell the goods, should the customer fail to repay the loan.

letter of indemnity 1. A document indemnifying a shipowner from any adverse consequences arising from a through clean bill of lading being issued irregularly. 2. A declaration of indemnity on the part of a third bank in the case of a provisional negotiation.

leu (plural **lei**) The standard currency unit of Moldova (formerly Moldavia) and Romania, divided into 100 bani.

lev The standard currency unit of Bulgaria, divided into 100 stotinki.

leverage An alternative, and mainly US, term for *gearing*.

levy An import duty applied by EU countries to agricultural products from countries outside the Union (thus bringing their prices in line with inter-EU prices).

Liberia currency: Liberian dollars (LRD), divided into 100 cents.

LIBID Abbreviation of *London Inter-Bank Bid Rate*.

LIBOR. Abbreviation of *London Inter-Bank Offer Rate*.

Libya currency: Libyan dinar (LYD), divided into 1000 dirham.

LIC Abbreviation of *local import control*.

licensed deposit taker (LDT) An organization authorized by the Bank of England to accept deposits (but not allowed to call itself a bank).

licensing Instead of manufacturing goods and exporting them, a licence may be granted by a company in one country for another company in another country to manufacture and sell goods on a royalty basis either under the other company's own brand name or its own.

Liechtenstein currency: Swiss franc (CHF), divided into 100 centimes.

lien A legal right over another's property to protect a debt charged on that property (OED).

LIFFE Abbreviation of *London International Financial Futures Exchange*.

LIFO Abbreviation of *last in, first out*.

light dues Sums levied on shipowners to help to pay for beacons, buoys, lights and other navigational aids in channels and rivers. In the UK they are paid through Customs and Excise to Trinity House.

lighter A boat, usually flat-bottomed, for transferring goods from a ship to a quayside, or farther inland by waterway, or to another ship.

lighter aboard ship (LASH) To avoid the payment of excessive *lighterage* charges, some ships carrying their own *lighter* on board to take their goods to the quayside or farther inland by waterway.

lighterage A charge for the use of a *lighter*, or barge, to take goods from an ocean-going vessel to the quayside or farther inland by waterway.

lilangeni (plural emalangeni) The standard currency unit of Swaziland, divided into 100 cents.

LIMEAN Abbreviation of *London Inter-Bank Mean Rate*.

limitations (OECD) The limitations on the terms and conditions of export credits that benefit from *official support* under the OECD's *arrangement* are as follows:

The *minimum cash down-payment* by the starting point of credit

L

required for each transaction is 15% of the export contract value.

The *maximum repayment terms* are 5 years (8½ after prior notification) for Category 1 countries, and 10 years for Category 2 countries (except that the maximum repayment term for conventional power plant is 12 years).

Countries are classified under two categories, based on the World Bank threshold: those that are graduated by the International Bank for Reconstruction and Development (IBRD) (GNP per capita above $5,445 based on 1997 data) are in *Category 1; Category 2* consists of all other countries.

limited Short form of *limited company (Ltd)*.

limited company (Ltd) Also called a limited liability company, a company formed from a group of people whose liability is limited to the extent of the investment they have made (usually to purchase shares in the company), although occasionally limited liability is limited by guarantee to a certain amount as specified in the company's memorandum. *See also public company*.

limited liability *See limited company*.

limit up/down The maximum and minimum limits within which the price of some commodity futures and financial futures are permitted to fluctuate in one day's trading.

line of credit (general) A fixed amount or limit of credit set up for a borrower. It is the amount of outstanding credit that may not be exceeded at any time. Such lines are usually set up for companies or countries.

line of credit (international trade) An arrangement between a bank in one country and a bank or other borrower in another country to make finance available for a number of different contracts. Normally the overall amount, currency (or currencies), minimum contract value, and any other conditions will be specified.

liner A ship or aircraft, etc. carrying passengers on a regular route at regular published times.

liner terms There is no authoritative definition of this popular phrase, but it is often taken as meaning carried on a liner (and hence on a regular route) and that the freight cost will include loading and discharge.

linked deal An international trader who has imported goods under a *compensation* agreement may sell his or her right to link subsequent *countersales* at a premium to another exporter who wants to deal with the same company/country concerned.

liquid assets Assets that consist of cash or can readily be converted into cash. They are also known by various other names, such as liquid capital, quick assets and realizable assets.

liquidate The closing out or cancelling a futures contract where the contract's owner has assets available for sale on the prescribed date, usually achieved by selling the assets.

liquidity The ease with which buying and selling takes place in a market, or an asset can be converted into cash.

liquidity ratio The ratio of a company's assets (not including stock) to its current liabilities. It is also called the acid test ratio or the quick test ratio.

lira (plural lire) The standard legacy currency unit of Italy, San Marino and the Vatican City, divided into 100 centesemi; the standard currency unit of Turkey and the Turkish Republic of North Cyprus, divided into 100 kurus; and Malta, divided into 100 cents.

lisente A subdivision (1/100) of the maluti (Lesotho).

listed security A security that is recognized for quotation and trading on a stock exchange.

litas The standard currency unit of Lithuania, divided into 100 centai.

Lithuania currency: litas, divided into 100 kopecks.

LKR (ISO) code Sri Lanka – currency: Sri Lankan rupee.

LLDCs Abbreviation of least developed countries (as distinguished from LDCs, lesser developed countries).

Lloyd's Short form of *Lloyd's of London*. *See also* **Corporation of Lloyd's**.

Lloyd's agents Agents appointed by Lloyd's of London throughout the world to report about shipping and aviation, and survey any damage or loss.

Lloyd's of London An incorporated association of insurers that specializes in marine insurance. Formally established by Act of Parliament in 1871, the Corporation developed from a group of 17th century underwriters who met at Edward Lloyd's coffee house in London. Lloyd's supervises about 20,000 individual insurers ("names") grouped into syndicates, each of which has unlimited liability and accepts a fraction of the risk

L

of business brought to them by one of more than 200 registered brokers. Lloyd's involvement in marine insurance currently comprises less than half the total business transacted by Lloyd's underwriters. Following disastrous losses between 1988-1994, limited liability companies are now allowed to become "corporate names".

LME Abbreviation of *London Metal Exchange*.

LNG Abbreviation of liquefied natural gas, usually applied to a ship specifically constructed to carry it.

loaded A note on a bill of lading recording that the cargo really has been loaded onto the named ship.

loading broker The employee or agent acting on a liner company's behalf at a given port.

loadline The line of a ship's submersion resulting from the extent to which it is loaded. It varies according to the voyage and season. *See also* ***Plimsoll line***.

loan A sum of money borrowed by one person or organization from another on condition that it is repaid, generally for a specified time and often at an agreed rate of interest.

loan rate The rate of interest charged for a loan, often expressed as a certain percentage above base rate.

loan selling The sale (usually at a discount) of outstanding loans by a lending bank to another financial institution, often involving underdeveloped countries with payment difficulties. The term also means the issue of debt instruments (such as Euronotes and floating-rate notes) in facilities for note issuance.

local currency The currency of a foreign country with which an exporter or trader is dealing.

LOC Abbreviation of *letter of credit*.

local export control A system of clearing goods through customs at an exporter's own premises.

local import control A system of clearing goods through customs at an importer's own premises.

local trader A trader on a futures or options exchange operating only for his own account.

locational arbitrage The dealing between two (international) financial centres to make a profit (or "turn") on rates of exchange, because of a temporary difference in the exchange rates quoted in the two centres.

locking The process of securing a cargo by fixing it rigidly or rendering it immovable.

lock-up On financial markets, an investment expected to yield profit only in the long term, and in which the capital will therefore be "locked up" for some time.

locus poenitentiae Latin for "opportunity to repent". It is an option open to the parties of an illegal contract, who may save it by deciding not to carry out that part which is against the law.

lo/lo Abbreviation of lift on/lift off, a reference to a ship that can load or discharge containers by crane.

London acceptance credit The credit of an exporter with a London bank or accepting house, on which bills of exchange may be drawn (within specified limits of amount and timing). The lender may requite security for such an arrangement.

London bank export credit A similar arrangement to London acceptance credit, although any bills of exchange are drawn on the foreign buyer and collected by the bank.

London Clearing House (LCH) An organization established in 1888 that clears futures, options and other forward contracts.

London Derivatives Exchange A financial exchange organization established in 1990 by the merging of the London International Financial Futures Exchange and the Traded Options Market.

London Fox Shortened name of the *London Futures and Options Exchange*.

London Futures and Options Exchange (London Fox) A commodity market established in 1987 that deals in futures and options. The Baltic International Freight Futures Exchange merged with London Fox in 1991.

London Inter-Bank Bid Rate (LIBID) The rate at which major London banks offer to take funds on deposit from other banks.

London Inter-Bank Mean Rate (LIMEAN) The average of the *London Inter-Bank Bid Rate* and the *London Inter-Bank Offered Rate*.

London Inter-Bank Offer Rate (LIBOR) The rate at which the principal

L

banks offer to lend currency (especially US$) to each other at a given moment and for a specified term. LIBOR is often used as a base rate for fixing interest rates on bank loans to non-bank customers (e.g. LIBOR plus a margin of 2%).

London Metal Exchange (LME) A market established in 1877 to deal in non-ferrous metals, including aluminium, copper, lead, nickel, tin and zinc.

long A market position in which the dealer has bought the market product in excess of immediate requirements, usually with a view to selling it at a higher price at a later date.

long bill A bill of exchange with more than 10 years to maturity.

long bond A bond with more than 15 years to maturity.

long credit A loan that may be repaid over a long period of time.

long-dated gilt A gilt-edged security with a redemption date of more than 15 years.

long hedge A hedge against a fall in the interest rate on the futures market.

long position A situation that arises when a dealer purchases more of a currency (spot or forward) than he requires for his selling needs. It is therefore an *overbought position*, with assets exceeding liabilities in the currency.

longs Fixed-interest securities with redemtpion dates more than 15 years in the future. It is also a US term for securities that somebody has bought and actually owns.

loss A disadvantage, forfeiture of money or goods, or negative profit (the amount by which expenses of a transaction or project exceed income).

loss adjuster A person who assesses loss and arranges payment of a claim to the policyholder on behalf of an insurer.

Loti The singular (plural maluti) of the standard currency unit of Lesotho.

low stowage factor Describing goods which are heavy in relationship to their bulk, e.g. marble.

LRD (ISO) code Liberia – currency: Liberian dollars.

LSM (ISO) code Lesotho – currency: maluti.

Ltd Abbreviation of *limited company*.

L

LUF (ISO) code Luxembourg – currency: Luxembourg franc. The 1999 legacy conversion rate was 40.3399 to the euro. It will fully change to the euro/cent from 2002.

lump sum A sum of money paid all at once, as opposed to being paid as a series of separate sums (instalments).

lump-sum freight A fixed charge payable for the charter of an ocean-going liner regardless of the tonnage or sort of cargo actually carried.

Luxembourg currency: Luxembourg franc (LUF), divided into 100 centimes. The 1999 legacy conversion rate was 40.3399 to the euro. It will fully change to the euro/cent from 2002.

LVR (ISO) code Latvia – currency: lat.

Lwei A subdivision (1/100) of the Angolan kwanza.

LYD (ISO) code Libya – currency: Libyan dinar.

L

M

Macedonia currency: denar.

MAD (ISO) code Morocco – currency: Moroccon dirham.

Madagascar currency: Malagasy franc (MGF); there is no subdivision. Also 1 ariary = 5 Malagasy francs.

made bills Bills of exchange traded in the UK but drawn and payable overseas.

maintenance The practice of preserving the service potential of an asset (which is different from improvement or repair).

maintenance bond A bond issued to support a maintenance contract to assure the buyer that the supplier will meet his obligations under the maintenance contract.

major trading currency One of the leading currencies in which most international trade is conducted, such as the US dollar, the Canadian dollar, the Japanese yen and the main West European currencies.

makuta A subdivision (1/100) of the zaire (Zaire Republic).

mala fide Latin for bad faith; fraudulent.

Malawi currency: Malawian kwacha (MWK), divided into 100 tambala.

Malaysia currency: ringgit (MYR), divided into 100 sen.

Malta currency: Maltese lira (MTL), divided into 100 cents.

maluti The standard currency unit of Lesotho, divided into 100 lisente.

managed currency A currency whose exchange rate is controlled (via a central bank) by the government. The intervention is also called managed floating.

managed float A situation that occurs when a government, through its central bank, intervenes in the foreign exchange market to stabilize the exchange rates of its currency, or to allow it to move in a required direction (appreciate or depreciate). *See also* **dirty float**.

managed floating exchange rate system *See managed currency*.

managing agent An overseas intermediary who represents a company in its dealings with a foreign government.

manat The standard currency unit of Azerbaijan and Turmenistan.

mandate A written authority empowering one person to act on behalf of another. Mandates are cancelled when the mandator dies, is declared bankrupt, or certified insane. Mandates are generally used to give access to the mandator's accounts (e.g. a banker's standing order is a mandate).

manifest A list of goods and/or passengers on a vehicle of any description.

manufacturer's agent An agent who agrees to market a company's products, usually in a specific geographical area, in return for a commission.

manufacturer's export agent A type of *manufacturer's agent* who seeks overseas customers.

margin On a futures or options exchange, a security deposit that must be put up by a person wishing to trade on that exchange.

margin call A broker's request for more funds from an investor who has not paid the full price for an investment.

margin loan Also known as a top-up loan, a loan generally made on limited security. For example, a group of several lenders may advance money secured on property to 75% of its value. A margin loan would then be secured on the remaining 25%. This would carry a higher risk and therefore attract a slightly higher rate of interest.

margin trading Practice of investing in the stock market using borrowed funds (subscribing only the *margin*).

marine insurance Insurance that covers three areas of risk: hull, cargo, and freight.

market 1. A place where goods and services are bought and sold. 2. Actual or potential demand for those goods or services. 3. An abstract expression denoting any area or condition in which buyers and sellers are in contact and able to do business together.

market clearing price The price for all goods or services that will find buyers in a given market.

market if touched (MIT) An instruction to a broker to sell shares as soon as the price reaches a designated level.

marketing The distribution, promotion and presentation of a product (goods or services).

market maker A market principal who encourages dealing by varying the price of stock to promote its sale or purchase. The term is used especially with reference to the stock market.

market order An order to buy or sell a security at the best available price. Most orders executed on the exchanges are market orders.

market rate The rate at which members of the London Money Market will discount first-class bills of exchange.

marking An identification mark on cargo being transported. To reduce pilferage and to make it readily identifiable a minimum of detail is given, but it usually contains the consignee's initials, the order number, its destination and the particular package identification number where there is more than one being sent at the same time.

markka The standard legacy currency unit of Finland, divided into 100 pennia.

marks of origin The name of the country of origin marked on imported goods, often a customs requirement.

mark-to-market A direction to revalue a position according to the prevailing market price.

marshalling yard A yard in which goods vehicles are assembled.

master document The template document from which other documents are either run off or adapted.

master franchise agreement A *franchisor* grants to a sub-franchisor the right to itself open *franchise* outlets and to franchise third parties described as sub-franchisees to open outlets within a specified or exclusive territory.

Master Guarantee Agreement (MGA) An umbrella document setting out the principal terms and conditions on which the ECGD guarantees payment to the banks making finance available under its supplier credit, line of credit, and loan contract for one-off transactions facilities.

matched sales technique A method of getting round foreign government-sanctioned price controls by linking the purchase of a price-controlled item with one that is not subject to such controls.

mate's receipt A declaration issues by a ship's officer in the name of the shipping company stating that certain goods have been received on board.

maturity date 1. The date on which an accepted-term bill of exchange becomes due for payment. 2. The day when a buyer and seller must effect settlement of a forward exchange contract.

maturity The length of time until a fixed income security is due for redemption.

Mauritania currency: ouguiya, divided into five khoums.

Mauritius currency: Mauritian rupee (MUR), divided into 100 cents.

maximum repayment terms (under the OECD's Arrangement) are 5 years (8½ after prior notification) for Category 1 countries, and 10 years for Category 2 countries (except that the maximum repayment term for conventional power plant is 12 years).

MCF (ISO) code Monaco – currency: French franc. It will adopt the Euro from 2002.

mean *See* **arithmetic mean**.

mean deviation A measure of statistical dispersion equal, for a group of numbers, the sum of the differences between each number and the arithmetic mean, divided by the number in the group.

measurement list A list of the dimensions of individual loaded cases and other packages.

measurement tonne A cubic metre.

median A statistical average used as an alternative to the arithmetic mean (when there are a few extreme values in a group of numbers). It is obtained by putting the group of numbers in ascending order and nominating the middle one as the median (or the average of the two middle ones if there is an even number in the group).

medium-term note (MTN) Euro commercial paper with several years' maturity.

merchandise Finished goods that are purchased by a wholesaler or retailer for resale.

merchandising business A business that purchases finished goods for resale (as opposed to a manufacturing business).

merchant A wholesaler who deals in a specific commodity or commodities as a principal. He or she may become the owner of the goods but need not necessarily take possession of them.

merchantable quality The quality of goods deemed fit for sale; also termed merchandisable quality.

merchant bank A bank that originally specialized in financing trade, but today offers long-term loans to companies, provides venture capital and the management of investments, and underwrites new share issues. Merchant banks also function as *acceptance houses*.

merchant's credit A letter of credit issued by a buyer and hence not containing any commitment whatsoever on behalf of any bank. Consequently, because it obviously lacks the backing of a bank, no great reliance can normally be placed on it and neither will there be any protection from the International Chamber of Commerce's Uniform Customs and Practice for Documentary Credits.

metical (plural meticais) The standard currency unit of Mozambique, divided into 100 centavos.

Mexico currency: Mexican peso (MXN); there is no subdivision.

mezzanine debt An alternative term for *mezzanine finance*.

mezzanine finance Money lent to a small and growing, but financially viable, company. It is so called because the risk of making the loan falls between that of advancing *venture capital* and the safer course of putting the finance into established debt markets. It is also known as quasi-equity.

MFN clause Abbreviation of *most favoured nation clause*.

MGA Abbreviation of *Master Guarantee Agreement*.

MGF (ISO) code Madagascar – currency: Malagasy franc.

MIA Abbreviation of maximum insured amount.

microcredit The World Bank provision of small loans for income-generating self-employment activities

microfinance project A World Bank project that aims to reduce poverty by stabilizing income and consumption as well as improving quality of life for millions of borrowers.

middleman An intermediary, usually a wholesaler, retailer or broker, who acts as an agent between a buyer and a seller. Middlemen tend to push up prices by adding their own profit margin to the difference between the buying and selling prices.

middle price The average of the buying and selling price of a currency.

MIGA Abbreviation of *Multilateral Investment Guarantee Agency*.

milliard One thousand million, which may be used in association with low-value currencies such as the yen or lire. It is also an old word for (American) billion, i.e. 1000 million.

millimes A subdivision (1/1000) of the Tunisian dinar.

minimum cash down-payment Under the OECD's Arrangement, the starting point of credit required for each transaction is 15% of the export contract value.

minimum fluctuation Also known as the basis point, the lower limit to which a price may fall in one day's trading on an exchange. As with the maximum fluctuation, it is fixed in advance and trading is halted for the day if the minimum fluctuation is reached.

minimum lending rate (MLR) The minimum rate at which the Bank of England, acting in its capacity of lender of the last resort, is willing to discount bills of exchange and at which it offers short-term loans. The MLR has a direct effect on bank interest rates.

mirror account Every bank dealing with a foreign correspondent bank keeps a record or "mirror" account of the transactions conducted in the other country, so that the mirror account of a nostro account will be kept in the UK and the mirror account of a vostro account will be kept in the other country.

MIT Abbreviation of *market if touched*.

mixed credit Development aid financed out of both public and private funds.

MLR Abbreviation of *minimum lending rate*.

MMO Abbreviation of multi-modal operator.

mode A statistical average equal to the number that occurs most frequently in a group of numbers, a measure of central tendency.

moengoe A subdivision (1/100) of the Mongolian tughrik.

Moldova (formerly Moldavia) currency: leu (plural lei), divided into 100 bani.

Monaco currency: French franc (MCF), divided into 100 centimes. It will adopt the euro/cent from 2002.

monetary compensation amounts (MCA) A temporary tax or subsidy meant to offset the differentials between the "green" and real exchange rates that arise because of the EU Common Agricultural Policy. It is being phased out.

monetary union An agreement between countries in an economic union to have a common currency, fixed exchange rates and free movement of capital between countries. It is a short-term aim of the EU.

money at call Loans that may be called in at short notice, and which therefore attract only low rates of interest.

money laundering *See laundering.*

moneylender A person licensed by the government to lend funds to others. The term is, however, used informally to describe anyone lending money independently of banks and other financial institutions, often at high rates of interest, and as such carries negative connotations.

money market The market for short-term financial instruments.

money market yield The discounted yield on a bond reformulated as the equivalent it would receive as interest. In the UK for non-UK securities it is worked out as:

$$\frac{\text{Discount}}{\text{Purchase price}} \times \frac{365}{\text{No. of days to maturity}}$$

See also **bond equivalent yield.**

money supply The total amount of money available at short notice in a given country. There are several categories of money supply, designated M0, M1, M2 and M3.

M0 is defined as notes and coins in circulation in bank tills, plus the operational balances that banks place with the Bank of England. M0 is the narrowest category and is sometimes called narrow money.

M1 is defined as notes and coin in circulation and money deposited in bank current accounts. It is the best gauge of money immediately available for exchange.

M2 is an obsolete definition of the money supply. It includes notes and coins in circulation and in bank accounts, together with funds saved in deposit accounts maintained with the clearing banks, National Giro Bank, Bank of England banking department and discount houses.

M3 is defined as M2 plus interest-bearing non-sterling deposit accounts held by British residents, and other certificates of deposit. M3 is the broadest definition of the money supply and may also be known as broad money. A subsidiary measure, £M3, excludes non-sterling deposit accounts.

Mongolia currency: tughrik, divided into 100 moengoe.

monitoring service A service provided by credit reference agencies to keep an up-to-date check on credit statuses of current interest.

monopoly Strictly, an industry with only one supplier. The term is also applied more widely to an industry controlled ("monopolized") by one company, which produces a sufficient proportion of the total output of that industry to effectively control supply and therefore price.

monopsony An industry in which there are many manufacturers but only one customer for the goods produced. By controlling demand the customer can, in theory, set the price.

Morocco currency: Moroccon dirham (MAD), divided into 100 centimes.

most favoured nation (MFN) clause A clause in a trading agreement between two countries specifying that each will grant the best available tariff and quotas to the other, usually because both are signatories of the *General Agreement on Tariffs and Trade*.

mountain A surplus of EU farm products (such as butter or apples; a surplus of wine is referred to as a lake). Such surpluses result mainly from the application of the *Common Agricultural Policy*, which specifies minimum selling prices for farmers.

Mozambique currency: metical (plural meticais), divided into 100 centavos.

MTL (ISO) code Malta – currency: Maltese lira.

MTN Abbreviation of *medium-term note*.

MTO Abbreviation of *Multilateral Trade Organization*.

multi-component Euronote facility A facility that allows Euronotes to be issued in a mixture of currencies of the issuer's choice.

Multilateral Investment Guarantee Agency (MIGA) The part of the World Bank organization that offers insurance cover with a low premium to investors in lesser developed countries (LDCs) up to 90% of the cost of any project.

Multilateral Trade Organization (MTO) An organization, established in 1993 as part of the *General Agreement on Tariffs and Trade*, which enforces the agreed rules for international trade.

multi-modal transport A system by which goods are carried by the most economical method of transport from door to door. It has been much improved by the development of *containerization*.

multinational Concerning more than one nation.

multinational company (MNC) Also called a multinational enterprise (MNE), a company that has facilities, such as those for production and marketing, in various countries other than its country of origin.

multinational corporation A corporation that has operations and offices in more than one country.

multinational trade Trade in which many countries are involved, thereby encouraging a general increase in trade the world over (i.e. it does not have to stop once one of two parties is satisfied, as would be the case with *bilateral trade*).

multiple exchange rate Variable currency exchange rate that some countries quote, often giving a more favourable rate to importers of wanted goods and to tourists.

MUR (ISO) code Mauritius – currency: Mauritian rupee.

MWK (ISO) code Malawi – currency: Malawian kwacha.

MXN (ISO) code Mexico – currency: Mexican peso.

Myanmar (formerly Burma) currency: kyat (BUK), divided into 100 pyas.

MYR (ISO) code Malaysia – currency: ringgit.

N

NAFTA Abbreviation of *North American Free Trade Agreement*.

naira The standard currency unit of Nigeria, divided into 100 kobo.

naked option An option to buy shares in which the seller of the option (the option writer) does not already own the shares. In this instance, the option writer hopes to buy back the option before it is exercised and so avoid having to supply the shares. If the option is exercised and the market price of the shares has risen, the option writer makes a loss.

narrow band Describing a currency whose exchange rate is allowed to float within set limits (typically 2.5% above and below the central rate), which if exceeded bring about central bank intervention.

National Association of Securities Dealers Automated Quotation (NASDAQ) A US computer-based system, established in 1971, that deals with orders and provides information for the US over-the-counter (OTC) market. More than 500 market makers dealing in actively traded securities of more than 4000 US companies.

national export licence All countries have some form of controlling what is exported from their country. The export of most goods from the UK is generally unrestricted, but nevertheless an exporter needs an individual licence for certain specified goods such as for military weapons, antiques, etc. *See also* **licensing** and **royalty agreement** for the use of licences under patent agreements.

National Freight Consortium (NFC) plc A privately-owned organization established in 1982 to buy the National Freight Corporation from the UK government. It now includes British Road Services, National Carriers and Pickfords. Now known as NFC plc, it also operates in Australia and the USA.

national import licence All countries have some form of controlling what is imported into their country. Although the majority of goods can be imported without restriction into the UK, individual licences are needed for some goods such as certain animals, drugs, etc.

national standard shipping note (NSSN) A six-part set of documents, copies of which are kept by those parties handling the goods until they are finally loaded on board and from which a "shipped bill of lading" is compiled. It has replaced the mate's receipt in most of the UK ports.

National Trade Data Bank (NTDB) A bank of data on international economic and export information, as supplied by 19 different US agencies.

natural monopoly A type of monopoly that arises where such is the scale of business operations that is sensible to have only one supplier of the service (such as nationalized or privatized water utilities).

natural rate of interest The interest rate at which the demand for and supply of loans is equal.

NCM Abbreviation of *Nederlandsche Credietverzekering*.

NCR Abbreviation of *no carbon required*.

nearby contract Describing the futures contract whose delivery date falls closest to the target hedge date.

nearby delivery In the commodity market, an indication that delivery will be made in the next calendar month.

nearby futures Futures contracts that are closest to maturity.

near money A liquid asset that can be transferred immediately (such as a bill of exchange or cheque), although not as liquid as cash. It is also known as quasi-money.

Nederlandsche Credietverzekering Maatschappij (NCM) A Dutch group which acquired the former short-term Insurance Services organisation of the ECGD in 1991 to form the largest private credit insurer in the world.

NEF (ISO) code Niger Republic – currency: CFA franc.

negative cashflow A cashflow in which the outgoings are greater than income.

negative equity An asset that is currently worth less than the money borrowed to pay for it.

negligence A breach of duty to take reasonable care. Professional people frequently guard against actions brought for negligence by taking out professional indemnity insurance.

negotiable bill of lading A bill of lading that can be negotiated by transfer or endorsement. Strictly speaking it is quasi-negotiable because it cannot pass on any better legal title (i.e. ownership) to the transferee than he or she already has.

negotiable instrument Any document that may be passed from one person to another either by mere delivery or by endorsement and delivery. It transfers a perfect title of ownership to the one (known as a *holder in due course*) taking it in good faith and for value, even though the transferor had no right to it. Examples include **bills of exchange** and *promissory notes*.

negotiable security A security that is easily passed from one owner to another by delivery. Very few instruments are negotiable in this way in the UK (*see* **negotiable instrument**).

negotiating bank A bank that makes an advance to the drawer of a term bill of exchange under a letter of credit after deducting from the face amount interest at the ruling rate for the period of time between the date of the advance and the date that the negotiating bank receives reimbursement from abroad.

negotiation In international finance, an action by which an advising bank buys the documents relating often to a letter of credit.

Nepal currency Nepalese rupee (NPR), divided into 100 paisa.

net An open-meshed fabric of cord, rope, fibre, etc. for lifting and carrying cargo.

Netherlands Antilles currency: Netherlands Antilles guilder (ANG), divided into 100 cents.

Netherlands currency: guilder (florin) (NLG), divided into 100 cents. The 1999 legacy conversion rate was 2.20371 to the euro. It will fully change to the euro/cent from 2002.

net registered tonnage (NRT) The gross registered tonnage of a ship less an allowance made for the space taken up by the engine room, crew accommodation and other non-profitable parts of the ship. It is used as the basis for the calculation of port and canal dues, etc.

netting The practice of offsetting payments against receipts and providing forward cover only for the net difference between payments and receipts.

net weight The actual weight of goods, ignoring the weight of any packaging. Of a vehicle, it is generally taken to mean its total empty weight but without any fuel in its tank. The inclusion of the weight of the fuel gives its kerb weight.

new sol The standard currency unit of Peru, divided into 100 centimos. It is also known simply as the sol.

N

New York Mercantile Exchange (NYMEX) A US commodity market established as the Butter and Cheese Market of New York in 1872. It changed its name to the New York Metals Exchange in 1887. It adopted its present name after merging with the Commodity Exchange (COMEX) in 1994. The NYMEX division deals mainly in futures in crude oil and oil products (including petrol), palladium and platinum; the COMEX division deals in other metals, such as aluminium, copper, gold and silver; it also trades in coal.

New Zealand currency: New Zealand dollar (NZD), divided into 100 cents.

NGN (ISO) code Nigeria – currency: naira.

NGO Abbreviation of *non-governmental organization*.

ngultrum The standard currency unit of Bhutan.

ngwee A subdivision (1/100) of the Zambian kwacha.

Niger Republic currency: CFA franc (NEF); there is no subdivision.

Nigeria currency: naira (NGN), divided into 100 kobo.

NLG (ISO) code Netherlands – currency: guilder (florin). The 1999 legacy conversion rate was 2.20371 to the euro. It will fully change to the euro/cent from 2002.

n.n. Abbreviation of not negotiable. It can refer to the copy of an ocean bill of lading.

no carbon required (NCR) A system of copying documents using coated paper rather than carbon paper to make multiple copies of a single document or aligned documentation.

no obligation A phrase inserted in some *incoterms* to make it unequivocal that the seller or buyer, as the case may be, does not owe a legal obligation to the other party. Nevertheless it may still be in the interest of the party without strict legal obligation to agree to do it anyway.

NOK (ISO) code Norway – currency: Norwegian krone.

non-business days Sundays and bank holidays when most financial institutions are closed for business. They are not included in days of grace, and bills of exchange that fall due on a non-business day are postponed until the following day.

non-governmental organization (NGO) A non-profit making organization in the private sector that assists developing countries through aid (financial and material), and the provision of skilled personnel and training.

non-negotiable receipt A receipt issued in lieu of a bill of lading for personal and household luggage.

non-recourse Buying a bill of exchange without recourse. (From the seller's point of view it is as good as cash.)

non-tariff barrier A hidden trade barrier, often achieved through regulations that are difficult for importers to comply with.

Norway currency: Norwegian krone (NOK), divided into 100 ore.

North American Free Trade Agreement (NAFTA) An agreement for the establishment of a free trade area established in 1989 between Canada and the USA, with Mexico joining in 1992 (coming into force in 1994).

nostro account (meaning our account) A UK bank's account with its overseas correspondent bank in the currency of the other country.

notary public An independent attested lawyer who evidences on a "deed of protest" why a bill of exchange has not been accepted or paid.

note of hand An alternative tem for a *promissory note*.

notify address An address referred to in a bill of lading or an air waybill that must be informed by the carrier as to when the goods are due to arrive.

notify party The party to whom an arrival notification form is sent.

noting The act of noting on a bill of exchange the failure of the drawee or other party either to accept it on presentation for acceptance or to pay it on presentation for payment on its due date.

noting and protest The first two stages in dishonouring a bill of exchange. The bill is first "noted", or witnessed, by a *notary public*, who thereby testifies to its existence but not necessarily to its validity. It is then presented again, and if refused for a second time it is protested by being returned to the notary, who then testifies to its refusal. Noting must be completed within one working day of the bill's' first being dishonoured.

not negotiable A description applied to a document to which a transferee has no better claim than any previous bearer. A bill of exchange may be crossed "not negotiable" as a safeguard against theft.

NPR (ISO) code Nepal – currency Nepalese rupee.

NRT Abbreviation of *net registered tonnage*.

NSSN Abbreviation of *national standard shipping note*.

NVOC Abbreviation of non-vessel owning (or non-operating) carrier. Such a carrier will issue bills of lading for cargo carried on ships that are neither owned nor operated by him or her.

NVOCC Abbreviation of non-vessel owning (or non-operating) common carrier. Such a carrier will issue bills of lading for cargo carried on ships that are neither owned nor operated by him or her.

NYMEX Abbreviation of *New York Mercantile Exchange*.

NZD (ISO) code New Zealand – currency: New Zealand dollar.

O

OBO Abbreviation of *oil-bulk-ore carrier*.

OBU Abbreviation of *offshore banking unit*.

obvious damage Describing goods damaged in transit where the damage can be seen by external examination (as opposed to hidden damage).

ocean bill of lading (OBL) A document that acts as a receipt for a cargo and a contract between the shipper and the carrier for its carriage. It may also be used to establish ownership of the cargo (and can be made negotiable).

ODDISSEY SITPRO Overall Departmental Information System. It is the concept or interface whereby any exporter, importer, or agent can communicate directly with any of the UK government departments such as the DTI or MAFF etc. through one window, i.e. just one means of communication being necessary for dealing with all of them.

OECD Abbreviation of *Organization for European Cooperation and Development*.

off-balance-sheet transaction A transaction that affects the assets or liabilities of an organization but which is not required by accounting standards to be reported as such.

offer price The price at which the market, or a particular market maker, is willing to sell.

official support Under the OECD's guidelines for officially supported export credits (the *Arrangement*) it covers direct credits/financing, refinancing, interest-rate support, aid financing (credits and grants), export credit insurance and guarantees.

offset The situation in which an importer only agrees to buy, say, a technologically advanced product provided that part of the payment is offset by having some of the manufacture/sub-assembly carried out in the importer's own country.

offshore Describing business carried out (in, e.g., London) between foreigners in foreign-denominated currency. The term is also used to describe a business that operates from a tax haven.

offshore banking unit (OBU) A foreign bank that deals in eurocurrency and foreign exchange settlements, located in a tax-favourable offshore banking centre.

offshore financing The raising of capital in countries other than one's own.

off-the-floor Refers to any transaction originating with brokers, as distinct from those off floor members dealing among themselves. The exchange rules will require that the off-the-floor order has to be carried out before those originated on the floor. *See also* **on-the-floor order**.

off-the-floor order An order to buy or sell an item that originates off the floor of an exchange.

OGL Abbreviation of *open general licence*.

OII Abbreviation of *Overseas Investment Insurance scheme*.

oil-bulk-ore carrier (OBO) A multipurpose bulk carrier specially constructed for alternating in use between bulk shipments oil, ore and grain, etc.

OKB Abbreviation of Oesterreichische Kontrollbank A.G., the Austrian credit insurance agency.

oligopoly An industry in which there are many buyers but few sellers. Such conditions give the producer or seller a certain amount of control over price, but leave him or her especially vulnerable to the actions of competitors.

Oman currency: Omani rial (OMR), divided into 1000 baiza.

OMR (ISO) code Oman – currency: Omani rial.

on board A note on a bill of lading recording that the cargo really has been loaded onto the named ship.

on board bill of lading A bill of lading that evidences that the goods have been loaded and accepted for the voyage, a normal requirement for a letter of credit.

on close order On some futures and options exchanges, a contract that is fulfilled during the closing period when there is a range of prices.

on consignment An international trading method whereby the goods are exported to an agent for sale on the best possible terms. *See also* *consignment stocks*.

on deck bill of lading It is generally less than satisfactory to have goods loaded on deck rather than in the hold because they are more exposed to weather damage or can be easily jettisoned. Sometimes, however, they have to be carried there because of their inherent dangerous or flammable nature or they are too bulky to store anywhere else; also some traders prefer paying less for an on deck rate. Unless it is unavoidable a letter of credit may possibly specifically prohibit it.

on demand Describing a bill of exchange or promissory note that is payable to the bearer immediately on presentation.

on demand bond A bond in which the buyer has the right to *call* the full amount of the bond for any reason, even if the exporter has satisfied his contractual obligations (although ultimately it will probably be sorted out satisfactorily, in the meantime it can cause unnecessary fears and complications).

on or about A phrase that banks interpret, in accordance with the ICC's Uniform Customs and Practice for Documentary Credits, as inclusively between five days before and five days after the date specified in a letter of credit.

OND Abbreviation of l'Office national du ducroire, the Belgian credit insurance agency.

one stop shop A business that can supply all of its customer's needs within a specific range of goods and/or services.

on-the-floor Phrase that refers to any transaction originating with members on the floor of an exchange when dealing among themselves, as distinct from transactions for their clientele, which are generally given precedence by the exchange rules. *See also* ***off-the-floor order***.

on-the-floor order An order to buy or sell an item that originates on the floor of an exchange. (The exchange rules will require that the off-the-floor orders have to be carried out first, before those originating on the floor.)

on-the-run (Treasury bond) In the US Treasury bond and note markets, one bond at each significant maturity (usually the most recently issued) is traded more heavily than any other and is known as the on-the-run or benchmark bond.

OOG Abbreviation of out of gauge, describing any goods being carried which exceed the size of what they are being carried in.

open account A situation in which an exporter sends goods and relevant commercial documents direct to an importer and then awaits payment. In other words it is just like any normal domestic transaction and just as dependent on the integrity of the buyer.

open cover An insurance agreement covering all of a shipper's shipments over a specified period with a maximum limit for any one ship.

open-ended guarantee A guarantee that has no fixed expiry date.

opener The applicant of a letter of credit (usually an importer).

open general licence (OGL) An export licence that allows most goods to be exported from the UK without the need for any individual licence.

open indent The situation in which an overseas customer has given an order to an export house and the export house is allowed to choose the supplier to be used.

opening bank The bank that opens a letter of credit on behalf of the opener/importer.

open outcry A trading system adopted on some exchanges where the traders are required to call out their price, which anyone in the pit may accept.

open position Uncovered or unhedged exposure to interest rate or currency movement. It refers to either a long or a short position. (For contrast, *see square position.*)

open-top container A container specially designed for carrying non-standardized goods, particularly those that are unwieldy. It may also be open-sided for maximum flexibility and is very suitable for unmanageable items such as timber.

operating ratio A measurement to test the practicability of a service. The operating costs are shown as a percentage of receipts. The lower the percentage the better, and if 100% is exceeded a loss will have been incurred.

operative clause Should an exporter have to agree to a bond to obtain an advance payment or progress payment, it is in the exporter's interests to ensure that it contains a clause (the operative clause) stating that the bond will become operative only upon receipt of that advance payment or progress payment. In other words it has not been unknown for some buyers to cheat and claim reimbursement for money they have not yet paid.

operator's licence A licence that in the UK a carrier must have in order to transport goods by road (in a vehicle of more than 1½ tons unladen weight).

OPIC Abbreviation of Overseas Private Investment Corporation, the US foreign investment insurance agency.

opportunity cost The implied cost of doing a transaction in terms of foregone opportunities. For example, the payment of a premium up front entails the opportunity cost of the interest that could have been received if the money had been placed on deposit.

option The right but not the obligation to buy or sell a specific quantity of a commodity or instrument at an agreed price for a specified period.

option contract A forward exchange contract in which the customer has the right to settle on any day within a specified period.

option holder The person having the right under an option contract to buy or sell the commodity in question. *See* **currency option**.

option writer A person or institution granting an option. *See* **currency option**.

ore A subdivision (1/100) of the Danish krøne, Norwegian krone and Swedish krona.

Organization for Economic Cooperation and Development (OECD) An intepnational organization established in 1961, mainly to coordinate aid to underdeveloped countries. Its members include the European countries, Australia, Canada, Japan, New Zealand and the USA.

Organization for International Economic Cooperation (OIEC) An organization of ex-Communist bloc countries that took over from the *Council for Mutual Economic Assistance* with the break-up of the Soviet Union in 1991.

Organization of Petroleum Exporting Countries (OPEC) An organization of African, Middle Eastern and South American oil-producing countries that act as a cartel to control the international price of crude oil.

originating bank In international transactions involving a foreign branch of a bank (with a head office in, say, London), the originating bank is the foreign branch at which the transaction originated.

OTC Abbreviation of over-the-counter, describing something not traded on an exchange.

OTC options Abbreviation of *over-the-counter options*.

ouguiya The standard currency unit of Mauritania, divided into five khoums.

outcry market On commodity markets, trading is recorded from the outcries of the traders on the floor, although deals are sealed by private contract. Markets on which trading is carried out in this noisy manner are known as outcry markets and the style of trading is known as open outcry.

out-of-the-money Describing an option whose strike price is worse than the current market price of the underlying instrument.

outright Describing a simple foreign exchange transaction involving either the purchase or the sale of a currency.

outright deal A forward exchange contract for the purchase or sale of a currency. It is distinguished from a swap deal.

overbought position A situation that arises when a dealer purchases more of a currency (spot or forward) than he requires for his selling needs. It is therefore a *long* position, with assets exceeding liabilities in the currency.

overdraft guarantee A guarantee given by a bank to cover the local borrowing requirements of a UK company (say, e.g., a building and construction contractor) engaged in a contract abroad.

over entry certificate A document issued by customs to acknowledge that too much duty was paid at prime entry.

overseas agent Having an overseas agent can be a very inefficient way of indirect of selling goods abroad, unless the appointee puts his or her interests first. It is therefore essential to take care over the agent's selection in the first place.

overseas branch office An office that uses local personnel trained by the exporter and supervised by resident managers.

overseas company A company that is incorporated outside the UK but with a British place of business.

overseas investment insurance scheme (OII) The ECGD provides cover against political risk (such as the main political risks of expropriation, war, restrictions on remittances and breach of government undertakings) on any equity or loan investment that a UK company may make overseas and for any guarantees that it might have to give to others concerning any overseas enterprise in which it has an interest. It will also cover bank loans to overseas companies.

overseas subsidiary company A subsidiary company established in the importing country.

oversold position A situation in which a dealer has bought less of a currency (spot or forward) than he requires for selling needs and consequently has it is a *short* position, with liabilities exceeding assets in the currency.

over-the-counter Not traded on an exchange. Dealing tends to be done nowadays over the telephone or on the Internet rather than on an exchange.

over-the-counter options (OTC options) Options that in practice are placed by telephone, fax or e-mail. They are issued and sold by a bank for a customer's specific requirements only and are not resaleable.

overvalued currency A currency whose rate of exchange is continuingly below its *parity* rate.

O/W Abbreviation of overwide. The description applies to any goods being carried that exceed the size of what they are being carried in.

P

pa'anga The standard currency unit of Tonga, divided into 100 seniti.

PACE Abbreviation of *Paying Abroad Cost Effectively*.

packing A colloquial term for the practice of adding (e.g. to the repayments on a loan) charges for services such as insurance etc. without the borrower requesting them, or indeed being fully aware that the charge is being made. It is illegal.

packing credit An alternative term for a red clause letter of credit. It deals with an advance granted by the importer's bank on behalf of its customer to the supplier to cover the latter's cost in assembling the cargo for shipment. The advance is secured by control over the stored goods and the assignment of the payment expected later under the documentary letter of credit.

packing list A list showing details of the goods contained in each individual container or case.

paisa A subdivision (1/100) of the Indian, Pakistani and Nepalese rupee; and of the Bangladeshi taka.

Pakistan currency: Pakistani rupee (PKR), divided into 100 paisa.

pallet A wooden frame on which goods are stacked and carried by fork-lift/pallet trucks.

palletization The transportation and storing of loads by means of putting them onto a wooden frame or pallet.

P & I Club Popular name for the Protection and Indemnity Association, which is a carrier's mutual liability insurer.

pan-European marketing The selling of the same products in the same manner throughout Europe, i.e. treating the whole of Europe as a single market.

paper loss A loss that has not yet been realized, i.e. the underlying security(ies) have not yet been sold.

paper profit A profit that has not yet been realized, i.e. the underlying security(ies) have not yet been sold.

Papua New Guinea currency: kina (PGK), divided into 100 toea.

P

par A forward exchange rate where there is no premium or discount, i.e. the spot rate and forward rate are the same.

para A subdivision (1/100) of the Bosnia-Herzegovina and the Yugoslavian dinar.

Paraguay currency: guarani.

parallel imports Imports that are taken into a country and sold at a lower price than the one that normally prevails there (because they are cheaper in the country of origin).

parallel trading *See counterpurchase.*

parity The equality of one currency with another; being at par (i.e. neither at premium nor at a discount).

part cash with order As a compromise to *cash with order* where a largish sum is involved, the exporter may accept an initial deposit with the buyer's promise to pay the rest once the goods are about to be shipped – known as balance due on notice of readiness to ship (in other words at a time when it would be much more difficult for either the seller or the buyer to pull out of the deal).

partial Describing a compensation agreement in which the compensation importer "pays" for his imported goods or services partly in cash and partly in goods.

partial shipment An incomplete order as requested by the purchaser (but which can be shipped if the purchaser agrees).

Participants (to the OECD's *Arrangement*) are: Australia, Canada, the European Community (Austria, Belgium, Denmark, Finland, France, Germany, Greece, Ireland, Italy, Luxembourg, the Netherlands, Portugal, Spain, Sweden, the United Kingdom), Japan, Korea (Republic of), New Zealand, Norway, Switzerland and the United States.

participation agreement Developing countries frequently insist that expatriates from other countries must share with their own home nationals by setting up a joint company or cooperating in any other approved way.

part load In the carriage of goods, a consignment that does not completely fill the transport but which shares the space with another part load going to the same (or a nearby) destination.

par value of currency In a system of fixed exchange rates, the amount or rate by which one country's currency is officially pegged to that of another country.

P

payable at the collecting bank's selling rate for sight drafts on London.
A traditional exchange clause for bills of exchange expressed in sterling.
The drawee pays the face value of the bill of exchange at the rate of
exchange set by the collecting banker. The drawer receives the face
value of the bill of exchange less collection charges.

**payable at the current rate of exchange for sight drafts on London, plus
all bank charges.** A traditional exchange clause for bills of exchange
expressed in sterling to determine that the current rate of exchange will
be the current rate on the day of payment and that the drawee has to
pay the bank charges, the drawer receiving the face value of the bill of
exchange in sterling.

payable to bearer A bill of exchange on which the payee or, if the bill has
been endorsed, the endorsee is not named. The bill is payable to the
bearer.

payable to order A bill of exchange payable to an existing payee or order
and not endorsed in blank. Only a bill payable to a payee or "bearer", a
fictitious payee or endorsed in blank will be payable to bearer and
therefore transferable by delivery without endorsements.

payee The person or people to whom money is paid (in the case of a
cheque also called the drawee).

payer The person who authorizes payment (in the case of a cheque also
known as the drawer, the person who signs it).

pay guarantee Foreign buyers often require that the fixed expiry date of a
bond or guarantee can be "extended or paid". The exporter should try
to resist such claims, but in practice may have difficulty in resisting
local pressures. Nevertheless acceptance of this practice could
jeopardie any insurance claim for the unfair calling of the bond or
guarantee.

Paying Abroad Cost Effectively (PACE) A NatWest software package
available to its customers to enable them to provide standard transfer
details for a low flat fee.

paying agent A bank or other institution that pays capital or interest to
holders of bonds, for which the agent may charge a fee.

paying bank The bank named in a letter of credit that is authorized to
release funds to the *beneficiary* if all the terms of the credit have been
complied with.

payload The proportion of the total load of a ship that earns freight or
fares.

payment 1. Remuneration in money or kind. 2. When applied to letters of credit and collections, bills/drafts payable at sight, i.e. for immediate reimbursement.

payment for honour supra protest The payment of a bill of exchange (that is not paid and is protested) by somebody who is not named on the bill.

payment in advance Method of payment in which the purchaser pays for goods or services before delivery, with all the attendant risks and cashflow problems.

payment on shipment As a compromise to *cash with order* where a largish sum is involved, the exporter may accept payment on shipment in full, although an initial deposit from the buyer is more usual. It would be relatively difficult for either the seller or the buyer to pull out of the deal at this stage.

payment trend profile A profile of a company that can be provided by a credit reference agency detailing its recent payment history and comparing its standing against similar firms within the same industry.

peculation Embezzlement, particularly the appropriation of public money or goods by an official.

penalty clause A clause in a contract stating that if one party breaks the contract (e.g. by late delivery of goods) it will be liable to pay a penalty, usually in money.

pence A subdivision (1/100) of the pound sterling, the Gibraltar pound, and the legacy currency the Irish punt.

pence per vehicle-mile The cost of operating a vehicle expressed in pence divided by the number of vehicle-miles, giving a standard costing unit.

pennia A subdivision (1/100) of the Finnish markka.

perfecting the sight Action of supplying the full details demanded on a *bill of sight*.

performance bond Also known as a contract bond, a bond delivered by a contractor to a public authority for a sum in excess of the value of a contract, and which is to be paid in the event of a breach of contract. It is therefore a form of guarantee.

period bill A fixed-period bill of exchange payable on a specified date, and not on demand.

perishable goods Goods that are likely to deteriorate over a relatively short period of time. The term is most frequently applied to foodstuffs.

perpetual floating rate note A type of *floating-rate note* that is not to be repaid, i.e. it has no maturity and is mainly used as an investment instrument.

per mille One in a thousand, i.e. 1/10% or expressed as ‰.

performance bond A guarantee to a buyer that the exporter will comply with the terms of the contract.

Peru currency: Peru new sol (PES), divided into 100 centavos.

PES (ISO) code Peru – currency: Peru new sol.

peseta The standard legacy currency unit of Spain (including the Canary Islands) and Andorra.

pesewa A subdivision (1/100) of the Ghanaian cedi.

peso The standard currency unit of Argentina, Chile, Colombia, Cuba, the Dominican Republic, Guinea-Bissau, Mexico, and the Philippines, divided into 100 centavos; and or Uruguay, divided into 100 centesimos. The latter is also known as the peso Uruguayo.

petrocurrency Money (usually US dollars) paid to the exporters of petroleum in exchange for their product.

petrodollars Petrocurrency denominated in dollars.

pfennig A subdivision (1/100) of the German legacy currency the Deutschemark.

PFF (ISO) code French Pacific Islands – currency: CFP (French Pacific Islands) franc.

PGK (ISO) code Papua New Guinea – currency: kina.

Phillipines currency: Phillipines peso (PHP), divided into 100 sentimos.

PHP (ISO) code Phillipines – currency: Phillipines peso.

physical distribution A comprehensive term covering all the different aspects of the carrying of goods, including handling, storing, warehousing, packing, etc.

phyto-sanitary certificate An official agricultural certificate that the plants being transported have been confirmed to be free from disease.

piastre A subdivision (1/100) of the Egyptian, Lebanese and Syrian pound, and of the Sudanese dinar.

piggy back Method by which a large-scale exporter (or importer) can help out one or more smaller exporters or importers by allowing them to share its overseas sales and/or distribution.

pilferage Theft, especially in small quantities, and included in basic cargo insurance cover.

pip Depending on context, either 1/32nd or on one basis point.

pipeline A long pipe for carrying oil, gas and other such commodities, normally underground.

pit The designated area in a futures market where trading in a particular commodity takes place.

pit trader A dealer on the floor of a commodity market or stock exchange that trades by open outcry.

PKR (ISO) code Pakistan – currency: Pakistani rupee.

P/L Abbreviation of partial (i.e. not complete) loss.

place of acceptance (POA) On a bill of exchange, the drawee's address, unless otherwise specified. In international trade, the point where a cargo is received ready for transit and where the carrier's liability begins.

platform/"tween" deck container A very flexible container suitable for sizes and weights beyond the normal container limits.

Plimsoll line (also *Plimsoll mark*) "A marking on a ship's side showing the limit of legal submersion under various conditions. [named after S. Plimsoll...promoter of the Merchant Shipping Act of 1876]"(OED).

Plimsoll mark Alternative term for *Plimsoll line*.

PLOC Abbreviation of *project line of credit* (an ECGD-supported finance facility).

PLZ (ISO) code Poland – currency: zloty.

POA Abbreviation of *place of acceptance*.

POD 1. Abbreviation of place of delivery, the point where a cargo is delivered and the carrier's liability ends. 2. Abbreviation of proof of delivery, where delivery is evidenced by a signed receipt.

P

point 1. A hundredth part of a cent or other currency sub-unit etc. (in quoted prices for foreign exchange). 2. A 1% interest rate.

Poland currency: zloty (PLZ), divided into 100 groszy.

political risk The potential for losses or reduced income arising from a change in government policy. It includes expropriation, war, restrictions on remittances and breach of government undertakings, etc.

political risk (ECGD cover) Serious political risks for which the ECGD provides cover to exporters include foreign political, economic or administrative events preventing the conversion or the transfer of payments due; actions of overseas governments and laws affecting the performance of the contract; the application of any law wrongfully discharging the buyer's obligation to pay; foreign hostilities, civil disturbances and natural disasters that affect the contract's performance; administrative or legislative measures occurring in the UK after the date of the contract that affect the contract, such as the cancellation or non-renewal of a UK export licence or the imposition of new export licensing restrictions, etc.

political union An agreement among nations to create a trading bloc with no trade, monetary or taxation barriers between the members.

POR Abbreviation of place of receipt, the point where a cargo is received ready for transit and where the carrier's liability begins.

port A place with a harbour where ships load or unload.

porterage A fee charged by a dock company for using its porters' services.

port of arrival The port at which goods sent for export are destined to land. Important in *incoterms* because within it can be the place where the risk passes from the seller to the buyer (e.g. **CFR** and **CIF** for over the ship's rail and **DEQ** not cleared for import on the quay, etc.). It is also important in letters of credit as the port that the importer stipulates because it is the most convenient to him or her. It is alternatively known as the port of destination.

port of departure The port from which goods sent for export leave the country. It is important in *incoterms* because as within it can be the place where the risk passes from the seller to the buyer (e.g. **FOB** for over the ship's rail, etc.).

port of destination Alternative term for *port of arrival*.

port of entry The port at which goods from overseas pass into the receiving country.

Portugal currency: Portuguese escudo (PTE), divided into 100 centavos. The 1999 legacy conversion rate was 200.482 to the euro. It will fully change to the euro/cent from 2002.

position sheet A document that shows how much of a given foreign currency a dealer holds.

postdate To put a future date on a document, e.g. a cheque, thereby delaying its validity until the specified date. ·

pound The standard currency unit of Cyprus, divided into 100 cents; Egypt, Lebanon, Sudan and Syria, divided into 100 piastres; and the Falkland Islands, Gibraltar and the United Kingdom, divided into 100 pence. *See also **punt**.*

pound sterling The standard currency unit of the United Kingdom, so called to distinguish it from other currencies called the pound (*see pound*).

pratique A health certificate issued to the master of a ship confirming that no infectious disease has been found on board.

pre-contract commercial interest reference rate (CIRR) Under the OECD consensus rates (the *Agreement*), a rate committed before the date of the contract.

predatory dumping The selling of an exported product on a foreign market at less than market value, to beat local competition. Once competition is eliminated, the price generally rises.

pre-entry The process of sending documentation to customs and excise prior to the clearance and shipment of goods.

preferential trade area (PTA) A region in which member countries have preferential tariff arrangements for good imported from certain other countries.

preliminary response An indication from export credit agencies in a cooperation agreement that they are initially agreeable to support it and the terms that they are likely to set, but they are not committing themselves to any formal offer of cover at this stage. *See also **final response**.*

prem. Abbreviation of premium

premium 1. A currency for future delivery that is more expensive than the currency for spot delivery. 2. An amount by which a forward currency is dearer than the spot currency. 3. The price of an option; *see currency option*.

P

presenting bank The collecting bank that specifically makes presentation to the drawee. For instance, the principal may nominate a collecting bank that is inconvenient to the buyer, but may agree to the latter's making payment to his or her own bank which can them transfer the payment to the original named collecting bank.

pre-shipment inspection certificate A document that certifies the quantity, quality, price, etc. of the goods that are being transported. Initially the certificate was introduced as a guarantee for unique and/or costly goods (letters of credit and collections, for instance, only at best guarantee the documents, not the goods themselves). An increasing number of shippers/freight forwarders and governments etc. are insisting on their use.

price elastic Describing goods or a service that sells in proportionately smaller quantities compared to the proportionate increase in its price; i.e. a price increase has a more serious effect on sales than might be expected. *See price elasticity*.

price elasticity A measure of the way in which a change in the price of goods or services affects the numbers sold. It is defined as the percentage change in numbers sold divided by the percentage change in price. The value of this ratio is greater than one for things that are *price elastic*, and less than one for those that are *price inelastic*.

price inelastic Describing goods or a service that sells in proportionately larger quantities compared to the proportionate rise in its price; i.e. a price increase has less serious effect on sales than might be expected. *See price elasticity*.

price value of a basis point (PVBP) The change in the price of a fixed-income security caused by a change in the security's yield of one basis point.

primage The cost of loading or unloading a vessel, normally part of freight charges.

primary market The market in new security issues, also known as the new-issues market.

prime rate The rate at which prime borrowers can borrow from banks.

principal (in foreign exchange or financing) 1.The main amount to or from which interest is added/subtracted. 2.The amount underlying an option.

principal (in the law of agency) The person who authorizes an agent.

principal (of a collection) The exporter who, after shipping the goods, gathers the documents together and sends them to his or her (the remitting) bank along with the *collection order*.

principal carrier The main carrier who issues a combined transport document, whether or not the cargo is subsequently carried on its or any other transport.

private carrier A carrier who transports goods only on specific contracts, i.e. does not make a general offer to carry to the public.

private limited company A company with share capital of at least £50,000 whose shares are not available to the general public through the medium of a stock exchange (i.e. it is unlisted), and whose members do not exceed 50 in number. The shareholders' liability is limited the value of their shareholding. *See also* **public company (plc)**.

private protocol A French *line of credit* arranged by banks.

private treaty A method of selling similar to **open outcry**, except that instead of shouting their bids and offers they are dealt with quietly and over a longer period.

privatization The practice of offering shares in previously state-owned industries or enterprises for sale to the general public. British Aerospace, British Rail and British Telecom are privatized companies in the UK. It may also be called denationalization.

pro forma invoice An invoice that has been created pro forma, i.e. payment of which is not intended. It is used:

1. As a preliminary invoice as well as a quotation;
2. To satisfy customs requirements pertaining to shipments of samples and advertising literature, etc.;
3. To satisfy exchange control regulations, if any.

progress payment One of several payments made in stages as a contract approaches completion.

progress payment bond A bond that guarantees repayment of the *progress payment* should the exporter/contractor fail to carry out the terms of the contract.

progress report A declaration by a buyer certifying the progress made by the supplier up to a specified point of time. It is employed where a percentage of a letter of credit sum is payable against a progress, or acceptance, report. If satisfied, the buyer will certify the supplier's

P

declaration that the contract conditions have been fulfilled and the object supplied is working properly.

project financing The financing of any large project from its revenues and the employment of its assets and contracts as security. The project owners usually take responsibility for its successful completion and operation. Because of their complexity, some projects take many years to complete and involve considerable expense.

project lines of credit (PLOCs) Specific cover by an ECGD's buyer credit guarantee for any major type of project supplied by a number of different UK exporters.

promissory note Similar to a bill of exchange, a note drawn by the buyer promising to pay the seller – like an IOU.

prompt date In a commodity futures contract, the delivery date.

proposal In insurance, an offer made by someone offering or seeking insurance.

proposal form A document drafted by an insurance company on which the *proposer* either makes a formal written offer or merely seeks a quotation from the insurer who is the one making the offer.

proposer An individual or company offering or seeking insurance.

protectionism A policy based on self-interest, for example one that shields an industry against foreign competition, usually by the imposition of selective or general quotas and tariffs.

protest A legal procedure that formally notes the refusal of the drawee of a bill of exchange to accept or pay it. It is essential in order to preserve the right of recourse on the endorser.

proven default bond A bond issued by a surety or insurance company which is a commitment to perform under a contract and/or pay a sum of money. There must be firm proof of the contract being defaulted on.

PSI Abbreviation of pre-shipment inspection.

PTA Abbreviation of *preferential trade area*.

PTE (ISO) code Portugal – currency: Portuguese escudo. The 1999 legacy conversion rate was 200.482 to the euro. It will fully change to the euro/cent from 2002.

P to P Abbreviation of port to port.

public company A company that is limited by guarantee or shares, which has more than £50,000 share capital and is referred to as a public company in its memorandum of association. It must be registered at Companies House and carry the words "public limited company" or the abbreviation "PLC" or "Plc" after its name. Its shares are available to the general public through a stock exchange.

public limited company (PLC) *See public company.*

pula The standard currency unit of Botswana, divided into 100 thebe.

pule A subdivision (1/100) of the afghani.

punt The standard legacy currency unit of Ireland, divided into 100 pence.

purchaser risk Alternative term for *buyer risk*. Serious purchaser risks for which the ECGD provides cover to exporters include the insolvency of their purchasers, and of any surety, where applicable; and their purchaser's (and surety's, again where applicable) failure to pay within six months of the due date; and also the purchaser's failure to meet its contractual obligations.

purchasing agent An agent who buys goods or services for large overseas buyers.

purchasing power parity Principle that exchange rates should adjust to equalize the price of a basket of goods and services across all countries.

pure option (currency option) Different from a forward exchange option contract in that it gives the holder the right, but not the obligation, to buy or sell a specified quantity of a foreign currency at a specified rate of exchange, either on or before the expiry date of the contract. The person or institution granting the option is called the option writer. The price of an option is known as the premium.

put An option to sell.

put option An option to sell. *See currency option.*

PVBP Abbreviation of *price value of a basis point.*

pya A subdivision (1/100) of the Myanmar (formerly Burmese) kyat.

P

Q

QAR (ISO) code Qatar – currency: Qatar rial.

Qatar currency: Qatar rial (QAR), divided into 100 dirham.

QC Abbreviation of *qualifying certificate*.

qindarka A subdivision (1/100) of the Albanian lek.

QR Abbreviation of *quantity restriction*.

qualifying certificate (QC) When an exporter ships or deliver goods or services under an ECGD-supported buyer credit contract, or reaches a certain stage of work, he or she can present a qualifying certificate to his or her bank for payment certifying that he or she has fulfilled that part of the contract with the buyer. It must be supported by evidence that the goods have been shipped or delivered, and may need to be countersigned by the buyer. Such certificates may be submitted throughout a contract, at various stages, if required.

quality of bills of exchange One of the three grades of bills of exchange: trade bills, agency bills or bank bills.

quantity restriction (QR) A limit to the amount of goods that can be imported or exported; a quota.

quanto option An option on a foreign security that is guaranteed to be free from exchange rate risk.

quantum meruit (Latin for as much as he has earned) If a supplier only half-completes the work he or she has been contracted to do, the supplier may in some cases claim payment in proportion to the amount of work completed, known as payment quantum meruit.

quasi-contract A contract judged by the Courts to be applicable (at least in part), even though no legal written contract exists.

quasi-negotiable Almost negotiable. It applies to a bill of lading because although it can be assigned to a third party by endorsement it is not, however, fully negotiable, because the transferor cannot pass on any better legal title (i.e. ownership) to the transferee than he or she has. *See also* **negotiable instrument**.

quick test ratio *See* **liquidity ratio**.

quota In international trade, a maximum quantity of goods that can officially be exported or imported.

quoted currency A rate of exchange determine by relating two currencies. The base currency is assigned the numerical value one; the other is the quoted currency. Thus if the exchange rate between sterling and the Deutschmark is quoted at 3.5, sterling is the base currency and the Deutschmark is the quoted currency.

quoted price The price of a security as it is quoted on an exchange. The quoted price may fluctuate from day to day, or even minute to minute.

Q

R

rahmenkredit A "frame" credit, a line of credit established by German, Swiss and Austrian banks.

rail waybill A duplicate copy of the rail freight document that is handed to the shipper of the goods.

rand The standard currency unit of South Africa, divided into 100 cents.

rate of exchange Also called exchange rate, the rate at which various currencies are exchanged for each other.

rate of interest *See interest.*

ratification Official approval, giving something (e.g. a document or an agreement) validity.

rating A method of classifying various financial instruments, based on an assessment of whether payments of capital and interest will be made when they are due. For example, Standard & Poor's ratings in the USA range from triple A (AAA), the best, to D (the worst: a debt that is in default).

rating agency An organization that rates the quality of issuers of securities or commercial paper (*see **credit rating; rating***).

real The standard currency unit of Brazil (also called cruzeiro real), divided into 100 centavos.

realignment Effectively a devaluation of a currency occurring under as fixed exchange rate system when one country's currency gets out of line (thus favouring its exports).

real interest rate An interest rate after taking into account the effects of inflation. For example, if an investment pays 5% interest and inflation is running at 4%, the real interest rate is only 1%.

realizable assets An alternative term for *liquid assets*.

realizable value An amount that can be obtained by selling an asset; market value.

realization The selling of assets for cash.

realize To dispose of goods or securities at the best price obtainable.

rebate A partial refund or a deduction from a sum to be paid. *See also discount.*

rebate of duty Also known as drawback, a government rebate of duty that was paid on imports that are later re-exported.

rebate rate A rate of interest that is deducted when a bill of exchange is paid in advance of its maturity date.

receivables Any collectibles, whether or not they are currently due, such as claims for goods, services or money.

received for shipment bill of lading A bill of lading that only certifies that the goods have been received, but because it does not evidence that they have been actually loaded on board it is not as acceptable to banks as a shipped bill of lading. However, with the advent of containerization and multi-modal transport this has less modern relevance, because many shippers use a house/combined transport/through bill of lading and accept responsibility at an earlier point of departure.

receiving date The date from which a consignment is accepted for shipment.

recession A stage in a trade cycle in which the decline in economic activity accelerates, causing investment values to fall, companies to have to deal with adverse trading conditions, and unemployment to rise and so income and expenditure to fall. A recession may end in a depression unless there is a recovery.

reciprocal deal An alternative term for a *countertrade* agreement.

reciprocal quote A quote divided by the direct quote of a rate of exchange (i.e. divided by the number of local currency units exchanged for one unit of the foreign currency).

reciprocity A reduction in import duties, quotas or tariffs in exchange for similar concessions from another country. Other similar mutual arrangements (such as thd setting up of financial institetions in two countries) are also termed reciprocity.

record account Every bank dealing with a foreign correspondent bank keeps a record or "mirror" account of the transactions conducted in the other country, so that the record account of a nostro account is kept in the UK and the record account of a vostro account is kept in the other country.

R

recourse The right to recover funds (plus interest where appropriate) from borrowers if lenders are not reimbursed as they expect to be.

recourse indemnity policy (ECGD) Type of policy meant for small or medium-sized companies which may otherwise have difficulties in providing recourse support to the ECGD for a larger project. The ECGD does not normally require recourse for a smaller export of capital goods. It is further supported by Lloyds of London.

recovery agent An agent acting on behalf of an insurance company who seeks to recover the money paid out in compensation to an insured person from the person responsible for the loss, damage or delay suffered.

red clause The clause in a documentary letter of credit that authorizes the paying bank to make advances to the beneficiary even before the stipulated shipping documents have been presented.

red clause credit Clause that deals with an advance granted by an importer's bank on behalf of its customer to a supplier to cover the latter's cost in assembling the cargo for shipment. The advance is secured by control over the stored goods and the assignment of the payment expected later under a documentary letter of credit.

redemption The repayment of an outstanding loan or debenture stock by the borrower.

redemption date The date on which a loan or debenture is to be repaid. Redemption dates (plural) are those on a stock which is redeemable at par. In the case of UK Treasury stocks, the precise date of repayment is decided by the government.

reduction clause A clause written into a bond stating that the guarantee value of it should be reduced in proportion to the performance of the contract (to prevent the buyer from claiming too much in the case of any subsequent dispute).

re-export To import goods from one country and then export them to another.

REF (ISO) code Reunion – currency: French franc. It will adopt the euro/cent from 2002.

referee in case of need A local employee or agent employed by an exporter to nag the importer into paying for or, failing that, to arrange for the disposal of the goods.

refinance credit A credit for a foreign buyer who does not wish to pay cash and who cannot obtain credit from the UK exporter, which is made available at a foreign bank in London. The deal is concluded using a sight draft (to pay the exporter) and a bill of exchange on the buyer (paid into the foreign bank).

reflation Government action that attempts to boost a country's economy. It is done by increasing the money supply, usually by reducing interest rates and taxation.

regiocentrism An exporting policy that recognizes the needs of regional markets.

regional trading arrangement An agreement about trade between countries in a given region, usually regarding common tariffs and the free movement of labour and currency.

reimbursement certificate After the initial down payment under an ECGD supported buyer credit contract, the buyer may possibly wish pay all other sums direct to the exporter. The buyer can then draw the loan money. The bank will make payment to the buyer when the latter has presented a reimbursement certificate supported by a receipt of payment from the exporter.

reimbursing bank The bank from which an advising bank requests repayment after negotiating a letter of credit.

RELAY A NatWest low-cost cross-border payment service covering most of the EU, North America and a few other countries.

release note (RN) A receipt signed and given to a carrier confirming that the goods have been delivered.

remittance The forwarding of bills of exchange and/or other documents.

remitting bank The bank that receives the documents of a collection from an exporter and forwards them to the collecting/presenting bank together with the collection order.

removal note A document certifying that goods have been cleared through customs.

repayment ability The ability of debtor to repay his or her loans. Creditors assess applicants' repayment ability on what they own or earn. Any outstanding loans are offset against this capacity. It is also called *debt capacity*.

rendu Form of contract by which an exporter pays to have goods

R

delivered to a buyer's warehouse. It is also known as a franco or free contract.

repatriation The act of transferring capital from overseas to the home market.

repo Abbreviation of repossession or of *repurchase agreement.*

repudiation The act of informing the other party in a contract that one does not intent to honour the contract. The term may also refer to the repayment of a debt, or to the termination of any form of agreement.

Republic of Yemen currency: Yemeni rial (YER), divided into 1000 fils.

repurchase agreement (repo) A transaction between a bond dealer and a bank. The dealer sells government securities while at the same time agreeing to buy them back at a specified time at a price high enough to allow the bank a profit margin. In this way the repo may be looked upon as a form of loan.

reserve currency Foreign currency held by a central bank in order to fund foreign trade.

restricted letter of credit A letter of credit whose negotiation is restricted to only a specified bank(s).

restrictions on remittances A type of insurance that covers the inability of a firm sending home currency by preventing it from converting locally acquired currency into stepling. The risk includes any adverse discriminatory rate of exchange set to deter an overseas investor. The ECGD provides a lot of cover for this.

restrictive endorsement An endorsement on a bill of exchange that limits the power of the endorsee to negotiate the bill.

retention bond A guarantee to a buyer that, if problems occur in a contract subsequent to its completion, retention funds will be callable.

retention money Part of a contracted price for a job kept back on completion of the work in case there is any faulty workmanship to be remedied.

retiring a bill Withdrawing a bill from circulation by having the acceptor pay it, either on or before the due date.

returned without action (RWA) A description applied to an export licence application that is incomplete or in respect of a product that cannot be granted a general licence.

return load A load sought by a carrier who has to carry goods to a particular place (rather than return with an empty vehicle).

Reunion currency: French franc (REF), divided into 100 centimes. It will adopt the euro/cent from 2002.

Reuters A worldwide news agency that also operates a screen-based information reporting system.

reverse arbitrage Paying off a bank loan by borrowing from the money market.

reverse repo Similar transaction to a *repurchase agreement* (repo) in which the dealer buys the bonds instead of selling them, so that in essence they are a security on bank loan.

revocable credit A type of credit that can be amended or cancelled at any time without the consent of the beneficiary or any other party. However a bank is entitled to be reimbursed for any payment, acceptance or negotiation made prior to receipt of notice of the modification or cancellation of the credit.

revolving credit A credit that, after utilization, is automatically reinstated for a further drawing and cannot be cancelled until the expiry date and/or maximum amount is reached.

rial The standard currency unit of Iran, divided into 100 dinars; Oman, divided into 1000 baiza; Qatar, divided into 100 dirham; and the Republic of Yemen, divided into 1000 fils.

riel The standard currency unit of Cambodia.

ring An exchange set-up in which traders face each other around a circle of curved benches and clerks stand behind them, outside the ring, to record contracts that have been agreed.

ringgit The standard currency unit of Malaysia, divided into 100 sen. It is also known as the Malaysian dollar.

ring trading The practice of trading in commodities when dealers assemble around a ring, calling out their bids and offers. It is thus a type of outcry market.

riot insurance A special *SR & CC* clause inserted in marine insurance for an extra premium to cover the risks of riots.

risk The possibility that the actual return from an activity will be less than had been anticipated.

R

risk-free interest rate The rate of interest payable for high-quality investments such as US Treasury bonds or UK gilts.

risk premium In the currency markets, the difference between the forward exchange rate and the expected future spot rate.

risk rating An analytical method of evaluating the likelihood of a borrower defaulting. The ratings range from AAA – assessing that it is extremely unlikely to default – down to a defaulter as D. Those rated below BB are generally considered to be too poor a risk.

risk reversal A combination of selling a call option and simultaneously buying a put option, to minimize potential loss.

riyal The standard currency unit of Saudi Arabia, divided into 100 halalas.

RN Abbreviation of *release note*.

road waybill A transport document issued for road haulage.

ROL (ISO) code Romania – currency: leu (plural lei).

roll-on/roll-off A ferry service, whereby vehicles can be driven directly on board and driven straight off the boat at the other end. It is specially designed for tourists' cars and container transport.

rollover date The date at which interest is reset on a *floating-rate loan*.

roll-over certificate of deposit (CD) A method of splitting a certificate of deposit's maturity period into shorter-term periods, for which other CDs are issued.

Romania currency: leu (plural lei) (ROL), divided into 100 bani.

ro-ro An alternative form of ro/ro.

ro/ro ship A roll/on roll/off ship with doors at each end through which vehicles can be driven on or off.

ro/ro terminal A berth constructed with special ramps and extensive marshalling areas for loading and discharging *ro/ro ships*.

rouble (US **ruble**) The standard currency unit of Belarus (also known as Belorussia, Byelorussia) and Russia, divided into 100 kopecks; and of Tajikistan, divided into 100 tanga.

round tripping On a futures market, the practice of buying and then selling the same investment, or vice versa.

round turn An entire futures transaction from start to finish.

royalty A payment to a patentee or copyright holder for the use of his or her patent/copyright.

royalty agreement Instead of manufacturing goods and exporting them, a licence may be granted by a company in one country for another company in another country to manufacture and sell the goods on a royalty basis either under the other company's own brand name or its own.

rufiya The standard currency unit of the Maldives, divided into 100 laari.

run A panic rush to withdraw money from a bank or sell currency or shares, because investors fear that there is to be a sudden significant fall in their value.

running days A number of consecutive *lay days* including weekends and public holidays.

run to settlement Describing the sale contract for a commodity that has run to the date when physical delivery is due.

rupee The standard currency unit of India, Pakistan and Nepal, divided into 100 paisa; and of Mauritius, the Seychelles and Sri Lanka, divided into 100 cents.

rupiah The standard currency unit of Indonesia, divided into 100 sen.

Russia currency: rouble, divided into 100 kopecks.

RWA Abbreviation of *returned without action*.

R

S

SACE Abbreviation of Sezione Speciale per l'Assicurazione del Credito all'Esportazione, the Italian credit insurance agency.

SAD Abbreviation of *single administrative document*.

sale or return An arrangement whereby a distributor or retailer takes goods from a manufacturer or wholesaler on the understanding that he or she may return them if they are not sold within a specified period of time.

sales documents The documents that relate to the fulfilment of customers' orders, including an order, delivery note and invoice.

samurai bond A bond denominated in yen and issued by a non-Japanese company in Japan.

sanction A type of embargo in which a country or group of countries refuse to trade with another country that is violating international law or endangering peace and security.

santimi A subdivision (1/100) of the Latvian lats.

São Tomé and Principe currency: dobra.

SAR (ISO) code Saudi Arabia – currency: Saudi Arabian riyal.

satang A subdivision (1/100) of the Thai baht.

Saudi Arabia currency: Saudi Arabian riyal (SAR), divided into 100 halalas.

SCF Abbreviation of *supplier credit facility* (an ECGD-supported finance facility).

Scheduled Territories Also known as the Sterling Area, a pre-1979 term for areas where sterling was the official currency (and so there were no exchange control restrictions). At the end it consisted only of Great Britain, the Channel Islands and the Isle of Man.

schilling The standard legacy currency unit of Austria, divided into 100 groschen.

SCP Abbreviation of *simplified clearance procedure*.

SCOUT Abbreviation of *shared currency option under tender*.

SDP (ISO) code Sudanese Republic – currency: Sudanese dinar.

SDR Abbreviation of *special drawing rights*.

seabee A system for carrying large barges that are loaded onto/discharged off a ship two at a time from the stern, developed by the American forces in World War II.

SEATO Abbreviation of *Southeast Asia Treaty Organization*.

secondary market A market in securities that have been listed for some time, rather than new issues. Secondary-market trading occurs in the eurobond and forfaiting markets, etc.

secured creditor A creditor (such as a bank) that has a legal charge on one of the debtor's assets.

secured liability A debt in which the lender is safeguarded because the borrower has put up sufficient assets as security in the event of non-payment.

secured loan A loan secured by specified assets that revert to the lender if the loan is not repaid. It generally attracts lower interest than an unsecured loan.

Securities and Futures Authority (SFA) A self-regulatory organization (SRO) established in the UK in 1991 to regulate the conduct of people who deal in debentures, futures, options and shares. It was formed by combining the functions of The Securities Association (TSA) and the Association of Futures Brokers and Dealers (AFBD).

security A negotiable certificate evidencing a debt or equity obligation.

SEK (ISO) code Sweden – currency: Swedish krona.

self-liquidating asset An asset that has a predetermined lifetime and liquidates itself at the end of that period.

self-propelled lighter aboard ship (SLASH) To avoid the payment of excessive *lighterage* charges, some ships carrying their own self-propelled *lighter* on board to take their goods to the quayside or farther inland by waterway.

sell at best An instruction to a broker to sell shares or commodities at the best price possible. Thus if the broker is selling, he or she must find the highest selling price; or if buying, the lowest price.

sellers' market A market that is more favourable to sellers than to buyers. Such a market often arises when demand is greater than supply.

S

sellers over A market condition on a stock exchange where there are more sellers than buyers.

selling directly A method of trading in which an exporter uses his or her own home firm to contact and deal with overseas customers directly.

selling short The practice of making a bargain to sell securities or commodities the seller does not own. The seller does this in the hope that before settlement is due, the price of the item will fall and he or she will be able to buy enough to cover the bargain at the lower price, thereby making a profit. It is also known as shorting or short selling.

sen A subdivision (1/100) of the Malaysian ringgit, the Indonesian rupiah and the Japanese yen.

sene A subdivision (1/100) of the Western Samoan tala.

Senegal currency: CFA franc (SNF); there is no subdivision.

senior debt The oldest existing debt owed by a person or company, hence the debt that should be paid first in normal circumstances.

seniti A subdivision (1/100) of the Tongan pa'anga.

sentimo A subdivision (1/100) of the Phillipines peso.

series Call or put options on the same underlying financial instrument with the same striking price and maturity.

set of bills An alternative term for bills in a set, foreign bills of exchange made out in triplicate and traditionally sent to the drawee separately to insure against loss. The copies are known as a set of bills.

settlement The payment of funds on maturity of a forward exchange contract.

settlement risk The probability that all the administrative procedures involved in delivery of financial instruments are not completed in time and the potential losses incurred thereby.

SFA Abbreviation of *Securities and Futures Authority*.

SFAFC Abbreviation of Sociétée Française d'Assurances pour Favoriser le Credit, a French private credit insurance company.

SGD (ISO) code Singapore – currency: Singapore dollar.

shared currency option under tender (SCOUT) In situations where a foreign currency contract is under tender from several companies, SCOUT allows them to share a single hedge in the form of a currency option.

S

shekel (shequel) The standard currency unit of modern Israel, divided into 100 agorot.

Sherman Antitrust Act One of the fundamental US Antitrust Laws, the pioneer federal statute in this field (passed 2 July 1890), and a cornerstone in the legal expression of public policy against restraint of trade and monopoly or attempts to monopolize.

SHEX Abbreviation of Sundays and holidays excepted. If *lay days* are exceeded, demurrage becomes payable, but Sundays and holidays are usually excepted.

shilling The standard currency unit of Kenya, the Somali Republic, the United Republic of Tanzania and Uganda, all divided into 100 cents.

ship-broker Also termed shipper's agent, a shipowner's agent who sells cargo space and obtains cargo for shipment.

shipment Formally, all cargo carried under one bill of lading. More generally, any cargo or freight carried by land, sea or air.

shipped bill of lading A bill of lading that is acceptable as evidence that the goods are actually on board the named vessel and hence very suitable to banks when checking letters of credit.

shipped on board (SOB) An endorsement on a bill of lading confirming that the goods have been loaded on the ship.

shipper A person responsible for shipping goods by ship, land or air, as named on the shipping document.

shipper's agent An alternative term for *ship-broker*.

shipping agent A general agent who deals with, among other things, the documentation concerning the import or export of goods.

shipping weight The gross weight of a cargo, including all wrappings and containers.

ship's husband An old term for a shipowner's agent who looks after a ship while it is docked.

ship's manifest A document that the master of a ship submits to a port authority detailing all the transport documents, such as bills of lading, relating to the cargo on board.

ship's master The captain of a merchant vessel.

ship's papers Various documents pertaining to a ship and carried on it,

S

such as the ship's articles, its certificate of registry, ship's log and manifest.

shogun bond A bond issued on the Japanese market by a non-resident and denominated in a foreign currency (i.e. not yen).

shoring The process of supporting a cargo by setting a prop or beam laterally against it to keep it pressed against the side of a ship.

short A market position in which a dealer has sold the market product, which he does not own, with a view to buying it back at a lower price at a later date.

short bill A bill of exchange that is payable on demand or on sight, or in less than 10 days.

short bond A bond with less than five years to maturity.

short covering When a person is *selling short*, the purchase of the security concerned in order to cover the bargain.

short credit A loan that must be repaid over a short timescale.

short-dated gilt A gilt-edged security with a redemption term of less than five years.

short-dated security A fixed-interest security that has a redemption date of less than five years.

short end That part of the market that deals with securities with relatively little time to go before payment is due. The amount of time varies from a few dais up to five years, depending on which security is being traded.

short form bill of lading A bill of lading on which the detailed conditions of transportation are not listed in full.

short hedge A hedge against a rise in interest rates on the futures market.

shorting An alternative term for short selling.

short interest The interest rate charged on loans over a period of three months or less.

short position A situation that occurs when a dealer has bought less of a currency (spot or forward) than he requires for selling needs. He is therefore **underbought** or **oversold**, with liabilities exceeding assets in the currency.

shorts An alternative term for *short-dated securities*.

short sale The sale of a security that the seller does not own, or any sale that is consummated by the delivery of a security borrowed by or for the account of the seller.

short shipment A situation that arises where any part of a consignment is *shut out*.

short-term monetary support (STMS) A European Monetary System (EMS) intervention mechanism by means of which a country with balance of payments difficulties gets its centbal bank to borrow (for three months) from other members' central banks. An extension to the agreed term is called a rallonge.

shrinkage A euphemism for theft (of goods or stock) by employees.

shrink wrap A method of packaging by enclosing goods in (usually transparent) film that shrinks tightly around it.

shunter A broker who deals on two different exchanges (usually a provincial exchange and a main exchange) in securities that are quoted on both.

shut out Describing goods that have missed the ship for which they were intended. They may have arrived too late, been overlooked, or simply there was no suitable space available.

SIAC Abbreviation of Società Italiana Assicurazione Crediti, an Italian private credit insurance company.

Sierre Leone currency: leone (SLL), divided into 100 cents.

sight bill of exchange A bill of exchange, or draft, that is payable on demand.

sight deposit Known in the USA as a demand deposit, money *at call*; or money deposited overnight.

sight draft A draft, or bill of exchange, that is payable on demand.

sight payment Describing a payment that is due immediately on either sight/presentation of the bill or (in some countries) on the arrival of the goods.

SIMEX Abbreviation of Singapore International Monetary Exchange.

simple cover (ECGD) ECGD cover that supports loans only in respect of goods supplied and/or services rendered. Any other sums that may be due, such as an arbitration award for example, would have to be claimed directly from the buyer by the exporter. An export insurance

S

policy (ECGD) provides credit insurance for the extra risks that might occur in respect of other elements.

simple interest A rate of interest that is calculated by keeping interest that has already accrued separate from the capital sum. In mathematical terms, simple interest equals $Atr/100$, where A is the amount invested or borrowed, t is the time in years and r is the interest rate as a percentage per annum. *See also* **compound interest.**

simplified clearance procedure (SCP) Goods for export not needing any special control can be submitted on streamlined documentation and the rest of the statistical information can be supplied within an agreed later time limit.

sine die Latin for indefinitely, usually relating to fixing a date for a future event.

Singapore currency: Singapore dollar (SGD), divided into 100 cents.

single administrative document (SAD) A document that is is required for trade between any members of the EU that are receiving special accessional rates for customs duties etc. while they are still in the transitional phase.

single currency An objective of the European Monetary System (EMS), as defined by the 1991 Maastricht Treaty, under which a sinele central bank would issue currency that could be used anywhere in the EU. The target date for its implementation, 1999, has already passed.

single-currency peg An exchange rate regime in which a country pegs its currency to the US dollar or some other stable currency and makes very few adjustments to the parity.

Single European Act European legislation of 1987 that planned for the establishment of the European single market by 1 January 1993.

single European market An agreement between EU member states to eliminate trading differences between them from 1 January 1993 (i.e. with no tariffs or customs controls and common taxation). It has yet to happen in its entirety.

SITC Abbreviation of Standard International Trade Classification.

SITPRO An organization that was set up to "guide, stimulate and assist the rationalization of international trade procedures and the documentation and information flows associated with them".

S

SLASH Abbreviation of *self-propelled lighter aboard ship.*

sling A strap or belt, etc. for hanging, supporting or raising any goods being transferred.

SLL (ISO) code Sierre Leone – currency: leone.

slot A space on board a vehicle occupied by or available for a container.

Slovakia currency: koruna, divided into 100 haleru.

Slovenia currency: tolar.

slump A period of time during which the economy is poor, with high levels of unemployment and reduced economic activity.

smaller exporters' package (ECGD) A new exports credits package launched in November 2000 for small and medium-sized companies exporting to countries outside Western Europe and North America. It includes improved and streamlined versions of its existing products, such as its supplier credit financing facility, more favourable margins for its fixed-rate export finance, and more flexible foreign content rules, as well as new features designed with the smaller exporter in mind. These include its *recourse indemnity policy*, a new fast-track system for processing applications for exporters with smaller contracts, drawing attention to its export insurance policy and its overseas investment insurance scheme and their relevance for the smaller exporter.

SMEs Abbreviation of small and medium-sized enterprises.

smurfing A colloquial term for the practice of transferring into a single (often offshore) account many small sums of money from many different bank accounts. It may be a device for *money laundering*.

snake A popular term for the European monetary system that links the following currencies: Belgian and French francs, Danish krøne, Irish punt, Dutch guilder, German Deutschmark and Italian lira. Its purpose is to control (within 2¼ %) day-to-day fluctuations in exchange rates against the US dollar.

SNF (ISO) code Senegal – currency: CFA franc.

SOB Abbreviation of *shipped on board*.

Society for Worldwide Interbank Financial Telecommunications *See SWIFT*.

soft arbitrage The movement of funds between the money market and bank deposits to benefit from the difference in interest rates.

soft currency A currency of which there is a surplus on the market and

S

which is therefore relatively cheap. It is also an alternative term for *weak currency*.

soft dollars Dollars traded on the foreign exchange markets for which demand is persistently low because of a US trade deficit. The value of soft dollars tends to fall.

soft-sided lorry A lorry with a hard top, but "soft" sides, such as tarpaulin or other synthetic material often fastened together by straps and hooks, used where ease of access, rather than full security, is the more desirable. It is also known as a *tilt*.

sola A bill of exchange that does not have a duplicate as in bills of a set.

sold contract note An alternative term for a *sold note*.

sold note A document sent by a broker to his or her client, confirming that a sale has been made. It is also known as a sold contract note.

sold short *See short position.*

sole agency An agreement by which one party (the agent) represents a principle either in a certain capacity or in a particular geographical area.

sol The standard currency unit of Peru, divided into 100 centimos. It is also called the new sol.

som The standard currency unit of Kyrgystan.

Somali Republic currency: Somali shilling (SOS), divided into 100 cents.

SOS (ISO) code Somali Republic – currency: Somali shilling.

soum The standard currency unit of Uzbekistan.

South Africa currency: rand (ZAR), divided into 100 cents.

Southeast Asia Treaty Organization (SEATO) A mutual defence pact signed in 1955 by Australia, France, New Zealand, Pakistan, the Philippines, Thailand, the UK and the USA. It was intended to resist Communist activity in the area, but was abandoned in 1977 through lack of support.

Spain currency: peseta (ESP); there is no subdivision. The 1999 legacy conversion rate was 166.386 to the euro. It will fully change to the euro/cent from 2002.

special agent An agent with authority to perform one particular action on behalf of another.

special drawing rights (SDR) A form of credit extended by the International Monetary Fund (IMF) to member countries as an addition to the credit they already hold.

special endorsement An endorsement in the name of a particular person on a bill of exchange.

special guidelines (relating to the OECD's *Arrangement*) Rules that apply to certain sectors only, such as ships and nuclear power plant ,etc.

specific letter of hypothecation A bank's general right to realize the money it is owed in full or part from specific property hypothecated (pledged) to it for that specific transaction only by its customer.

speculation 1. The act of buying or selling a currency forward, in the hope that before the settlement date a favourable exchange rate movement will have taken place, allowing the speculator to make a profit by buying or selling spot. 2. The act of buying or selling currency in the expectation of an exchange rate movement so as to make a profit.

spoilage An alternative term for *wastage*.

spot An exchange deal where the exchange rate is determined at "today's prices", for settlement in, usually, two working days' time (as opposed to the forward rate). The settlement date is only one day for North American dollars. *See also* **value date**.

spot deal A deal for currency exchange that must be completed within two business days of signature (at the rate prevailing at that time).

spot exchange rate An alternative term for *spot rate*.

spot goods As opposed to futures, commodities that are available for immediate delivery, rather than forward delivery.

spot market A market in which the goods sold are available for immediate delivery. It is also known as the non-contract market.

spot price A price quoted for goods available for immediate delivery, usually higher than the forward price because it takes into account all costs except delivery.

spot rate The current exchange rate of a currency for settlement in two business days (as opposed to the *forward rate*).

spot transaction Dealing for cash (rather than credit) or in futures.

spread A difference in prices or yields, often between a market maker's bid and offer rates.

S

square position Situation that occurs where a dealer has his purchases and sales in balance, and therefore has no position, long or short.

SR & CC A special clause inserted in marine insurance for an extra premium to cover the risks of wars, strikes, riots, and civil commotions.

Sri Lanka currency: Sri Lankan rupee (LKR), divided into 100 cents.

SSN Abbreviation of standard shipping note.

staggered closing A method by which shippers sort out their cargoes for loading according to the discharge port rota, in other words logically the cargo that will be the last to be discharged will be entered first and placed at the bottom/back, so that the nearer-to-hand cargo can be unloaded more easily first, and so on.

STAGS Abbreviation of *sterling accruing government securities*.

stale bill of lading A bill of lading that has been presented so late that it could be rejected in connection with, say, a letter of credit.

stale bull A dealer who has bought in the expectation that prices will rise but cannot then sell at a profit, either because prices have remained static or fallen, or because nobody wants to buy.

standard "exchange traded" options Options in certain currencies and for standard amounts of currency traded in future/option exchanges.

Standard International Trade Classification (SITC) The classification of all the types of goods that are subject to a *tariff*.

standard shipping mark The identification mark on any package consisting of the initials of the consignee or the consignee's abbreviated name, the reference number, the destination and the number of the particular package.

standby credit A form of back-up credit guaranteed by a Euronote facility or other note issuance facility

standby letter of credit A credit that acts as a form of security for an advance. 1. It provides a guarantee to a beneficiary that he will receive payment if the importer has not met his obligations to pay by some other means, such as by open account or by bill of exchange. 2. It is used when a guarantee cannot be obtained, for example in the USA.

state protocol A *line of credit* arranged by the French government and supported by its banks.

state trading enterprises (STEs) Government-established organizations

S

that produce, export and/or import certain products (with various exclusive or special trading privileges).

status report A report from a credit reference agency estimating a borrower's suitability to receive commercial credit.

step-lock option An alternative term for *ladder option*.

sterling accruing government securities (STAGS) A form of zero-coupon bonds, denominated in sterling and backed by Treasury stock.

sterling area *See Scheduled Territories.*

sterling bloc The countries of the British Commonwealth that fixed the exchange rate of sterling to favour trade within the bloc. *See Scheduled Territories.*

stevedore A person who loads and unloads ships.

STMS Abbreviation of *short-term money support*.

stockbroker Formal name agency broker, somebody who gives advice and buys and sells stocks and shares on a stock exchange on behalf of clients.

stockjobber An alternative term for *jobber*.

stop for freight A shipowner's or broker's instruction to a dock authority not to permit delivery of goods until freight is paid.

stop-loss Describing an automatic selling price assigned to a security that prevents any further losses to an investor.

stop-loss order An instruction given by a client to a stockbroker to sell securities should they fall below a certain price.

stop-loss selling The sale of shares or futures contracts in a declining market, usually at a predetermined price, in order to prevent further loss.

stop order An alternative term for *stop-loss order*.

stopover A pre-agreed break in a carrier's journey.

stoppage in transitu The repossession of goods from a carrier by a seller because their buyer has become insolvent.

stotinki A subdivision (1/100) of the Bulgarian levi.

stowage order A shipowner's instruction to stevedores on how to stow

S

fragile, valuable or dangerous goods and to the shipper as to where and when he is to deliver the goods ready for stowing.

straddle The practice of simultaneously buying forward and selling forward a futures contract or an option in the same security in order to make a profit if the price of the security moves in either direction.

straight bill of lading A bill of lading issued to the name of a specified party and which cannot be transferred by endorsement.

strangle The practice of buying out-of-the-money call and put options that are close to expiry at a relatively low premium. If the price of the underlying future rises or falls suddenly, the buyer makes a profit.

strike insurance A special **SR & CC** clause inserted in marine insurance for an extra premium to cover the risks of strikes.

strike price The rate at which an option may be exercised (also known as the exercise price).

Stubbs Gazette A publication that provides weekly information of legal actions adversely affecting the credit ratings of borrowers.

subcontractor A person or company that makes part of all of a final product on behalf of another company. Some manufacturing contracts specifically do not permit the use of subcontractors.

subcontractor cover (ECGD) The ECGD insures against risks relating both to a main contractor (if based overseas) and to an overseas buyer. If a subcontractor's right to payment under the contract is unconditional he or she needs insurance only against the main contractor. However, if he or she has a conditional contract (such that payment is dependent on the main contractor being paid) then he or she can choose whether to cover the risks relating to the buyer only, or to both the buyer and the main contractor.

subject bid/offer A bid/offer that is subject to stated conditions (as opposed to a firm bid).

subrogation The substitution of one person for another so that an insurance company, for instance, can stand in the shoes of its client and sue the perpetrator of the damage etc. having already compensated its client for the loss.

subsidiary A company that is wholly or partly owned by another – the parent company.

S

sucre The standard currency unit of Ecuador, divided into 100 centavos.

Sudanese Republic currency: Sudanese dinar (SDP), divided into 100 piastres.

supplier credit facility (SCF) An ECGD-supported financial facility providing non-recourse (occasionally, alternatively, with recourse) finance to exporters of capital and semi-capital goods.

supply risk In limited recourse financing of a construction project, the risk that the materials required may not be available some time after the project has been started.

support agreement under ECGD-supported buyer credit If a buyer fails to repay any instalment under an ECGD-supported buyer credit in full or to pay any interest due, the ECGD will guarantee to pay the bank 90 days after the date on which the buyer should have paid.

supporting a currency The practice of actively buying securities or foreign exchange by an "official" in order to stop their market value from falling. This most often happens when a central bank buys its own securities to stop the price falling and thus forestall a rise in interest rates.

support level A price level at which to expect buying to take place to prevent the price breaking through that level.

supranational An entity that cannot be classified as belonging to one particular country, e.g. the World Bank.

surcharge An extra charge imposed on certain goods, such as an added tax on imported goods (when it may be referred to as surtax).

survey report A report by an independent expert, often required in bond and guarantee finance to certify the work of builders and constructors, etc.

sushi bond A bond denominated in a foreign currency and issued by a Japanese institution, when it then counts as a domestic bond.

swap A contract for exchange of interest obligations (fixed/floating, currency or other bases) and on occasion principal amounts.

swap deal 1. A simultaneous spot sale and forward purchase of a currency, or vice versa. 2. A simultaneous spot purchase and forward sale of a currency.

Swaziland currency: lilangeni (plural emalangeni) (SZL), divided into 100 cents.

S

Sweden currency: Swedish krona (SEK), divided into 100 ore.

SWIFT Abbreviation of Society for Worldwide Interbank Financial Telecommunications, a private company based in Belgium that transfers monetary and other financial messages electronically.

swing A degree of imbalance, which may arise on a bilateral clearing agreement.

switch trading The purchase by a third party in hard currency, but at a discount, of an imbalance that has arisen on a bilateral clearing agreement.

Switzerland currency: Swiss franc (CHF), divided into 100 centimes.

syndicate A combination of individuals or commercial enterprises created to promote some common interest.

syndicate manager In an investment-banking context, the official responsible for handling and managing new bond-issuing business and liasing with the other members of the syndicate.

SYP (ISO) code Syria – currency: Syrian pound.

Syria currency: Syrian pound (SYP), divided into 100 piastres.

systematic risk The general price risk applicable to all securities arising from changes in the overall economic environment.

SZL (ISO) code Swaziland – currency: lilangeni (plural emalangeni).

S

T

Taiwan currency: Taiwanese dollar (TWD), divided into 100 cents.

Tajikstan currency: rouble, divided into 100 tanga.

taka The standard currency unit of Bangladesh, divided into 100 paisa.

tala The standard currency unit of Western Samoa, divided into 100 sene.

tambala A subdivision (1/100) of the Malawian kwacha, divided into 100 tambala.

tanga A subdivision (1/100) of the Tajikstan rouble.

tangible assets Literally, assets that may be touched, such as buildings or stock; also called tangibles. They may be contrasted with intangible (or invisible) assets, such as a company's goodwill or the expertise of its staff. *See also fixed asset.*

tangibles Another term for *tangible assets*.

tank container A container specially designed for carrying a single/range of specific good of all types from beer to flour, etc.

Tanzania currency: Tanzanian shilling (TZS), divided into 100 cents.

TAPS Abbreviation of Transcontinental Automated Payment Service, the Bank of Scotland's economic cross-border payment system.

tare 1. The weight of a vehicle or container without its fuel and/or load. 2. An allowance made for the weight of the packing or wrapping around goods.

target price Theoretical selling price set annually on farm produce under the *Common Agricultural Policy (CAP)* of the *European Commission (EC)*. It may be achieved by purchasing goods at the intervention price (see *intervention mechanism*).

tariff A duty imposed on a particular class of imports or exports.

tariff anomaly A situation in which the tariff on raw materials or semi-manufactured goods is larger than that on the finished product.

tariff barrier A tariff imposed by an importing country that restricts or prevents the free flow of such goods. It is also called a customs barrier.

T

tariff quota The imposition of a higher tariff on imported goods once a specified quantity has been imported (at a lower tariff).

tariff suspension The cancellation of a tariff to protect domestic industry from foreign competition.

TBL Abbreviation of *through bill of lading*.

TDF (ISO) code Chad – currency: CFA franc.

technical analysis Statistical analysis to predict market movements.

Technical Help to Exporters (THE) A service provided by the British Standards Institution for the British Overseas Trade board to collect information about the technical standards and regulations in other countries, so that exports can be modified accordingly, if necessary.

telecommunication Any communication by cable, telegraph, telephone, broadcasting or any specifically electronic means. *See transmission of messages*.

Telerate A screen-based information reporting system.

tender bond *See bid bond*.

tender to contract (TTC) Cover provided by the ECGD for the exchange risk involved in tendering for contracts quoted in foreign currencies. Banks normally provide foreign exchange cover only once the commercial contract has been signed.

tenge The standard currency unit of Kazakhstan.

terminal date Also called terminate date, the date of expiry of a futures contract.

terminal market The financial market in futures.

terminate date An alternative term for *terminal date*.

terms of trade An indication of a county's trading prospects, based on a comparison of its imports and exports.

territorial waters The area of sea around a country over which it claims jurisdiction. The distance from shore varies widely among countries. For example, the UK claims up to 12 nautical miles (Territorial Sea Act 1987) for general purposes, but up to 200 miles for fishing rights.

TEU Abbreviation of twenty foot equivalent unit, a container measurement. Thus a container 40ft by 8 ft is 16 TEU.

TGF (ISO) code Togo Republic – currency: CFA franc.

Thailand currency: baht (THB), divided into 100 satang.

THB (ISO) code Thailand – currency: baht.

THE Abbreviation of *Technical Help to Exporters*.

The Maldives currency: rufiya, divided into 100 laari.

thebe A subdivision (1/100) of the Botswana pula.

theta The rate of change of an option premium with respect to time.

threshold price A price fixed under the Common Agricultural Policy (CAP) of the European Commission, below which the price of agricultural imports from non-member states is not allowed to fall.

through bill of lading (TBL) A bill of lading covering goods being transhipped en route. It covers the whole voyage from the port of shipment to their final destination.

through transport operator A carrier who carries goods that are also handled by other operators as well in the course of its journey. Legally, he or she is the principal while acting on his or her own behalf, but only an agent otherwise.

TIndemnity Company. A British private credit insurance company.

tick The minimum price fluctuation of a future or an option.

tied aid Foreign aid tied to the purchase of goods and/or services from the donor country.

tied aid credit Foreign aid that is financed exclusively out of public funds for development aid.

TIF Abbreviation of *Transport Internationaux par Chemin de Fer* (International Rail Transport).

TIFFE Abbreviation of Tokyo International Financial Futures Exchange.

tilt A fabric covering secured to a lorry's bodywork. To comply with *TIR* regulations it must be sealable and undamaged.

time bill of exchange A bill of exchange, or draft, payable either on a definite date or at a fixed time after sight or demand.

time charter The hiring of all or part of a ship for a specified period of time (during which any number of voyages may be made).

T

time draft A draft, or bill of exchange, payable either on a definite date or at a fixed time after sight or demand.

time spread The buying and selling of similar options having the same strike prices but maturing at different times to try to make a profit should the market price rise. It is also known as a *calendar spread or horizontal spread*.

time value What remains of an *option premium* when the *intrinsic value* has been deducted.

TIPAnet Abbreviation of *Transferts Interbancaires de Paiements Automatises*.

TIR Abbreviation of *Transport Internationaux par Route*.

T/L Abbreviation of total loss.

TND (ISO) code Tunisia – currency: Tunisian dinar.

today/tomorrow Describing the simultaneous buying and selling of currency for value same day against the next, or vice versa.

toea A subdivision (1/100) of the Papuan New Guinea kina.

Togo Republic currency: CFA franc (TGF); there is no subdivision.

tolar The standard currency unit of Slovenia.

toman 1 toman = 10 Iranian rials.

tomorrow/next Describing the simultaneous buying and selling of a currency for delivery the following day and selling for the next day, or vice versa.

Tonga currency: pa'anga, divided into 100 seniti.

tonnage The size of a ship based on its cubic capacity, where 1 tonne equals 100 cubic feet. It is not the vessel's carrying capacity.

tonne-miles The weight of a load or cargo multiplied by the distance carried.

TOPFORM An aligned paper-based documentation system.

total distribution cost The economic and efficient costing of the whole system of handling, transporting and storing goods from door to door rather than treating each individual action in isolation.

towage A charge for towing a ship.

trade acceptance A bill of exchange drawn by an exporter/seller on the importer/buyer. It is distinguished from a bankers' acceptance in that the buyer's credit is not normally held in the same high esteem.

trade agreement An agreement between two or more countries or two groups of countries regarding general terms of trade.

trade association An organization that represents the interest of companies within a particular industry, especially in discussions with government.

trade barrier Something that restricts or discourages trade, such as high levels of import duty or low import quotas.

trade bill A bill of exchange between traders. The value and acceptability of a trade bill depends on the standing of the accepting trader.

trade credit The credit one company or business gives to another, usually in the form of time to pay for goods or services supplied.

trade creditor A company or person to whom money is owed as a result of normal trading.

trade facilitation The aim to eliminate procedures that add cost without adding value. The UK's main agency is *SITPRO*.

trade gap In an adverse balance of trade, the difference between the values of imports and exports.

Trade Indemnity A British company that provides export credit insurance.

trade investment A company investment in capital goods relating to another (usually associated) existing business, or in a new business in an established sector.

trade war A retaliatory action, such as an embargo, by one government against another that has imposed tariff barriers against its exports.

trading after hours Trading on official exchanges outside normal trading hours. Prices might thereby change considerably between the previous day's closing and the beginning of the next.

trading association An organization whose members are people or companies in the same sort of business, formed to represent them in, for example, dealings with local and national government.

trailer A vehicle that is towed by another vehicle, particularly referring to the rear section of an articulated lorry.

T

tramp A ship that is chartered (i.e. distinct from a liner), often but not necessarily carrying bulk cargo.

transaction envelope A batch of international payment messages packaged together.

transaction risk Interest-rate risk arising from the fact that a transaction is priced in a foreign currency.

Transcontinental Automated Payment Service (TAPS) Offered by the Bank of Scotland, a system designed specifically for regular, low-value payments to specific countries where the banking details of the beneficiary are known (such as standing order payments).

transferable letter of credit A letter of credit in which the specified beneficiary has the option of instructing his bank to transfer it fully or in part to another beneficiary. It can be transferred in parts, but can be transferred once only in total.

transfer risk The risk that a transfer cannot take place from one currency area to another, particularly if foreign exchange restrictions are introduced.

Transferts Interbancaires de Paiements Automatises (TIPAnet) The Co-operative Bank's cheaper international money transfer service operating between the UK, Belgium, France, Germany, Italy and Canada.

translation Banks assume no liability or responsibility for errors in the translation of telecommunication transmissions when using these for letters of credit and collections, etc.

translation risk Exchange-rate risks arising from the revaluation of assets and liabilities, which are denominated in a foreign currency.

transmission of messages Banks assume no liability or responsibility arising from delays, loss, or other errors in telecommunication transmissions when using these for letters of credit and collections, etc.

transportation bond A bond that covers transporting goods imported to be used by an exporter undertaking an overseas contract, from where they land to the work site.

Transport Internationaux par chemin de Fer (TIF) The international railway customs procedure similar to TIR for road haulage, but by international rail carnet. Goods can be sent in approved sealed vehicles or containers to cross frontiers without being impeded by unnecessary

T

customs inspections. The seals must remain unbroken and any *tilts* undamaged. The purpose is to put such transport on a par with air and sea transport, i.e. normally goods are inspected by customs only at the port of departure and the port of destination and so the fact that they are travelling through, rather than over and round, countries by rail should not make any difference. Intra-EU transport does not need TIR carnets anyway – only if and when the goods enter or leave the EU.

Transport Internationaux par Route (TIR) (International Road Transport) The international road carnet system. Goods can be sent in approved sealed vehicles or containers to cross frontiers without being impeded by unnecessary customs inspections. The seals must remain unbroken and any *tilts* undamaged. The purpose is to put such transport on a par with air and sea transport, i.e. normally goods are inspected by customs only at the port of departure and the port of destination and so the fact that they are travelling through, rather than over and round, countries by road should not make any difference. Intra-EU transport does not need TIR carnets anyway – only if and when the goods enter or leave the EU.

trans-ship To transfer goods from one ship or form of transport to another.

trans-shipment entry Customs entry for entrepot trade, i.e. where goods are imported and immediately re-exported.

Treasury bills Short-term securities (one year or less) issued by the US Government at a discount.

Treasury bonds Coupon-bearing securities issued by the US Government with an original maturity of more than 10 years.

Treasury notes Coupon-bearing securities issued by the US government with an original maturity of 10 years or less.

treasury risk The risks inherent in the money market operations of an organization.

TREAUARBEIT Short form of Treauarbeit Aktiengesellschaft, the German foreign investment insurance agency.

TREM card A HAZCHEM card issued with detailed information about the particular goods being carried and how they are to be handled in the event of an emergency.

triangular deal A *compensation* trade involving a third party.

trim chart A chart displaying the weight distribution of an aircraft before take off.

T

trimming Adjusting the balance of a ship by spreading the cargo evenly.

TRL (ISO) code Turkey – currency: Turkish lira.

trucking The transportation of containers and/or lorries etc. between container terminals and other transport bases.

trust receipt A declaration issued by a customer that the ownership of goods remains with the bank, even after the goods have been released to him or her, i.e. the customer has received the goods in trust only.

TTC Abbreviation of *tender to contract*.

TTO Abbreviation of *through transport operator*.

tughrik The standard currency unit of Mongolia, divided into 100 moengoe.

Tunisia currency: Tunisian dinar (TND), divided into 1000 millimes.

Turkey currency: Turkish lira (TRL), divided into 100 kurus.

Turkish Republic of North Cyprus currency: Turkish lira (TRL), divided into 100 kurus.

Turkmenistan currency: manat.

turnkey project A project in which ownership is usually transferred from the original builder/operator only after ensuring that everything is "turned on" and running properly. *See also* **build-own-operate-transfer** scheme.

TWD (ISO) code Taiwan – currency: Taiwanese dollar.

two-way price A price for which both a bid and an offer are quoted.

TZS (ISO) code United Republic of Tanzania – currency: Tanzanian shilling.

U

UA (ISO) code Ukraine – currency: hryvna

UCP or **UCPDC** Abbreviation of *Uniform Customs and Practice of Documentary Credits*.

UDEAC See *Central African Customs and Economic Union*.

Uganda currency: Ugandan shilling (UGS), divided into 100 cents.

UGS (ISO) code Uganda – currency: Ugandan shilling.

UIACP Abbreviation of Uniform International Authentication and Certification Practices, an International Chamber of Commerce (ICC) statement of best practice for certification authorities.

Ukraine currency: hryvna (plural hryvni) (UA).

ULCC Abbreviation of ultra large crude carrier (such as an oil tanker).

ULD Abbreviation of unit load device (in the consolidation of air freight).

ullage The difference between the capacity of a cask and the volume of its present contents (now called vacuity by Customs officials); or the actual contents of a cask (as used by Customs officials).

umbrella document A unifying document summarizing the purpose and contents of the other documents in a series.

umpirage In cases of arbitration, there may be more than one arbitrator. A group of arbitrators is governed by an umpire and in the event that the arbitrators are unable to reach a unanimous decision, the umpire's decision is always final. The act of referring to the umpire in this way is known as umpirage.

UNCITRAL Abbreviation of United Nations Commission on International Trade and Law.

UNCON Abbreviation of *uncontainerable goods*.

unconditional bond A bond in which the buyer has the right to **call** the full amount of the bond for any reason, even if the exporter has satisfied his contractual obligations (although ultimately it will probably be sorted out satisfactorily, in the meantime it can cause unnecessary fears and complications).

uncontainerable goods (UNCON) Goods that cannot be put into containers because they are too big or the wrong shape.

UNCTAD Abbreviation of United Nations Conference on Trade and Development.

UNCTAD MMO Abbreviation of United Nations Conference on Trade and Development's multi-modal transport convention.

underbought position Situation in which a dealer has bought less of a currency (spot or forward) than he requires for selling needs and consequently has liabilities exceeding assets in the currency.

underlying instrument The instrument on which an option is based. For example, an option on a future has an underlying futures contract.

under reserve An advising bank may credit the account of a beneficiary of an unconfirmed letter of credit, even before it has itself been reimbursed, by noting the payment as being "under reserve". This means that the beneficiary must repay the credited amount plus interest, charges and exchange rate difference if the issuing bank should(fail to reimburse it for any reason.

under usual reserve An advising bank may credit the account of a beneficiary of an unconfirmed letter of credit, even before it has itself been reimbursed, by noting the payment as being "under usual reserve". This means that the beneficiary must repay the credited amount plus interest, charges and exchange rate difference if the issuing bank should fail to reimburse it for any reason.

undervalued currency A currency whose rate of exchange is continuingly above its *parity* rate.

UNDP Abbreviation of *United Nations Development Programme*.

unfair calling insurance An insurance that protects an exporter against a bond being called without good reason.

Uniform Customs and Practice of Documentary Credits (UCP or **UCPDC)** The International Chamber of Commerce's rules and regulations governing the banks and other parties dealing with letters of credit and accepted, subject to different national minor amendments, as having the full authority of mercantile law.

uniform order bill of lading A negotiable bill of lading that is made to the shipper's order.

Uniform Rules for Collections The International Chamber of

Commerce's rules and regulations governing the banks and other parties dealing with collections and accepted, subject to different national minor amendments, as having the full authority of mercantile law.

Uniform Rules for Contract Guarantees The International Chamber of Commerce's rules and regulations governing the practice of the parties involved in a bond or guarantee and attempting to provide a fair balance between their conflicting interests.

unit load A large load can be assembled and/or separated by treating each small part of it as a standardized unit (for use in pallets and condainers).

United Arab Emirates currency: dirham (AED), divided into 100 fils.

United Kingdom currency: pound sterling (GBP), divided into 100 pence.

United Nations Development Programme (UNDP) A programme that helps to sustain existing ecosystems while also promoting viable income-earning development activities. The programme uses environmental conservation as a catalyst to alleviate poverty and improve quality of life, foster regional cooperation, etc.

United Republic of Tanzania currency: Tanzanian shilling (TZS), divided into 100 cents.

United States of America currency: US dollar (USD), divided into 100 cents.

universal agent An agent with unlimited authority to close contracts on behalf of the principal. *See also* **special agent**.

unlimited company A company that consists of members who are all liable for the total of the company's debts. *See* **limited company**.

unlimited liability The liability of the members of an unlimited company, or of the general partners in a partnership, or of the sole proprietor of a sole proprietorship. *See* **limited liability**.

unlisted company Also called an unquoted company, a company whose shares are not traded on a major stock exchange.

unrealized loss A loss that has not yet been realized, i.e. the underlying security(ies) have not yet been sold.

unrealized profit A profit that has not yet been realized, i.e. the underlying security(ies) have not yet been sold.

unrestricted letter of credit A letter of credit that can be negotiated through any bank of the beneficiary's own choice.

Uruguay currency: peso Uruguayo (UYP), divided into 100 centesimos.

usance The extra time allowed for the payment of foreign bills of exchange where credit has been permitted.

usance credit A letter of credit that authorizes the beneficiary to draw a time draft on a specified bank (be it the issuing, advising, or a third bank). He or she can discount immediately after it has been accepted, although the buyer will still be called upon to pay it only on its maturity.

USD (ISO) code United States of America – currency: US dollar.

US prime rate The rate at which US banks will lend to their prime corporate customers.

usufruct The right to the use of property belonging to someone else, but not the right to diminish its value in such use.

u.u.r. Abbreviation of credit under usual reserve.

UYP (ISO) code Uruguay – currency: peso Uruguayo.

Uzbekistan currency: soum.

V

validity date The date on which a bond or guarantee expires.

valuation trade An options trade that aims to profit from the difference between the theoretical option price and its actual price in the market.

value date The maturity date of a spot or forward contract, when funds change hands.

value quota An import restriction by value, e.g. a maximum of £200 million.

value spot An exchange deal in which the exchange rate is determined at "today's prices", for settlement in two working days' time.

Vanuatu currency: vatu.

variation margin Funds required to be deposited with an exchange by a buyer or seller of a futures contract where the price movement on the contract has caused the initial margin to fall below the designated maintenance level.

vatu The standard currency unit of Vanuatu.

VEB (ISO) code Venezuela – currency: bolivar.

vega The rate of change of an option premium with respect to volatility.

vehicle currency A currency that is used to make payments and quotations in international investment and trade, most often the US dollar.

Venezuela currency: bolivar (VEB), divided into 100 centimos.

ventilated container A specialized container for carrying foods that need to be kept fresh, such as vegetables, beverages etc.

venture capital Also known as risk capital, capital invested in a venture (usually a young company, often in high-technology areas) that presents a risk.

VER Abbreviation of *voluntary export restrictions*.

vertical diversification The diversification into industries or businesses at different stages of production to the diversifying company. *See also horizontal diversification.*

vertical integration The amalgamation of companies involved in different stages of production in the same industry, for example to form one company capable of extracting raw materials, using them to produce goods and then distributing and selling the manufactured product.

vertical spread The buying and selling of similar options having different strike prices but expiring at the same time, to try to make a profit should the market price rise.

vessel A large ocean-going ship or boat frequently used as a relatively cheap means of sending goods long distances abroad.

Vienna Convention A United Nations Convention governing contracts for the international sale of goods.

Vietnam currency: dong, divided into 100 xu.

VISA An international credit card company that has also developed a cross-border payment service that utilizes its international network.

visible exports Also known as visibles, goods sold to foreign buyers and shipped abroad. The difference between the value of visible exports and visible imports is the balance of trade.

visible imports Tangible products that are imported; imports of goods rather than of services.

visibles An alternative term for visible exports.

visible trade The trade in *visible exports* and *visible imports*.

VLCC Abbreviation of very large crude carrier (such as an oil tanker).

volatility A measure of price fluctuations.

volume quota An import restriction by volume, e.g. a maximum of 100,000 cars.

voluntary export restriction (VER) A limitation on certain types of exports from one country to another (or group of countries) in order to forestall the imposition of import quotas or other restrictions by importing countries. It is often preceded by a voluntary restraint agreement, stating that this is what the exporting country intends to do.

vostro account i.e. "your account", a UK bank's account with its overseas correspondent bank in sterling.

voyage charter A charter agreement (relating to a ship or its cargo space) for a particular voyage.

VTL Abbreviation of Vientitakuulaitos, the Finnish credit insurance agency.

W

warehouse receipt Also termed a depository receipt, a document that gives details of goods (commodities) delivered to a warehouse

warehouse to warehouse clause An insurance clause evidencing that a cargo is insured from the seller's warehouse to the buyer's warehouse.

warehousing 1. With reference to shipping, it is the business of storing, examining and sorting imported goods, which takes place in a warehouse before they are released into the country in question. 2. In more general terms, it is the storage of goods on behalf of a manufacturer, distributor or retailer.

war insurance A special **SR & CC** clause inserted in marine insurance for an extra premium to cover the risks of wars.

warrant A collateral certificate used in some countries for lending on the security of goods.

warranty A legal term meaning an implied condition, express guarantee or negotiation contained in a contract.

warranty bond A bond financially guaranteeing the satisfactory performance of the goods or equipment etc. supplied during the agreed maintenance or warranty period specified in a contract.

war, revolution or insurrection insurance Insurance that covers losses due to war in which the host government is a participant, or due to revolution or insurrection in the host country. It covers not only damage to, or removal of, all or part of overseas property but also the inability of an overseas enterprise to operate the covered project due to war.

wastage Also known as spoilage, the materials lost during a production process. Normal loss is an acceptable level of wastage.

waybill A document acknowledging the receipt for goods and the contract of their carriage. It is not a document of title (in other words it is not proof of ownership).

weak currency A currency that is expected to devalue or depreciate against many other currencies, or whose exchange rate must be supported by central bank intervention or exchange controls.

weather working days Working days (particularly in the construction industry or at a port) when work can be done because the weather conditions are favourable.

WebElecTra A *SITPRO* web-based system allowing international traders to complete, save, and send their documentation.

wedging The process of securing a cargo by tightening, securing, or fastening it to keep it immobile against a container's sides.

weight list A list of all the weights of individual packages contained in one consignment.

Western Samoa currency: tala, divided into 100 sene.

wharf A level quayside area for the mooring, loading and unloading of ships.

wharfage A fee charged for the use of a wharf to load or unload cargo.

wharfinger An owner or manager of a wharf.

wharfinger's receipt A receipt for goods warehoused prior to shipment.

what if The prediction of what would result *if* or what would it matter *if* etc. if a possible predicted event were to happen.

WHO Abbreviation of *World Health Organization.*

with particular average (WPA) An obsolete term (yet one still occasionally seen) meaning the insurance cover of the total loss of individual packages, each being treated as a separate insured risk. Now referred to as an *Institute Cargo Clause B.*

with recourse The right to recover funds (plus interest where appropriate) from borrowers if lenders are not reimbursed as they expect to be.

without recourse A note on a bill of exchange indicating that in the event of non-payment of the bill, the current holder may not blame the person from whom he or she bought it.

won The standard currency unit of North Korea, divided into 100 zeuns; and South Korea, divided into 100 chon.

working days In shipping, each weekday except Sunday and bank holidays; in some places Saturday is also excluded.

World Health Organization (WHO) A United Nations agency that provides country support, develops standardized technical guidelines and training materials, conducts operational research, and acts as secretariat of the Global Alliance and other health organizations.

World Trade Organization (WTO) An international organization that promotes freedom of trade and hence the reduction and ultimate removal of trade barriers.

Worldpay The HSBC(UK)'s cheaper international money transfer service operating between a wide group of countries.

WPA Abbreviation of with *particular average*.

writer The seller of an option.

WTO Abbreviation of *World Trade Organization*.

X

XEU (ISO) code European Monetary Cooperative Fund – currency: ecu.

xu A subdivision (1/100) of the Vietnamese dong.

Y

yankee A colloquial term of the London Stock Exchange for a US security.

yankee bond A bond that is written in dollar denominations to attract US investors.

yen The standard currency unit of Japan, divided into 100 sen.

YER (ISO) code Republic of Yemen – currency: Yemeni rial.

yield The rate of return on a security.

yield curve A chart that shows the relationship between yields and maturities for a set of similar securities or interbank deposits.

York-Antwerp Rules A voluntary code, drawn up as long ago as 1877, for those involved in shipping cargo by sea.

yuan The standard currency unit of China, divided into 10 jiaos.

YUD (ISO) code Yugoslavia – currency: Yugoslavian new dinar.

Yugoslavia currency: Yugoslavian new dinar (YUD), divided into 100 para.

Z

Zaire Republic currency: zaire (ZRZ), divided into 100 makuta.

zaire The standard currency unit of the Zaire Republic, divided into 100 makuta.

Zambia currency: Zambian kwacha (ZMK), divided into 100 ngwee.

ZAR (ISO) code South Africa – currency: rand.

zero-coupon bonds Eurobonds that, instead of accruing interest, mature at a higher value.

zeun A subdivision (1/100) of the North Korean won.

Zimbabwe currency Zimbabwean dollar (ZWD), divided into 100 cents.

zloty The standard currency unit of Poland, divided into 100 groszy.

ZMK (ISO) code Zambia – currency Zambian kwacha.

ZRZ (ISO) code Zaire Republic – currency: zaire.

ZWD (ISO) code Zimbabwe – currency Zimbabwean dollar.